Beiträge zum
ausländischen öffentlichen Recht und Völkerrecht

Edited by

the Max Planck Society
for the Advancement of Science
represented by Prof. Dr. Armin von Bogdandy
and Prof. Dr. Anne Peters

Volume 312

Yota Negishi

Conventionality Control of Domestic Law

Constitutionalised International Adjudication and Internationalised Constitutional Adjudication

Nomos

The Deutsche Nationalbibliothek lists this publication in the Deutsche Nationalbibliografie; detailed bibliographic data are available on the Internet at http://dnb.d-nb.de

ISBN 978-3-8487-8562-9 (Print)
978-3-7489-2983-3 (ePDF)

British Library Cataloguing-in-Publication Data
A catalogue record for this book is available from the British Library.

ISBN 978-3-8487-8562-9 (Print)
978-3-7489-2983-3 (ePDF)

Library of Congress Cataloging-in-Publication Data
Negishi, Yota
Conventionality Control of Domestic Law
Constitutionalised International Adjudication and
Internationalised Constitutional Adjudication
Yota Negishi
252 pp.
Includes bibliographic references.

ISBN 978-3-8487-8562-9 (Print)
978-3-7489-2983-3 (ePDF)

1st Edition 2022

Published by
Nomos Verlagsgesellschaft mbH & Co. KG
Waldseestraße 3–5 | 76530 Baden-Baden
www.nomos.de

Production of the printed version:
Nomos Verlagsgesellschaft mbH & Co. KG
Waldseestraße 3–5 | 76530 Baden-Baden

ISBN 978-3-8487-8562-9 (Print)
ISBN 978-3-7489-2983-3 (ePDF)
DOI https://doi.org/10.5771/9783748929833

Onlineversion
Nomos eLibrary

For Righteousness, Happiness, Grace and Manna

Acknowledgement

The very first book for me is the crystal of encounters with persons in different times and spaces. My academic career started at the School of Law, Waseda University, Tokyo, Japan. I had dived into the world of international law through moot court competitions such as Japan/Asia Cup in Tokyo and Jessup Cup in Washington DC. Having got caught up in the appealing power of international law, I then joined the seminar held by Professor Shuichi Furuya. For more than ten years from Bachler (2007–2011) through Master (2011–2013) to Doctoral (2013–2017) courses (and even now), his extraordinary skills and tenderness have shaped my personality as a researcher. Professor Hiroyuki Banzai is another mentor during the Master course, whose training programmes have stylised my attitude in accordance with the academic standard in the field. In their seminars, I was greatly helped by my senior colleagues, especially, Makoto Minakawa, Shinya Tazunoki, Makoto Seta, and Kenta Hirami, all of whom kindly gave precious advice for not only public matters but also private lives. I am especially grateful to Toshiki Mogami, professor of international law at the School of Political Science and Economics. It is no exaggeration to say that his professionalism has influenced my academic life entirely. He also wrote a recommendation letter for a research environment abroad. Without his gracious supports, my research would have lacked sensibility and rigorousness.

The second stage of my research life was at the Max Planck Institute for Comparative Public Law and International Law, Heidelberg, Germany. It has been my fortunes to meet splendid academic staffs and guest researchers there. My stay in the Institute was facilitated by Director Professor Anne Peters, for whom my thankfulness is beyond description. Her careful attention to every member of the Institute including me has been the model to follow in my professional tasks. I deeply thank Peter's research team members, particularly, Milan Tahraoui, Raffaela Kunz, Christos Kypraios, and Yueyao Zhang, to whom I am indebted for many things. The interaction with members of the *Ius Constitutionale Commune en América Latina* project in the Institute was essential for expanding and deepening my research. Mariela Morales Antoniazzi, project coordinator of *Ius Constitutionale Commune en América Latina*, deserves to receive my distinguished appreciation for her lovely generosity. I also appreciate project members, especially, Director Professor Armin von Bogdandy, Simon Hentrei, Ximena Soley, Pedro Villarreal, Franz Ebert, and Davide Paris. Such a wonderful stay was supported by the Institute's library and office staffs – my special gratitude goes to Anette Kreutzfeld who had cooperated with logistical matters.

Thanks to the fund for the status as Research Fellow of the Japan Society for the Promotion of Science (JSPS) (2013–2017), I was granted opportunities to visit various cities in Europe, Latin America, Africa and Asia, and engage in a multitude of dialogues with distinguished scholars. In the Italian public law school, Diletta Tega, Antonia Baraggia, Giuseppe Martinico, and Fulvio Maria Palombino should be mentioned for their suggestive comments on my work. For the theoretical problems of international adjudication, I gained inspiration from the interviews with André Nollkaemper, Laurence Burgorgue-Larsen, and Andreas Føllesdal. I also appreciate Eduardo Ferrer MacGregor's generosity in facilitating a short stay at the Inter-American Court of Human Rights. Dialogues with Pablo González-Domínguez and Norberto Garay Boza in San José were quite suggestive for understanding the doctrine of *control de convencionalidad*. Japanese public law scholars, especially, Koji Tonami, Takao Suami, Hajime Yamamoto, Akiko Ejima, Kaoru Obata, Hiromichi Matsuda, and Hinako Takata, made critical comments on my work. I express my sincere gratitude to Jean d'Aspremont who not just influenced my theoretical framework but also has offered guidelines in decisive moments in my research career.

All these experiences enabled me to elaborate and publish the essential parts of this book in distinguished journals and books including *European Journal of International Law*. My Ph.D. thesis itself was also highly evaluated and granted 2016 VASEDA VNIVERSITAS PALMA IN MEMORIAM AZVSAONO and 6th Ikushi Prize by the JSPS with the Endowment from Emperor Akihito. I could finalise the edition of this book in the third and current location in my research life, Seinan Gakuin University, Fukuoka, Japan. The research environment supported by library and office staffs at the university is comfortable, in which it has been easily possible to update the relevant case-laws and teachings (until December 2020). For the English language review, the author would also like to thank Enago (www.enago.jp). I hope this book contributes to the world of public law.

I conclude with personal debts. My parents Masami (Righteousness) and Sachiko (Happiness), my grandmother Yoshiko, and my sister Megumi, are always lovely and generous to my decisions. It is also literally graceful that I was led by the invisible hands to Fukuoka to meet my wife Megumi

(Grace). My daughter Manna sheds fresh light on my world every day. I again thank everyone involved in the research, without any of whom the crystal cannot keep shining forever.

Inhaltsverzeichnis

Abbreviation

American Convention on Human Rights (ACHR)
Articles on the Responsibility of States for Internationally Wrongful Acts (ARSIWA)
Andean Tribunal of Justice (ATJ)
Charter of Fundamental Rights of the European Union (CFREU)
Committee of Ministries (CoM)
Council of Europe (CoE)
Court of Justice of the European Union (CJEU)
Deutsche Bundesverfassungsgericht (BVerfG)
Economic Community of West African States (ECOWAS)
European Convention on Human Rights (ECHR)
European Court of Human Rights (ECtHR)
European Social Charter (ESC)
European Union (EU)
Human Rights Committee (HRC)
Inter-American Commission on Human Rights (IACHR)
Inter-American Court of Human Rights (IACtHR)
International Court of Justice (ICJ)
International Criminal Court (ICC)
International Covenant on Civil and Political Rights (ICCPR)
International Covenant on Economic, Social and Cultural Rights (ICESCR)
International Law Association (ILA)
International Law Commission (ILC)
International Labour Organisation (ILO)
Organisation of American States (OAS)
Permanent Court of International Justice (PCIJ)
Southern African Development Community (SADC)
Treaty on European Union (TEU)
Treaty on the Functioning of the European Union (TFEU)
United Nations (UN)
Vienna Convention on the Law of Treaties (VCLT)

Introduction

1. Research Problems

A. Systemic Human Rights Violations Caused by Unconventionality of Domestic Law

Patients are considered to have the ultimate say regarding their health condition. Although doctors may play a crucial role in providing medical treatment, their capacity is ultimately complementary to patients' right to self-determination. What if, however, patients fail to recover by themselves due to permanent problems stemming from physical dysfunctionality? Should doctors be limited to examining patients' conditions just by touching their skin and telling them the name of their disease, and providing ointment or a pill that is only superficially effective for the affected area? Or can medical experts identify the affected areas through intense scrutiny, prescribe drugs to eliminate the root cause of the problem, and if the situation requires it, open a surgical resection of their bodies to directly stimulate individual organs that may be the source of the identified causes? If the health of patients is restored through such medical interventions, should their autonomy continue to be restricted based on expert advice?

This analogy helps set out the research problems of this monograph, namely, the issue of systemic violations of international human rights law caused by the defections of domestic legal orders. Within the Westphalian system, nation States with sovereignty have primary powers and duties to implement international obligations, and international institutions remain in principle subsidiary for that purpose.[1] This idea of subsidiarity has been structurally embedded in international human rights law, in which the primary authorities and responsibilities of States Parties are complementarily supervised by treaty bodies.[2] What if, however, human rights violations occur not in single cases but rather in a systematic way due to the lack of ability and/or willingness of States Parties to align their domestic

---

1 Gerald L Neuman, 'Subsidiarity' in Dinah Shelton (ed), *The Oxford Handbook of International Human Rights Law* (Oxford University Press 2013) 360–378, 363–365.

2 Paolo G Carozza, 'Subsidiarity as a Structural Principle of International Human Rights Law' (2003) *American Journal of International Law* 38–79.

legal orders with treaty standards? Should the experts on human rights mandated under treaties refrain from exerting their authority beyond the original meaning of subsidiarity? Or should they reconfigure the meaning of subsidiarity to proactively enforce the primary responsibilities of States Parties? If States Parties follow the decisions of treaty bodies, should their autonomy remain bound to the supervision of human rights experts? These questions are not just figurative or hypothetical but rather exist in reality before the European and Inter-American human rights systems.

The original members of the Council of Europe, mostly western European countries, have retained their domestic legal orders for the effective protection of human rights in accordance with the established criteria, such as the rule of law and democracy. Due to their fidelity to a trinity of values (human rights and democracy and the rule of law), ECtHR jurisprudence deferred to States Parties, and only moderately exercised its remedial power for granting only monetary compensation or declaratory relief to victims.[3] The Strasbourg Court's cautious attitude seemed to reflect how effectively the States Parties have performed their primary duties for the protection of human rights. Despite its past effectiveness, the present European system faces a major challenge that has emerged due to the admission of new members from Central and Eastern Europe whose domestic systems do not necessarily conform to the criteria established by the original members.[4] Consequently, the unconventionality of their domestic laws has resulted in repetitive cases in which vast numbers of victims make similar claims like 'clones' on the same factual basis.[5]

On the other side of the Atlantic, the Inter-American human rights system experienced systemic human rights violations caused by unconventional domestic law even earlier. During the birth of the system, the historical background of Latin American states heavily weighed against the optimism for protecting human rights in this region. That is, these States were 'simply not ready for a system that vests individuals with basic rights under international law and provides judicial machinery for

3 Rudolf Bernhardt, 'Just Satisfaction under the European Convention on Human Rights' in Maurizio Ragazzi (ed), *International Responsibility Today: Essays in Memory of Oscar Schachter* (Martinus Nijhoff Publishers 2005) 243–252, 246–249.

4 For the problems relating the admission of new members from Central and Eastern Europe, see in general Wojciech Sadurski, *Constitutionalism and the Enlargement of Europe* (Oxford University Press 2012).

5 Ed Bates, *The Evolution of the European Convention on Human Rights: From its Inception to the Creation of a Permanent Court of Human Rights* (Oxford University Press 2010) 485–486.

the vindication of those rights'.[6] It should be noted, additionally, that dictatorship had historically remained endemic in the political life of Latin American States, and violence continued to be the principal vehicle for the attainment of political power in too many states.[7] As a result, widespread and grave violations of human rights in these states, such as forced disappearances, torture and extrajudicial killings were conducted under authoritarian regimes and in internal wars. In addition to these circumstances, amnesty laws and military jurisdiction were abused within their domestic legal orders in favour of those responsible for these violations. As a result, a culture of impunity spread over this region and most of the victims were systemically denied access to remedies.[8]

Figuratively speaking, doctors cannot deal with patients' internal dysfunction by simply touching their skin and telling them the name of their disease or providing an ointment that only superficially treats affected areas. Likewise, regional courts originally tended to provide individual relief to injured persons.[9] However, such case-by-case decisions would lead to difficulty in addressing systemic human rights violations caused by dysfunction within domestic legal systems.[10] To fundamentally address such violations, regional courts 'should view individual cases that are emblematic of persistent or structural human rights problems as opportunities to stimulate broader change on relevant issues'.[11] When States Parties do not comply with conventions standards by engaging in systemic violations, the collective mechanism of human rights protection manifests as a feature of *international law as intervention*, which allows treaty-based institutions

6 José A Cabranes, 'Human Rights and Non-Intervention in the Inter-American System' (1967) 65 *Michigan Law Review* 1147–1182, 1175–1176.

7 Ibid.

8 Laurence Burgorgue-Larsen, 'Exhaustion of Domestic Remedies' in Laurence Burgorgue-Larsen and Amaya Úbeda de Torres (eds), *The Inter-American Court of Human Rights: Case Law and Commentary* (Oxford University Press 2011) 129–145, 138.

9 *Velásquez-Rodríguez v Honduras*, IACtHR, Series C No 4, Judgment on Merits of 29 July 1988, paras 134; *Karner v Austria*, ECtHR, App no 40016/98, Judgment on Merits and Just Satisfaction of 24 July 2003, para 26.

10 With regard to the meaning of 'structural problem', see in general Mart Susi, 'The Definition of a "Structural Problem" in the Case-Law of the European Court of Human Rights Since 2010' (2012) 55 *German Yearbook of International Law* 1–51.

11 James L Cavallaro and Stephanie Erin Brewer, 'Reevaluating Regional Human Rights Litigation in the Twenty-First Century: The Case of the Inter-American Court' (2008) 102 *American Journal of International Law* 768–827, 770.

to 'intervene' in the domestic legal order to eradicate the root causes of systemic problems.[12]

Just as doctors must take a step further to solve organic dysfunctions of patients, regional courts have developed remedial jurisprudence not only for individual *reparation* but also collective *restoration*. Within the international legal order, if a State commits an internationally wrongful act against other subjects of international law, that State is obliged to discharge its international responsibility by making reparations to the injured parties, as dictated in the *Factory at Chorzów* case concerning 'reparation' under Article 36(d) of the Statute of the PCIJ.[13] According to Dionisio Anzilotti, who was influential in the PCIJ era, however, '[t]he violation of the international legal order committed by a State subject to that order thus gives rise to a duty of reparation in general consisting of the restoration [*rétablissement*] of the disrupted legal order'.[14] A remedy for an internationally wrongful act is therefore 'not confined solely to reparation of the material damage on a basis of *restitutio in integrum*' but '[m]ore broadly, it aims at *restoration* of the situation, both legal and material, that existed, before commission of the act giving rise to it'.[15] Such 'aspects of the restoration and repair of the legal relationship affected by the breach'[16] are significant particularly when international wrongful acts result due

12 Syuichi Furuya, 'The Image of International Legal Order in International Criminal Adjudicative System: The Exteriorisation of "International Law as Intervention" [Kokusai Keiji Sisutem no Kokusaiho Chitsujozo: "Kainyu no Kokusaiho" no Kenzaika]' (2013) 11 *Horitsu Jiho* 32–36 (in Japanese). For the concepts of *international law of coexistence and co-operation*, see Wolfgang Friedmann, The Changing Structure of International Law (Columbia University Press 1964).

13 *Factory at Chorzów (Germany vs Poland)*, PCIJ, Series A No 9, Judgment on Jurisdiction of 26 July 1927, 21.

14 Dionisio Anzilotti, 'La responsabilité internationale des États à raison des dommages soufferts par des étrangers' (1906) 13 *Revue générale de droit international public* 5–29 and 284–309, 13. In this respect, the Anzilotti's logic still possesses the 'contemporaneity' even for the present international legal order includes obligations *erga omnes (partes)*. See, Separate Opinion of Judge Cançado Antonio Augusto Trindade, *Ahmadou Sadio Diallo (Compensation owed by the Democratic Republic of the Congo to the Republic of Guinea) (Republic of Guinea v. Democratic Republic of Congo)*, Meirts, Judgment, ICJ Reports 2010, paras 22–24, 41–59.

15 Pierre-Marie Dupuy, 'Dionisio Anzilotti and the Law of International Law' (1992) 3 *European Journal of International Law* 139–148, 146 [emphasis added].

16 Commentary to Articles on the Responsibility of Sates for Internationally Wrongful Acts (hereinafter, Commentary to ARSIWA), *Report of the International Law Commission on the work of its fifty-third session*, A/56/10 (2001), Art 30, para 1.

to the incompatibility between the domestic legal order in question and international law.[17]

Regional human rights courts have, remarkably, started to exert their *remedial powers* for systemic violations of *general obligations* and *rights to domestic remedies* under the conventions, all of which reflect the subsidiarity principle. It follows, then, that these reparative and restorative measures have a *caractère hybride* because their legal bases are found in both primary rules (establishing an obligation under international law for a state) and secondary rules (on state responsibility).[18] More specifically, based on the different categories of primary rules (obligation to *respect and ensure* and obligation to *harmonise*), the different content of secondary obligations (the past-oriented, remedial *reparation* and the future-oriented, preventative *restoration*).[19] Such an essential connection between primary and secondary norms serves 'to coordinate and ensure some degree of convergence between two [international and domestic] legal systems'.[20]

B. Conventionality Control of Domestic Law

This monograph's main topic, the doctrine of *conventionality control of domestic law*, indeed emerged to restore the unconventional defections of domestic legal orders, which cause systemic human rights violations. The doctrine of conventionality control appeared for the first time in the leading case of *Almonacid-Arellano and Others v Chile*, in which the compatibility between the self-amnesty law in the Pinochet regime and the ACHR

17 *Arrest Warrant of 11 April 2000 (Democratic Republic of the Congo vs Belgium)*, Judgment, ICJ Report 2002, paras 75–76; *LaGrand (Germany vs United States of America)*, Judgment, ICJ Report 2001, para 125; *Avena and Other Mexican Nationals (Mexico vs United States of America)*, Judgment, ICJ Report 2004, para 121.

18 Hélène Tigroudja, 'La satisfaction et les garanties de non-répétition de l'illicite dans le contentieux interaméricain des droit de l'homme' in Elisabeth Lambert Abdelgawad and Kathia Martin-Chenut (eds), *Réparer les violations graves et massives des droits de l'homme: la Cour interaméricaine, pionnière et modèle?* (Société de Législation Comparée 2010) 69–89, 77. As to the distinction between primary and secondary rules, Working Paper Prepared by Roberto Ago, Yearbook of International Law Commission, 1973 Vol. II, A/CN.4/SER.A/1973/Add.1, 253.

19 Letizia Seminara, *Les effets des arrêts de la Cour interaméricaine des droits de l'homme* (Bruylant/Nemesis 2009) 61–66.

20 André Nollkaemper, 'The Power of Secondary Rules to Connect the International and National Legal Order' in Tomer Broude and Yuval Shany (eds), Multi-Sourced Equivalent Norms in International Law (Hart 2011) 45–67, 59–64.

was challenged. In this decision, the IACtHR dictated that the amnesty law, which left victims defenceless and perpetuated impunity for crimes against humanity, was 'manifestly incompatible with the wording and the spirit of the American Convention, and undoubtedly affect rights embodied in such Convention', and therefore, did 'not have any legal effects and cannot remain as an obstacle for the investigation of the facts inherent to the instant case, or for the identification and punishment of those responsible therefor' and '[n]either can it have a like or similar impact regarding other cases of violations of rights protected by the American Convention which occurred in Chile'.[21] According to this interpretation, the Court determined the violation of Article 2 ACHR (obligation to harmonise) by formally keeping the amnesty law within the *legislative corpus*, and that of Article 1(1) thereof (obligation to respect and ensure) by the *judicial* application of the amnesty law.[22] In this context, the San José Court took a monumental step towards the regional integration of international and domestic legal orders:

> [W]hen a State has ratified an *international treaty* such as the American Convention, *its judges*, as part of the State, are also bound by such Convention. This forces them to see that all the effects of the provisions embodied in the Convention are not adversely affected by the enforcement of laws which are contrary to its purpose and that have not had any legal effects since their inception. In other words, *the Judiciary* must exercise a sort of '*conventionality control*' between the domestic legal provisions which are applied to specific cases and the American Convention on Human Rights. To perform this task, the Judiciary has to take into account not only the treaty, but also the interpretation thereof made by the Inter-American Court, which is *the ultimate interpreter* of the American Convention.[23]

The conventionality control doctrine initiated in *Almonacid-Arellano* embraces at least two implications for rethinking the relationship between international and domestic law. The first implication is what the present author calls the *constitutionalisation of international adjudication*. Just as the San José Court characterises itself as 'the ultimate interpreter' of the

---

21 *Almonacid-Arellano and Others v Chile*, IACtHR, Series C No. 154, Judgment on Preliminary Objections, Merits, Reparations and Costs of 26 September 2006, para 119.

22 Ibid. para. 122.

23 Ibid. paras 123–125 (emphases added).

ACHR, a human rights court behaves as a regional constitutional court that makes authoritative interpretations and conducts judicial review of national acts within Convention orders.[24] Alternatively, human rights courts are expected to 'focus more on the public, even *constitutional* aim of the regime in which they operate than they do on dispute settlement'.[25] In this context, human rights courts 'exercise *constitutional* functions in the sense that they may interfere significantly with activities of national legislative, executive, and judicial national organs'.[26] There is, in fact, the *constitutionalisation* of the Inter-American law phenomenon, in which the IACtHR performs 'much like a constitutional court, to "invite itself" into the member States' legal systems in order to force them to conform to the Convention'.[27] Similarly, the ECtHR has increasingly engaged in *constitutional justice* beyond individual justice to the extent that '[s]tates are routinely required to reform their internal law and practices in response to findings of violations by the Court'.[28]

---

24 Alec Stone Sweet, 'Sur la constitutionalisation de la Convention européenne des droits de l'homme : cinquante ans après son installation, la Cour européenne des droits de l'homme conçue comme une cour constitutionnelle' (2009) 77 *Revue trimestrielle des droits de l'homme* 923–944; Catherine Van de Heyning, 'Constitutional Courts as Guarantees of Fundamental Rights: The Constitutionalisation of the Convention through Domestic Constitutional Adjudication' in Patricia Popelier, Armen Mazmayan and Werner Vandenbruwaene (eds), *The Role of Constitutional Courts in Multilevel Governance* (Intersentia 2013) 21–48; Laurence Burgorgue-Larsen, 'La Corte Interamericana de Derechos Humanos como tribunal constitucional' in Armin von Bogdandy, Héctor Fix-Flerro and Mariela Morales Antoniazzi (eds), *Ius Constitutionale Commune en América Latina: Rasgos, Potencialidades y Desafíos* (Universidd Nacional Autótonoma de México 2014) 421–457; Ariel Dulitzky, 'An Inter-American Constitutional Court? The Invention of the Conventionality Control by the Inter-American Court of Human Rights' (2015) 50 *Texas International Law Journal* 45–93.

25 Dinah Shelton, 'Form, Function, and the Powers of International Courts' Chin. J. Int'l L. 9 (2009), 537–571, 564 (emphasis added).

26 Geir Ulfstein, 'The International Judiciary' in Jan Klabbers, Anne Peters and Geir Ulfstein, *The Constitutionalization of International Law* (Oxford University Press 2009) 126–152, 127 (emphasis added).

27 Ludovic Hennebel, 'The Inter-American Court of Human Rights: The Ambassador of Universalism' (2011) *Quebec Journal of International l Law (Special Edition)* 57–97, 71–76 (emphasis added).

28 Keller, Helen and Stone Sweet, Alec, 'Assessing the Impact of the ECHR on National Legal Systems' in Helen Keller and Alec Stone Sweet (eds), *A Europe of Rights: The Impact of the ECHR on National Legal Systems* (Oxford University Press 2008) 677–710, 703 (emphasis added).

The second implication is, in contrast, what the present author terms the *internationalisation of constitutional adjudication*. As predicted based on Georges Scelle's *dédoublement fonctionnel* theory, the institutional deficiencies that affect global governance still require domestic courts to promote international goals.[29] In the context of European integration, the *Simmenthal* judgement mandated that all national judges as the ordinary judges of Community law set aside national law that conflicted with EU law.[30] The *Simmenthal* doctrine may be applied to characterise domestic courts as the ordinary judge of international law.[31] Indeed, international law increasingly designates domestic judges as 'natural judges' of international law to ensure the opportunity for the state to comply with its international obligations.[32] Domestic courts specifically assume an important role in 'review[ing] the legality of national acts in the light of international obligations and ensuring rule-conformity'.[33] According to this statement, domestic courts are required to reconcile the traditional domestic task of constitutionality control and the new international mission of conventionality control. Human rights conventions are in reality becoming integrated into national constitutions, and thereby, domestic courts are becoming empowered to exercise constitutionality control by applying both national and international criteria.[34] In line with the *Simmenthal* doctrine, the conventionality control doctrine purports to convert domestic judges into 'primary and authentic guardians' of the legal orders established by human rights treaties.[35]

---

29 Yuval Shany, '*Dédoublement fonctionnel* and the Mixed Loyalties of National and International Judges' in Filippo Fontanelli, Giuseppe Martinico and Paolo Carrozza (eds), *Shaping Rule of Law Through Dialogue* (Europa Law Publishing 2010) 27–44, 36.

30 Case 106/77, *Amministrazione delle Finanze dello Stato v. Simmenthal SpA* [1978] ECR 629, at paras 21–22. See also, Monica Claes, *The National Courts' Mandate in the European Constitution* (Hart 2006) 102.

31 El Boudouhi, 'The National Judge as an Ordinary Judge of International Law? Invocability of Treaty Law in National Courts' (2015) 28 *Leiden Journal of International Law* 283–301, 283–286.

32 Antonios Tzanakopoulos, 'Domestic Courts in International Law: The International Judicial Function of National Courts' (2011) 34 *Loyola of Los Angeles International and Comparative Law Review* 133–168, at 152.

33 André Nollkaemper, *National Courts and the International Rule of Law* (Oxford University Press 2012) 10.

34 Carlos Ayala Corao, *Del diálogo jurisprudencial al Control de Convencionalidad* (Editorial Jurídica Venezolana 2012) 90.

35 Concurring Opinion of Judge *ad hoc* Eduardo Ferrer MacGregor, *Cabrera Garcia and Montiel Flores v Mexico*, IACtHR, Series C No 220, Judgment on Preliminary

Can existing theories sufficiently elucidate such a dynamic synergy between 'constitutionalised international adjudication' and 'internationalised constitutional adjudication' illuminated by the doctrine of conventionality control? As is well known, dualist and monist scholars have debated the *validity* of international and domestic law. *Dualism* presupposes the independent character of the international and domestic orders.[36] Nevertheless, complete and reciprocal independence between these two orders has also been challenged, particularly in relation to the field of State responsibility that necessitates appreciation of the conformity between international and domestic law.[37] *Monism* alternatively perceives a hierarchical unity between the international and domestic legal orders.[38] In reality, however, these two legal orders differ from each other in terms of validities because the legal effects of domestic law cannot be denied directly due to its incompatibility with international law.

To avoid such dogmatic confusion, scholars have suggested practice-oriented approaches that examine 'the relationship between international and domestic law'. Sir Gerald Fitzmaurice noted that what may occur between international and domestic law is not a conflict of 'systems' but a conflict of 'obligations', which are regulated by the rules of State responsibility.[39] From a practical viewpoint, Başak Çalı has recently advocated a *reflexive authority* of international law before domestic courts to overcome the limits of the traditional monism–dualism debate by categorising in greater

---

Objection, Merits, Reparations and Legal Costs of 26 November 2010, para. 24. As regards the relationship between the *Simmenthal* doctrine and the *control de convencionalidad* doctrine, see Jânia Maria Lopes Saldanha and Lucas Pacheco Vieira, 'Controle jurisdictional de convencionalidade e reenvio prejudicial interamericano: Um diálogo de ferramentas processuais em favor da efetivação do direito internacional dos direitos humanos' (2013) 19 *Anuario de derecho constitucional latinoamericano* 435–460, 438–440.

36 Heinrich Triepel, 'Les rapports entre le droit interne et le droit international' (1923) 1 *Recueil des cours* 73–122, 82–87; Dionisio Anzilotti, (traduit par Gilbert Gidel), *Cours de droit international, Premier Volume: Introduction : Théorie génerales* (Sirey 1929) 51.

37 Paul Guggenheim, *Traité de droit international public*, 2e éd., (Tome I, Librairie de l'Université, Georg & Cie S. A. 1967) 53–54.

38 Hans Kelsen, *Principles of International Law*, 2nd ed. (Revised and Edited by Robert W Tucker) (Holt, Rinehart and Winston 1967) 562.

39 Gerald Fitzmaurice, 'The General Principles of international Law: Considered from the Standpoint of the Rule of Law' (1957-II) 92 *Recueil des cours* 1–228, 79–80. See also, Charles Rousseau, 'Principes de droit international public' (1958-I) 93 *Recueil des cours* 369–550, 473; James Crawford, *Brownlie's Principles of Public International Law*, 8th ed (Oxford University Press 2012) 50, 110–111.

detail the scope and extent (strong, weak or rebuttable) of the authority claim of international law.[40] Domestic judges are under the duty to disregard domestic law manifestly incompatible with a strict international legal obligation.[41] Moreover, they are given a certain amount of discretion to implement international law when confronted with a weak obligation of international law, or even may set aside a rebuttable international legal mandate.[42]

However, the doctrine of conventionality control has an uncharted potential to resurrect theoretical debates beyond considering practical tasks. Indeed, conventionality control does not simply denote, as the 'coordination' doctrine explains, each practice of coordinating a specific conflict that arises between international and national law; it more fundamentally involves, as the 'validity' doctrine such as dualism and monism argued, the theoretical momentum to reconstruct the overall relationship between the international and national legal orders. To cite the famous *Barrios Altos* and *La Cantuta* judgements against Peru concerning the self-amnesty or blanket amnesty laws by which perpetrators or responsible regimes grant themselves or their members immunity from prosecution, the IACtHR declared that '[o]wing to the manifest incompatibility of self-amnesty laws and the ACHR, the said laws lack legal effect'.[43] Antonio Cassese insightfully put forward Alfred Verdross' *moderate monism* theory by considering the IACtHR's jurisprudence of conventionality control in these decisions invalidating domestic law that is inconsistent with international law.[44] However, former judge Sergio García-Ramírez retained the dualistic position in his separate opinion, stating, '[i]t is not the inter-American Court's but the State's place to answer this question [concerning the means through which the State should do away with any unconventional laws], *i.e.* to analyse and implement the decision that will lead to the intended end, which is the elimination of any potential effect of a legal

40 Başak Çalı, *The Authority of International Law: Obedience, Respect, and Rebuttal* (Oxford University Press 2015) 146–157.

41 Ibid.

42 Ibid.

43 *Barrios Altos v Peru*, IACtHR, Series C No. 75, Judgment on Merits of 14 March 2001, para 44.

44 Antonio Cassese, 'Towards a Moderate Monism: Could International Eventually Acquire the Force to Invalidate Inconsistent National Law?' in in Antonio Cassese (ed), *Realizing Utopia: The Future of International Law* (Oxford University Press 2012) 187–199, 198.

provision that is incompatible with the Convention'.[45] The doctrine of conventionality control, therefore, cannot be accurately grasped by either the *static validity* theory or the *practical coordination* theory but rather by the *dynamic process* theory.[46]

In essence, the present volume analyses the doctrine of conventionality control that exposes a parallel dynamism between 'constitutionalised international adjudication' and 'internationalised constitutional adjudication'. The adoption of normative settings of constitutionalism does not mean that the book conducts a purely value-oriented analysis that might lead to an unrealistic utopia. Rather, practical moments are evaluated to the maximum extent 'as an empirical point of departure for mapping specific normative claims as well as identifying the actorship involved in raising these claims'.[47] This book therefore takes an approach that integrates both empirical and normative viewpoints because its ultimate aim is to capture the dynamic process where observable judicial practices suggest the value-oriented convergence of different legal orders.[48] Put differently, this project aims at establishing one normative model of conventionality control that is based on the currently existing human rights adjudicatory practices at the international and domestic levels, and will be subject to further elaboration in view of future empirical developments.

---

45 Separate Opinion of Judge Sergio García-Ramírez, *La Cantuta v Peru*, IACtHR, Series C No 162, Judgment on Merits, Reparations and Costs 29 November 2006, para 4.

46 For the three types of theory, Teraya, Koji, 'Shijinkan Koryoku to "Kokusaiho" no Siko Yoshiki: Kenpogaku to Kokusaihogaku no Dosyoimu [Horizontal Application Theories and "International Law" Thinking: Strange Bedfellows in the Disciplines of Constitutional Law and International Law]' (2012) 23 *Kokusai Jinken [Human Rights International]* 9–15, 11 (in Japanese).

47 In the context of pouvoir constituant 'unbound' by the State, Antje Wiener and Stefan Oeter, 'Introduction: Who recognizes the emperor's clothes anymore?' (2016) 14 *International Journal of Constitutional Law* 608–621, 611–614.

48 For the necessity to integrate both empirical and normative analyses, see Anne Peters, 'Realizing Utopia as a Scholarly Endeavour' (2013) 24 *European Journal of International Law* 533–552, 551–552.

2. *Research Materials and Frameworks*

A. International and Constitutional Adjudications in Europe and Latin America

Against the background of the above-mentioned research problems, the following section demarcates the limits of research materials based on which empirical analyses are conducted. It is notable for this purpose that the San José Court does not restrict the doctrine of conventionality control only mandated to *judges* under the *American Convention*; rather, it broadly formulates an obligation of *a contracting state as a whole* under *international treaty law in general*:

> When a State has ratified an international treaty such as the American Convention, the judges are also subject to it; this obliges them to ensure that the *effet util* of the Convention is not reduced or annulled by the application of laws contrary to its provisions, object and purpose.[49]

The general statement corresponds to the recommendations contained in the *Guidelines* of the ILA Committee on International Human Rights Law that '[c]onstitutional and supreme courts develop and practice *control of conventionality*'.[50] Although this book admits that the potential of conventionality control needs to be comprehensively studied, it consciously limits its scope to *judicial* practices in *regional* human rights systems, particularly in *Europe* and *Latin America*, for the following reasons.

Through gaining lessons from the doctrine of *constitutionality control*, the book deals principally with conventionality control achieved by judicial adjudicators. In most constitutional systems worldwide, judicial bodies are explicitly empowered to guarantee respect for their constitutional pro-

---

49 *The Dismissed Congressional Employees (Aguado-Alfaro and Others) v Peru*, IACtHR, Series C No 158, Preliminary Objections, Merits, Reparations and Costs, Judgment of 24 November 2006, para 128.

50 Guidelines: The Obligations of a State and Its Domestic Courts with Respect to a Decision Issued by an International Judicial or Quasi-judicial Body Involving International Human Rights Law, annexed to *Johannesburg Conference Resolution No. 2/2016*, the Committee on International Human Rights Law, the 77th Conference of the International Law Association, held in Johannesburg, South Africa, 7–11 August 2016, para 9(a).

visions and principles.[51] Generally speaking, the purposes of constitutional adjudication by national courts include ensuring that the legislature does not overstep constitutional boundaries; protecting the fundamental rights of individuals in specific cases; resolving institutional disputes; and ensuring the integrity of political office and related issues.[52] Therefore, it can be concluded that conventionality control aimed at protecting human rights and maintaining a treaty-based legal order is primarily entrusted to judges who assume the function of maintaining the law.

The author is fully aware that focusing on judicial conventionality control may be subject to the criticism of international adjudication-centrism. Yasuaki Onuma questions the *judiciary-centric culture* as a corollary of international legal studies based on the domestic model.[53] Despite there still being a significant gap between norms of adjudication and conduct at the international level in contrast to the domestic systems of developed countries, international legal scholars tend to unconsciously regard international law as a set of norms of adjudication.[54] Nevertheless, these criticisms do not necessarily discourage the approach taken in this monograph but rather promote its significance in analysing the parallel phenomena of international and constitutional adjudication. In fact, Onuma does not reject the increasing roles played by norms of adjudication against the backdrop of the recent pluralisation of international courts and tribunals.[55] His idea also has parallels with the present monograph in his warning that we should not overlook the important roles of international judicial bodies for various functions other than dispute settlement.[56]

In confining this discussion to judicial practices, the author does not intend to disregard the political competences for attaining conventionality control. Even at the national level, in accordance with the constitutional principle of separation of powers, the roles and responsibilities for constitutionality control are allocated to political organs as well as national

---

51 Tom Ginsburg, 'The Global Spread of Constitutional Review', in Gregory A Keleman, R Daniel Kelemen and Keith E Whittington (eds), *Oxford Handbook of Law and Politics* (Oxford University Press 2008) 81–98.

52 Maartje de Visser, *Constitutional Review in Europe: A Comparative Analysis* (Hart 2014), Chapter 3.

53 ONUMA Yasuaki, *International Law in a Transcivilizational World* (Cambridge University Press 2017) 22–25.

54 Ibid.

55 Ibid 579–587.

56 Ibid.

tribunals.[57] The same is equally true of conventionality control, as represented by the second category of general obligations to harmonise domestic law with human rights conventions that is directed at the political sector. Despite its significance, political conventionality control is ultimately characterised as supplementary to judicial conventionality control for the purpose of protecting human rights.

The book furthermore narrows its focus to the judicial control of national law within *regional* human rights systems, precisely, two human rights courts, the *European Court* and the *Inter-American Court of Human Rights*. These two regional courts have developed ample jurisprudence as regards conventionality control, which falls within the scope of analytical objects here. The limited range of the empirical analysis entails three exclusive implications. First, the book does not include the African Court on Human and People's Rights because, albeit theoretically and practically interesting, it has not necessarily accumulated sufficient case law with regard to the conventionality control of national acts of States Parties in comparison to the ECtHR and IACtHR.[58] Second, the author does not directly deal with courts and tribunals established in the context of regional integration, although they often behave as human rights courts to protect the fundamental rights of regional communities (e.g. the ATJ in the Andean Community,[59] the Caribbean Court of Justice of the Caribbean Community,[60] the Central American Court of Justice, the ECOWAS Com-

57 In Japan, for example, when the Diet introduces a statute, the Legislation Bureau of the Cabinet Office checks the bill's compatibility and consistency with the Constitution, existing law, and international obligations. See Hiromichi Matsuda, 'International Law in Japanese Courts' in Curtis Bradley (ed), *The Oxford Handbook of Comparative Foreign Relations Law* (Oxford University Press 2019) 537–548, 541.

58 Amos O Enabulele 'Incompatibility of National Law with the African Charter on Human and Peoples' Rights: Does the African Court on Human and Peoples' Rights Have the Final Say' (2016) 16 *African Human Rights Law Journal* 1–28.

59 Karen J Alter and Laurence R Helfer (eds), *Transplanting International Courts: The Law and Politics of the Andean Tribunal of Justice* (Oxford University Press 2017).

60 Salvatore Caserta, *International Courts in Latin America and the Caribbean: Foundations and Authority* (Oxford University Press 2020).

munity Court of Justice,[61] the East African Court of Justice,[62] the SADC Tribunal[63]). Exceptionally, due to its close relationship with the ECtHR, the CJEU jurisprudence regarding fundamental rights protection is considered.[64] Third, the book does not refer to the practices of human rights committees established under UN-related treaties. Although those treaty bodies may exercise quasi-judicial powers through the procedure of individual complaints, the non-legal binding nature of their view should be examined from a theoretically different viewpoint from the jurisprudence of human rights courts.[65]

The crucial problem for the present aim of the book is the *comparability* or *commensurability* between regional human rights systems, which have created different epistemic communities.[66] In his seminal paper, Oscar Schachter wrote that 'the professional community of international lawyers [...], though dispersed throughout the world and engaged in diverse occupations, constitutes a kind of invisible college dedicated to a common intellectual enterprise'.[67] Such an invisible college as the 'homeland of the people of international law' allows international lawyers to imagine themselves as the *conscience juridique* of everyone else.[68] In the process of

---

61 Obiora C Okafor and Okechukwu J Effoduh, 'The ECOWAS Court as a (Promising) Resource for Pro-Poor Activist Forces: Sovereign Hurdles, Brainy Relays, and "Flipped Strategic Social Constructivism"' in James Thuo Gathii (eds), The Performance of Africa's International Courts: Using Litigation for Political, Legal, and Social Change (Oxford University Press 2020) 106–148; Olabisi Akinkugbe, 'Towards an Analysis of the Mega-Political Jurisprudence of the ECOWAS Community Court of Justice' ibid 149–177.

62 Andrew Heinrich, 'Sub-Regional Courts as Transitional Justice Mechanisms: The Case of the East African Court of Justice in Burundi' ibid 88–105.

63 Frederick Cowell, 'The Death of the Southern African Development Community Tribunals Human Rights Jurisdiction' (2013) 13 *Human Rights Law Review* 153–165.

64 Gráinne de Búrca, 'After the EU Charter of Fundamental Rights: The Court of Justice as a Human Rights Adjudicator?' (2013) 13 *Maastricht Journal of European and Comparative Law* 168–184.

65 General Comment No 33 on Obligations of States parties under the Optional Protocol to the International Covenant on Civil and Political Rights, HRC, UN Doc CCPR/C/GC/33 (2009), para 11.

66 On the notion of commensurability in comparative international law, see Jean d'Aspremont, 'Comparativism and Colonizing Thinking in International Law' (2019) 57 *Canadian Yearbook of International Law* 89–112.

67 Oscar Schachter, 'The Invisible College of International Lawyers' (1977–78) 72 Northwestern University Law Review 217–226.

68 Zoran Oklopčić, *Beyond the People: Social Imaginary and Constituent Imagination* (Oxford University Press 2018) 223–226.

co-constituting their home, however, international lawyers also have the transgressive experience of 'divisible college', as coined by Anthea Roberts in opposition to Schachter's 'invisible college'.[69] The relativist term describes the diversity of epistemic communities, 'whose members hail from different states and regions and often from separate, though sometimes overlapping, communities with their own understandings and approaches, as well as their own distinct influences and spheres of influence'.[70] Similarly, Lauri Mälksoo asks an interesting question: 'are international lawyers globally really all in the same college or temple? Perhaps instead there are a number of fragmented colleges, epistemic communities, speaking each a different language or at least dialect of the same language, and thinking they are "predominant" while being relatively ignorant about the others'.[71]

Maintaining a consciousness of distinctive epistemic communities, the monograph reflects an appreciation of the situationality of regional human rights systems. In the context of international law, as a result of the ultimate denial of solipsism, 'an international lawyer is faced with the entire situational interconnectedness—both in terms of other disciplines of scholarship and in terms of his own personal being'.[72] With such a situationality, as Martti Koskenniemi says, 'a serious comparative study of international law would contribute to [...] seeing all players as both universal and particular at the same time, speaking a shared language, but doing that from their own, localizable standpoint'.[73] Put another way, in the determined words of Andrea Leiter, 'international law is a practice that cannot provide such comfort' but rather 'holding on to the uncertainty in decision-making and the multiple means of meaning-making available at any given moment, holding on to the situatedness of the practice without

69 On the notion of Divisible College, see Andrea Carcano, 'Uses and Possible Misuses of a Comparative International Law Approach' (2018) 54 *Questions of International Law* 21–38; Miriam Bak McKenna, 'Decentering the Universal: Comparative International Law and Decolonizing Critique' (2018) 12 *ESIL Conference Paper Series* 1–25.

70 Anthea Roberts, *Is International Law International?* (Oxford University Press 2017) 2.

71 Lauri Mälksoo, 'International Legal Theory in Russia: A Civilizational Perspective, or: Can Individuals Be Subjects of International Law?' in Florian Hoffmann and Anne Orford (eds), *The Oxford Handbook on the Theory of International Law* (Oxford University Press 2016) 257–275, 273.

72 Outi Korhonen, 'New International Law: Silence, Defence or Deliverance?' (1996) 7 *European Journal of International Law* 1–28, 14.

73 Martti Koskenniemi, The Case for Comparative International Law' (2009) 20 *Finnish Yearbook of International Law* 1–8.

resorting to nihilism, is the task of the international lawyer'.[74] Therefore, the dialect between universality and particularity denotes 'the role of international lawyers as a discursive bridge, passing back and forth to facilitate interaction and understanding between the national and transnational'.[75]

Significant disparities have existed between the European and Inter-American human rights systems. As the following explanation summarises, one of the most crucial differences is the political context within which the two mechanisms operate: 'Whereas the European system has during its forty year history generally regulated democracies with independent judiciaries and governments that observe the rule of law, the history of much of the Americas since 1960 has been radically different, with military dictators, the violent repression of political opposition and of terrorism and intimidate judiciaries for a while being the order of the day in a number of countries'.[76] Consequently, the European system has principally dealt with 'qualified' rights (Articles 8–11), the interference in which is justified through the balance between individual and community interests in relatively consolidated democratic countries.[77] The Inter-American system, in contrast, has had to address gross and systematic human rights violations, such as forced disappearances, arbitrary detentions, extrajudicial executions and torture in the context of dictatorship and internal armed conflicts.

Notwithstanding such a historical discrepancy, we should not overlook the recent convergence of political contexts. Christina Cerna detects the *Europeanisation of the Inter-American system*, in which 'petitions presented in recent years concern problems common to most democratic states, such as violations of due process, delays in judicial proceedings, disputes over property rights, and status questions (e.g. loss of employment, decrease in pension, and the like)'.[78] At the same time, Cerna rightly identifies the

74 Andrea Leiter, 'Review Essay: Is International Law International? by Anthea Roberts' (2018) 19 *Melbourne Journal of International Law* 413–422, 421.

75 Gleider Hernández, '*E Pluribus Unum?* A Divisible College?: Reflections on the International Legal Profession' (2018) 29 *European Journal of International Law* 1003–1022, 1021–1022.

76 Henry J Steiner, Philip Alston and Ryan Goodman, *International Human Rights in Context: Law, Politics, Morals : Text and Materials*, 3rd ed (Oxford University Press 2008) 1027.

77 Sarah Maringele, *European Human Rights Law: The Work of the European Court of Human Rights Illustrated by an Assortment of Selected Cases* (Anchor Academic Publishing 2014) 44.

78 Christina M Cerna, 'The Inter-American System for the Protection of Human Rights' (2004) 16 *Florida Journal of International Law* 195–212, 201–203.

Latin-Americanisation of the European system, which 'deal[s] with different violations due to the composition of the newly democratic governments of the new member states of the Council of Europe [...] such as the conflict in Russia with Chechen rebels, and the incidents of torture in Turkey'.[79] As a result of such a coming together, as will be demonstrated in the following chapters, the number of comparative analyses between the European and Inter-American human rights systems has actually been increasing in the academic literature.

Against the similar backgrounds of systemic human rights violations caused by unconventional domestic law, domestic and regional courts have engaged in conventionality control. As a fundamental similarity, both systems aim at the collective enforcement of human rights beyond the reciprocal exchange of rights for the mutual benefit of the Contracting States.[80] As Strasbourg judge Lech Garlicki highlights, there have been certain instances where the European Court faced the question of the conventionality of domestic legal norms, and therefore, had to establish whether a national norm conformed with the European Convention.[81] Because the existing literature on the national implementation of human rights treaties has centred on European practices, the concept has been only fragmentarily examined. Although Latin American scholars have been interested in this notion, their analyses are generally limited to the regional context and ignore any comparability beyond the Americas.[82] Only a few authors in the existing literature have attempted to compare the Inter-American doctrine of conventionality control with the European practice; therefore, the research remains embryonic.[83] This monograph, then, fills the gap in

79 Ibid.

80 *Ireland v the United Kingdom*, ECtHR (Plenary), App no 5310/71, Judgment on Merits of 18 January 1978, para 239; *"Other Treaties" Subject to the Consultative Jurisdiction of the Court (Art. 64 American Convention on Human Rights)*, IACtHR, Series A No 1, OC-1/82, Advisory Opinion of 24 September 1982, para 29.

81 Lech Garlicki, 'Contrôle de constitutionnalité et contrôle de conventionnalité : sur le dialogue des juges' in *La conscience des droits : Mélanges en l'honneur de Jean-Paul Costa* (Dalloz 2011) 271–280, 278–280.

82 Pablo González-Domínguez, *The Doctrine of Conventionality Control: Between Uniformity and Legal Pluralism in the Inter-American Human Rights System* (Intersentia 2018).

83 Gonzalo Aguilar Cavallo, 'El control de convencionalidad; análisis en derecho comparado' (2013) 9 *Revista Direito GV* 721–754; Néstor Pedro Sagüés, 'El "control de convencionalidad" en el sistema interamericano, y sus anticipos en el ámbito de los derechos económico-sociales: concordancias y diferencias con el sistema europeo' in Armin von Bogdandy, Héctor Fix-Fierro, Mariela Morales

comparative law research on international and constitutional law by empirically analysing the regional and domestic practice of conventionality control and normatively envisions a model thereof.[84]

B. Conventionality Control Parameters and Powers

To elaborate the structure of conventionality control, the book returns once again to the jurisprudence of the San José Court as the principal advocate of this international legal obligation. In the *Dismissed Congressional Employees* case, the IACtHR further clarified the manner and scope of conventionality control as follows:

> [T]he organs of the Judiciary should exercise not only a control of constitutionality, but also of 'conventionality' *ex officio* between domestic norms and the American Convention; evidently in the context of their respective spheres of competence and the corresponding procedural regulations.[85]

This explanation is highly suggestive for establishing analytical frameworks as regards to conventionality control. Concretely speaking, the Court refers to the control of domestic law following both the constitutional and the conventional *parameters*, which is achieved through the *powers* of domestic courts and a human rights court. As **Chart 1** below indicates, the book accordingly establishes the frameworks of *parameters* (Chapter 1) and *powers* (Chapter 2) of conventionality control in relation to the 'constitutionalisation of international adjudication' (Part I) and the 'internationalisation of constitutional adjudication' (Part II). After empirically inspecting the judicial practices in question (Section 1), each chapter makes normative claims in terms of constitutionalism and legal pluralism (Section 2).

Antoniazzi and Eduardo Ferrer Mac-Gregor (eds), *Construcción y papel de los derechos sociales fundamentales: Hacia un ius constitucionale commune en América Latina* (Instituto de Investigaciones Jurídicas 2011) 993–1030.

84 Anja Seibert-Fohr, 'Judicial Engagement in International Human Rights Comparativism' in August Reinisch, Mary E Footer and Christina Binder (eds), *International Law and...: Select Proceedings of the European Society of International Law*, Vol 5, (Hart 2014) 7–24.

85 *The Dismissed Congressional Employees (Aguado-Alfaro and Others) v Peru* (n 49) para 128.

The first analytical framework concerns the relationship of norms: the *parameters* as the yardstick by which conventionality control of domestic law is achieved. To elucidate the criteria, it is useful to borrow the concept of *block* that the French *Conseil constitutionnel* has developed as the parameter for constitutionality control. The concept *bloque de constitutionalidad* has been subsequently used by several constitutional courts in Latin America.[86]

Part 1 – Chapter 1: The first aspect of the constitutionalisation of international adjudication is that human rights courts are authorised to interpret the parameters through which the compatibility between national legislation and the Conventions is assessed. Since they originated, human rights courts had been limited to the interpretation and application of the provisions of the Conventions (and relevant protocols). Notwithstanding these *formal* limits, the ECtHR and the IACtHR have broken away from the *closed* position of adhering to the regional framework. As guardians of conventions-based constitutional orders, human rights courts are responsible for interpreting the conventionality block that is generally applied to all States Parties beyond individual contentious cases. In the practice of human rights courts, it is remarkable that external international instruments are referred to, to expand the rights and freedoms of Conventions.

Part 2 – Chapter 1: The first aspect of the internationalisation of constitutional adjudication is that domestic judges are required to exercise control of domestic law in accordance with not only national constitutions but also regional conventions. At the domestic level, the supremacy of international law over domestic law cannot duly answer the question of whether domestic courts can utilise human rights conventions in judicial review. Moreover, human rights conventions and national constitutions share analogous catalogues of rights and freedoms for the most part. Therefore, a judicial review involving fundamental rights would indicate the inevitable coexistence of conventionality control and constitutionality control. When domestic courts find certain domestic provisions incompatible with a treaty and abstain from enforcing them, conventionality control may replace constitutionality control, and the latter's ultimate aim of

86 Manuel Eduardo Góngora Mera, 'La diffusion del bloque de constitucionalidad en la jurisprudencia latinoamericana y su potencial en la construcción del *ius constitutionale commune* latinoamericano' in Armin von Bogdandy, Héctor Fix-Fierro and Mariela Morales Antoniazzi (eds), *Ius constitututionale commune en América Latina: Rasgos, potencialidades y desafíos* (UNAM —IIJ/Institut Max Planck de Derecho Público comparado y Derecho Internacional 2014) 301–324.

ensuring the *supremacy of constitution* may also be undermined. Against this background, national judges have attempted to integrate human rights treaties into national constitutions to converge the parallel judicial control mechanisms.

The second analytical framework deals with the relationship among organs: the *powers* allocated to each organ to achieve conventionality control. To explain the allocation of competence, we can gain inspiration from the categorisation of *centralised* and *decentralised* models of constitutional review.[87] The centralised system confers upon a special institution, mostly the constitutional court, the exclusive authority to settle constitutional matters, and therefore, the powers of ordinary judges are limited to applying and interpreting parliamentary legislations. Following the theoretical foundations provided by Hans Kelsen, the concentrated model of constitutionality review has spread widely in Europe and Latin America. The *decentralised* or *diffused* system grants all judges the power to declare legislation unconstitutional. As a typical example, Chief Justice John Marshall in the 1803 *Marbury v Madison* decision introduced the diffused model of judicial review in the United States.

Part 1 – Chapter 2: The second aspect of the constitutionalisation of international adjudication is that human rights courts perform judicial review of national acts against the yardstick of conventions' parameters. As the structural principle of international human rights law, subsidiarity presumes that the *primary* responsibilities are incumbent on States Parties and that treaty mechanisms are essentially *subsidiary* to domestic systems. As the primary guardians of human rights, States Parties are required to perform general obligations to respect and ensure treaty rights and to align their domestic law and practice in line with treaty criteria. As a literal meaning, the subsidiarity principle governing the allocation of public authority in systems of multilevel governance shows a preference for functions at the lowest level of governance. Inversely, however, subsidiarity reallocates authority to the higher level if, and to the extent that, the higher level is better placed to fulfil the task in question. Considering these *negative* and *positive* aspects, this study demonstrates the dual pattern of power allocation (*centralisation* and *diffusion*) for conventionality control through subsidiarity.

Part 2 – Chapter 2: The second aspect of the internationalisation of constitutional adjudication is that the distribution of powers between con-

87 In general, Mauro Cappelletti, 'Judicial Review in Comparative Perspective' (1970) 58 *California Law Review* 1017–1053.

stitutional and ordinary courts is reallocated in accordance with regional conventions as well as constitutional mandates. In the subsequent jurisprudence, the IACtHR elaborated that the judiciary, at all levels, must exercise *ex officio*, a sort of conventionality control between the domestic legal provisions and the American Convention, evidently within the framework of their respective competence and the corresponding procedural rules. This position embraces both *restrictive* and *permissive* aspects concerning the distribution of competences for conventionality control among domestic courts. As for the *restrictive* aspect, conventionality control must be performed by *all judges*, regardless of their formal membership in the judiciary branch, and regardless of their rank, grade, level or area of expertise. Regarding the *permissive* aspect, States Parties are granted certain discretions to exclusively entrust conventionality control to the *constitutional court* in line with its concentrated powers for constitutionality control.

	Chapter 1 Conventionality Control Parameters	**Chapter 2 Conventionality Control Powers**
Part I Constitutionalisation of International Adjudication	**Interpretation of conventionality control parameters**	**International distribution of conventionality control powers**
Part II Internationalisation of Constitutional Adjudication	**Application of conventionality control parameters**	**Domestic distribution of conventionality control powers**

Chart 1. Research Framework: Conventionality Control Parameters and Powers

Part I
Constitutionalised International Adjudication

Chapter 1
Interpretation of Conventionality Control Parameters

The first aspect of the constitutionalisation of international adjudication is that human rights courts are authorised to interpret the parameters through which the compatibility of national legislation with the Conventions is assessed. In this respect, human rights courts develop a *bloque de convencionalidad* just as a constitutional court interprets a *bloque de constitucionalidad*.[88] More concretely, like other powerful constitutional courts, human rights courts perform an *oracular* function: the nature and scope of Convention rights are identified, clarified and expanded through the Court's pronouncements, over time as circumstances change.[89] The oracular function of human rights courts is primarily based on the *living instrument* doctrine of the *evolutionary interpretation* of treaties.[90] Pierre-Marie Dupuy sharply distinguished the evolutionary interpretation supported by past-oriented memory from the evolutionary interpretation towards future-oriented prophecy.[91] In the latter case, an international judge 'brings to mind the constitutional judge in domestic legal orders' and 'uses individualized disputes to remind all parties of the route that each one of them must follow in order to achieve the collective goal'.[92]

In the practice of human rights courts, it is noteworthy that external international instruments are referred to for the purpose of expanding Convention rights and freedoms. Originally, human rights courts were limited to the interpretation and application of the provisions of the Conventions (and relevant protocols) (Article 32(1) ECHR/Article 62(3) ACHR). Notwithstanding these *formal* limits, the ECtHR and the IACtHR have broken away from the *closed* position of adhering to the regional

88 Burgorgue-Larsen (n 24) 441.

89 Stone Sweet (n 24) 930.

90 See in general, Eirik Bjorge, *The Evolutionary Interpretation of Treaties* (Oxford University Press 2014); Katharina Böth, *Evolutive Auslegung völkerrechtlicher Verträge: Eine Untersuchung zu Voraussetzungen und Grenzen in Anbetracht der Praxis internationaler Streitbeilegungsinstitutionen* (Duncker & Humbolt 2013).

91 Pierre-Marie Dupuy, 'Evolutionary Interpretation of Treaties: Between Memory and Prophecy' in Enzo Cannnizzaro (ed), *The Law of Treaties Beyond the Vienna Convention* (Oxford University Press 2011) 123–137, 131–132.

92 *Ibid.* (both quations).

framework. Instead, both human rights courts demonstrate an *open-minded* attitude towards integrating human rights standards with more protective *substance* established at the universal level. Such a human-centric interpretative method is based on the *pro homine* approach, which offers high priority to the most favourable protection of persons.[93]

Taking this recent trend as a backdrop, the chapter begins by describing recent interpretative practices that bridge regional conventions as living instruments with human rights standards accumulated at the universal level (Section 1-A). It goes on to prove that this practice that extends beyond state consent requires a shift in the source of legitimacy from regional consensus to universal consensus (Section 1-B). To normatively justify such practices, the following section invokes the *pro homine* principle that is reflected in 'more favourable' clauses of human rights conventions. As the horizontal functions regulating regional and universal human rights standards, the *pro homine* principle contributes to the global constitutionalist unification (Section 2-A) and to the legal pluralist diversification (Section 2-B) of international human rights law.

1. Relationship between Regional Conventions and Universal Standards

A. Evolutionary Interpretation of Regional Conventions

(i) Evolutionary Interpretation of Living Instruments

General rules of treaty interpretation are codified in Section 3 (Articles 31–33), Part III of the VCLT. In the metaphor of *playing the game of interpretation*, '[t]he rules contained in the VCLT, and the cluster of concepts therein – including "ordinary meaning", "context", and "object and purpose" – have long provided a focal point for interpretation in international law, and a source of constancy for the international legal profession'.[94] These game rules of treaty interpretation enshrined in the VCLT are characterised as either *volontariste* or *objectiviste*. Alternatively, the voluntarist

---

93 Malgosia Fitzmaurice, 'Interpretation of Human Rights Treaties' in Shelton (n 1) 739–771, 765–767.

94 Daniel Peat and Matthew,' Windsor, Playing the Game of Interpretation: On Meaning and Metaphor in International Law' in Andrea Bianchi, Daniel Peat, and Matthew Windsor (eds), *Interpretation in International Law* (Oxford University Press 2015) 3–33, 3–4.

position emphasises Article 31(3)(a) and (b) that permit interpreters to take into account States Parties' subsequent agreement and practice respectively; and Article 31(4) that provides that '[a] special meaning shall be given to a term if it is established that the parties so intended'.[95] Conversely, the objectivist approach focuses on the terms 'object and purpose'; and the hierarchy between Article 31 and Article 32, the latter of which prescribes the recourse to 'subjective' *supplementary* means of interpretation, that is, the preparatory work of the treaty and the circumstances of its conclusion.[96]

In contrast to the voluntarist approach prioritising the original intent of States Parties, the objectivist approach leads to an evolutionary or dynamic interpretation on the basis of temporal changes in societies. Famously, in *Namibia*, which concerned the self-determination and independence of the people and the *corpus iuris gentium*, the ICJ was 'bound to take into account the fact that the concepts embodied in Article 22 of the Covenant [of the League of Nations – "the strenuous conditions of the modern world" and "the well-being and development" of the peoples concerned] – were not static, but were by definition evolutionary'.[97] Evolutionary interpretation is also recognised in the ILC's topic in the Conclusions on *Subsequent Agreements and Subsequent Practice in Relation to Interpretation of Treaties*. Conclusion 8 stipulates that subsequent agreements and subsequent practice under Articles 31 and 32 may assist in determining whether or not the presumed intention of the parties upon the conclusion of the treaty was to give a used term a meaning that is capable of evolving over time.[98]

The objectivist evolutionary interpretation has been widely accepted in the context of human rights conventions as living instruments. The Human Rights Committee in *Judge v. Canada* states that the ICCPR 'should be interpreted as a *living instrument* and the rights protected under it

95 Olivier Corten, 'Les techniques reproduites aux aritlces 31 à 33 des conventions de Vienne : approche objectivistte ou approche volontariste de l'interprétation?' (2011) 115 *Revue Générale de Droit International Public* 351–366, 352–359.

96 Ibid.

97 *Legal Consequences for States of the Continued Presence of South Africa in Namibia (South West Africa) notwithstanding Security Council Resolution 276 (1970), ICJ Reports 1971*, para 53. See also, *Dispute regarding Navigational and Related Rights (Costa Rica v Nicaragua)*, Judgment, ICJ Reports 2009, para 64.

98 *Report of the International Law Commission*, 70th sess, UN Doc A/73/10, 64–70.

should be applied in context and in the light of present–day conditions'.[99] As is well known, the ECtHR in *Tyrer* characterised that the Convention as '*a living instrument* which [...] must be interpreted in the light of present–day conditions', and therefore, could not 'but be influenced by the developments and commonly accepted standards in the penal policy of the member States of the Council of Europe in this field'.[100] The subsequent *Loizidou v. Turkey* ruling further clarified that the living instrument doctrine 'is not confined to the substantive provisions of the Convention, but also applies to those provisions, such as Articles 25 and 46, which govern the operation of the Convention's enforcement machinery'.[101] In Advisory Opinion OC-16/99 regarding the right to information on consular assistance, the Strasbourg jurisprudence was cited by the IACtHR to articulate that 'human rights treaties are living instruments whose interpretation must consider the changes over time and present–day conditions'.[102]

(ii) Regional Consensus

Within the traditional framework, the legitimate authority of international law has derived from the international system having been composed of the *voluntary association* among States under the *state consent* model.[103] Because such a voluntarist approach to international law may encounter the natural objection that the consent of some states does not reflect the interests of most people in those states, another alternative *democratic association* is currently being pursued under the *democratic state consent* model.[104] The collective systems of human rights protection are based on international law; therefore, human rights bodies necessarily encounter

---

99 *Judge v Canada*, HRC, Communication No 829/1998, UN Doc CCPR/C/78/D/829/1998, View of 13 August 2003, para 10.3 (emphasis added).

100 *Tyrer v the United Kingdom*, ECtHR, App No5856/72, Judgment on Merits of 25 April 1978, para 31.

101 *Loizidou v Turkey*, ECtHR (Grand Chamber), App No 15318/89, Judgment on Preliminary Ojbections of 23 March 1995, para 71.

102 *The Right to Information on Consular Assistance in the Framework of the Guarantees of Due Process of Law*, IACtHR, Series A No 16, Advisory Opinion OC-16/99 of 1 October 1999, para 114.

103 Thomas Christiano, 'Democratic Legitimacy and International Institutions' in Samantha Besson and John Tasioulas (eds), *The Philosophy of International Law* 119–138, 122–126.

104 Ibid 126–137.

the conflict of *interpretación extensiva versus el consentimiento del Estad.*[105] It is therefore necessary to strike an appropriate balance between evolutionary interpretation and *the principle of consent* that has been enshrined as the 'cornerstone' of international law.[106] In practice, when adopting an evolutionary interpretation in the previously mentioned *Judge* case, the HRC was 'mindful of the fact that the above-mentioned jurisprudence was established some 10 years ago, and since that time there has been a broadening international consensus in favour of abolition of the death penalty, and in States which have retained the death penalty, a broadening consensus not to carry it out'.[107]

In Europe, the Strasbourg Court has also justified the adoption of evolutionary interpretation by proving the existence of *consensus* among States Parties. As a paradigmatic explanation, the judgement in *A, B and C v Ireland* stated that '[t]he existence of a consensus has long played a role in the development and evolution of Convention protections beginning with *Tyrer v the United Kingdom* the Convention being considered a "living instrument" to be interpreted in the light of present–day conditions. Consensus has therefore been invoked to justify a dynamic interpretation of the Convention'.[108] Thus, consensus may be conceptualised as an 'updated state consent' that reflects the current state of practice and law in States Parties, and as another legitimising factor for the Court's activities.[109] Judge Ineta Ziemele suggests the interchangeability between *opinio juris* and consensus by noting that the ECtHR is in fact exploring a particular regional custom and subsequent practice when it examines domestic laws and practices.[110]

---

105 Álvaro Franciscco Amaya Villarreal, 'El principio *pro homine*: Interpretación extensiva vs. el consentimiento del Estado' (2005) *Revista Colombiana de Derecho Internacional* 337–380.

106 Hugh Thirlway, *The Sources of International Law* (Oxford University Press 2014) 10–11.

107 *Judge* (n 99) para 10.3.

108 *A, B and C v Ireland,* ECtHR, App No 25579/05, Judgment on Merits and Just Satisfaction of 10 December 2010, para 234.

109 Kanstantsin Dzehtsiarou, *European Consensus and the Legitimacy of the European Court of Human Rights* (Cambridge University Press 2015) 149–155.

110 Concurring Opinion of Judge Ziemele, *Rohlena v Czech Republic*, EctHR (Grand Chamber), Appl. no. 59552/08, Judgment on Merits and Just Satisfaction of 27 January 2015, para 2. See also, Ineta Ziemele, 'European Consensus and International Law' in Anne van Aaken and Iulia Motoc (eds), *The European Convention on Human Rights and General International Law* (Oxford University Press 2018) 23–39.

In contrast, the IACtHR has been reluctant to emphasise the existence of consensus among States Parties in attempting to spell out an evolutionary interpretation of the ACHR. Antonio Augusto Cançado Trindade, former president of the San José Court, insists that 'the majority of the cases before the Court have involved alleged violations to non-derogable rights where no invocation of a margin of appreciation could be conceived'.[111] Gerald Neuman describes the particular situation of Latin America as follows: 'One evident reason for the less frequent reliance on "regional consensus" in the Americas is the comparative prevalence of systematic human rights abuses directed against the core of the protected rights. Setting international standards by reference to actual national practice would risk the adoption of very low targets'.[112] In recent cases, however, the IACtHR has occasionally examined the consensus or generalised practices of States Parties, particularly in cases involving sensitive political decisions, such as access to public information,[113] healthcare[114] and refugees.[115]

B. Interpreting Regional Conventions Through Universal Standards

(i) Evolutionary Interpretation through Universal Standards

A recent remarkable trend in the jurisprudence of human rights courts as regards evolutionary interpretation is that the standards of regional conventions are elevated according to those of external legal sources. In the European system, the ECtHR has robustly established that the provisions of the ECHR are never considered as the sole framework of reference for

---

111 Antonio Augusto Cançado Trindade, *Reflexiones sobre el Futuro del Sistema Interamericano de Protección de los Derechos Humanos*, in Juan E Méndez and Francisco Cox (eds), El futuro del sistema interamericano de protección a los derechos humanos (IIDH 1998) 573–603, 582.

112 Gerald L Neuman, 'Import, Export and Regional Consent in the Inter-American Court of Human Rights' (2008) 19 *European Journal of International Law* 101–123, 107–108.

113 *Claude Reyes v Chile*, IACtHR, Series C No 151, Judgment on Merits, Reparations and Costs of 19 September 2006, para 78.

114 *Artavia Murillo and Othres ('in vitro Fertilization') v Costa Rica*, IACtHR, Seiries C No 257, Judgement on Preliminary Objections, Merits, Reparations and Costs of 28 November 2012, paras. 254–256.

115 *The Pacheco Tineo Family v Plurinational State of Bolivia*, IACtHR, Series C No 272, Judgment on Preliminary Objections, Merits, Reparations and Costs of 25 November 2013, para 158.

the interpretation of the rights and freedoms enshrined therein.[116] One of the most prominent instances in this context is the *Demir and Baykara v Turkey* judgement concerning the rights of municipal civil servants under Article 11 of the ECHR. As a starting point, the ECtHR confirmed the necessity not only to 'promote internal consistency and harmony between its various provisions' but also to 'take into account any relevant rules and principles of international law applicable in relations between the Contracting Parties'.[117] The Court then examined in detail the precedents where other international instruments were relied on for illuminating the content of Convention rights.[118] Eventually, the following passage was presented as a conclusion:

> The Court, in defining the meaning of terms and notions in the text of the Convention, can and must take into account elements of international law other than the Convention, the interpretation of such elements by competent organs, and the practice of European States reflecting their common values.[119]

Based on this statement, the Court induced the general principles concerning the substance of the right of association in light of international law, including ILO Conventions, the ESC (which Turkey had not ratified) and the European Union's Charter of Fundamental Rights.[120]

The *Demir and Baykara* ruling stimulated scholars to reconsider the relationship between the ECHR and other sources of international law in the name of *interprétation globalisante*[121] or *globalisation des sources.*[122] As a particularly notable view, Laurence Burgorgue-Larsen coined the term *décloisonnement des sources* to express the dichotomy between regionalism and universalism:

---

116 *Cyprus v Turkey*, ECtHR (Grand Chamber), App No 25781/94, Judgment on Just Satisfaction of 12 May 2014, para 23.

117 *Demir and Baykara* v. *Turkey*, ECtHR (Grand Chamber), App No 34503/97, Judgment on Merits and Just Satisfaction of 12 November 2008, paras 65–68.

118 Ibid paras 69–84.

119 Ibid para 85.

120 Ibid paras 140–170.

121 Patrick Wachsmann, 'Réflexions sur l'interprétation 'globalisante' de la Convention européenne des droits de l'homme' in *Mélanges en l'honneur de Jean-Paul Costa* (n 81) 667–676.

122 Frédéric Sudre, 'L'interpretation constructive de la liberté syndicale, au sens de l'article 11 de la Convention EDH' (2009) 5 *JCP/La semaine juridique, édition générale* 30–33.

> The use of universal trends generally leads to enrichment of the Convention in relation to its stated objective and purpose; in other words, interpretive enrichment results in benefits for individuals. Interpretation is systematically *pro homine*. [...] *Decompartmentalisation of sources* is far distant from such a static, if not to say conservative, approach. The Convention is, now more than ever, a 'living instrument'. Individual rights are reinforced and *universalism is revisited*.[123]

The IACtHR adopted a more radical approach of evolutionary interpretation. A passage from *Advisory Opinion OC-16/99* in the context of consular assistance manifestly shows the Court's sympathy towards international instruments outside the regional framework:

> The *corpus juris* of international human rights law comprises a set of international instruments of varied content and juridical effects (treaties, conventions, resolutions and declarations). Its dynamic evolution has had a positive impact on international law in affirming and building up the latter's faculty for regulating relations between States and the human beings within their respective jurisdictions. This Court, therefore, must adopt the proper approach to consider this question in the context of the evolution of the fundamental rights of the human person in contemporary international law.[124]

The pursuance of evolutionary interpretation in terms of *corpus juris* of international law is especially significant for people or groups in a situation of *vulnerability*.[125] In the context of migration, for example, *Vélez Loor v Panama*, in line with Advisory Opinion OC-16/99, gave 'essence to the rights enshrined in the Convention, according to the evolution of the international *corpus juris* existing in relation to the human rights of migrants, taking into account that the international community has recognized the

---

123 Laurence Burgorgue-Larsen, '*Nothing is Perfect* : Libres propos sur la méthodologie interpretative de la Cour européenne' in *L'homme et le droit : En hommage au Professeur Jean-François Flauss* (Pedone 2014) 129–143, 131–134.

124 *The Right to Information on Consular Assistance in the Framework of the Guarantees of Due Process of Law* (n 102) para 115.

125 On the concept of vulnerability in the IACtHR jurisprudence, see in general Romina I Sijniensky, 'From the Non-Discrimination Clause to the Concept of Vulnerability in International Human Rights Law: Advancing on the Need for Special Protection of Certain Groups and Individuals' in Yves Haeck, Brianne MacGonigle Leyh, Clara Burbano-Herrera and Diana Contreras-Garduño (eds), *The Realization of Human Rights: When Theory Meets Practice: Studies in Honour of Leo Zwaak* (Intersentia 2013) 259–272.

need to adopt special measures to ensure the protection of the human rights of this group'.[126] Another pertinent example is *Pacheco Tineo Family v Bolivia*, in which the San José Court took 'into account the significant evolution of the principles and regulation of international refugee law, based also on the directives, criteria and other authorized rulings of agencies such as United Nations High Commissioner for Refugees'.[127]

A similar trend occurred in the development of social, economic and cultural rights of indigenous people. At the early stage in *Mayagna (Sumo) Awas Tingni Community v Nicaragua*, the IACtHA deduced an evolutionary interpretation that 'Article 21 of the Convention protects the right to property in a sense which includes, among others, the rights of members of the indigenous communities within the framework of communal property, which is also recognized by the Constitution of Nicaragua'.[128] Subsequently, this decision was reaffirmed in *Yakye Axa Indigenous Community v Paraguay*, with explicit reference to ILO Convention No 169 and the respondent's legislation for its national implementation.[129] *Saramaka People v Suriname* further extended Article 21 to include safeguards (consultation and benefit-sharing) against restrictions on the right to property that deny survival, on the basis of the 2007 United Nations Declaration on the Rights of Indigenous Peoples.[130]

Advancement as regards internally enforced displacement that deserves to be mentioned here. Initially, the IACtHR in *'Mapiripán Massacre' v Colombia* simply adopted an evolutive interpretation that 'Article 22(1) of the ACHR protects the right to not be forcefully displaced within a State Party to the Convention'.[131] In *Ituango Massacres v Colombia*, however, the San José Court explicitly referred to the Guiding Principles on

---

126 *Vélez Loor v Panama*, IACtHR, Series C No 218, Judgment on Preliminary Objections, Merits, Reparations, and Costs of 23 November 2010, para 99.

127 *The Pacheco Tineo Family* (n 115) para 143.

128 *The Mayagna (Sumo) Awas Tingni Community v Nicaragua*, IACtHR, Series C No 79, Judgment on Merits, Reparations and Costs of 31 August 2001, para 148.

129 *The Yakye Axa Indigenous Community v Paraguay*, IACtHR, Series C No 125, Judgment on Merits, Reparations and Costs of 17 June 2005, para 130; Sawhoyamaxa Indigenous Community v Paraguay, IACtHR, Series C No 146, Judgment on Merits, Reparations and Costs. Judgment of 29 March 2006, para 117.

130 *The Saramaka People v Suriname*, IACtHR, Series C No 172, Judgment on Preliminary Objections, Merits, Reparations and Costs of 28 November 2007, paras 129–140; *Kichwa Indigenous People of Sarayaku v. Ecuador*, IACtHR, Series C No. 245, Judgment on Merits and Reparations 27 June 2012, paras. 159–176.

131 *The Mapiripán Massacre v Colombia*, IACtHR, Series C No 134, Judgment on Merits, Reparations and Costs of 15 September 2005, para 188.

Internal Displacement issued by the Representative of the United Nations secretary-general and Protocol II to the 1949 Geneva Conventions as an especially useful instrument for defining the content and scope of Article 22 of the ACHR concerning internal displacement.[132] As a recent example, *Operation Genesis v Colombia* added Article 3, which is common to the Geneva Conventions and customary international humanitarian law, as relevant rules in this context.[133]

The *corpus juris* of international law has been a driving force to enhance the status of economic, social and cultural rights enshrined in Article 26 of the ACHR. In practice, the content of the relevant rights to just and favourable conditions of work[134] and the right to social security[135] were determined in light of special standards, such as the ILO Conventions and the ICESCR's and the CESCR's general comments. In *Indigenous Communities of the Lhaka Honhat Association*, the Inter-American judges again invoked the international *corpus juris* to demarcate the scope of the rights to a healthy environment, adequate food and water, and participation in cultural life under Article 26 of the ACHR.[136]

As these decisions show, the IACtHR, as one of 'regional drivers of the universal',[137] has raised regional Convention standards against the yardstick of the universal *corpus juris* of international law in question.

---

132 *The Ituango Massares v Colombia*, IACtHR, Series C No 148, Judgment on Preliminary Objections, Merits, Reparations and Costs of 1 July 2006, paras 207–210.

133 *The Afro-descendant Communities Displaced from the Cacarica River Basin (Operation Genesis) v Colombia*, IACtHR, Series C No 270, Judgment on Preliminary Objections, Merits, Reparations and Costs, Judgment of 20 November 2013, paras. 217–226.

134 *The Employees of the Fireworks Factory of Santo Antônio de Jesus v Brazil*, IACtHR, Series C No 407, Judgment on Preliminary Objections, Merits, Reparations and Cost of July 15, 2020, para 156. See also, *Lagos del Campo v Peru*, IACtHR, Series C No 340, Judgment on Preliminary Objections, Merits, Reparations and Costs of 31 August 2017, para 145.

135 *The National Association of Discharged and Retired Employees of the National Tax Administration Superintendence (ANCEJUB-SUNAT) v Peru*, IACtHR, Series C No 394, Judgment on Preliminary Objections, Merits, Reparations and Costs of 21 November 2019, para 158.

136 *The Indigenous Communities of the Lhaka Honhat Association (Our Land) v Argentina*, IACtHR, Series C No 400, Judgment on Merits, Reparations and Costs of 6 February 2020, paras 194–198.

137 Chaloka Beyani, 'Reconstituting the Universal: Human Rights as a Regional Idea' in Conor Gearty and Costas Douzinas (eds), *The Cambrdige Companion to Human Rights Law* (Cambridge University Press 2012) 173–190.

From a different angle, Hélène Tigroudja argues convincingly that 'even if the Inter-American Court was established to control the implementation of a specific treaty, the ACHR, its task is *formally* bound by this regional Convention, but from a *material* point of view the Court perceives itself as a *Human Rights* Tribunal before being a *Regional* Body'.[138] It should be reminded that even in the initial Advisory Opinion OC-1/82, the San José Court showed the inherent sign of such an approach of bridging regional and universal standards. This opinion contained two conflicting interpretations about the meaning of 'other treaties' subject to the Court's consultative jurisdiction under Article 64: the narrowest interpretation that leads to the conclusion that only those treaties adopted within the framework or under the auspices of the Inter-American system are deemed within the scope; and the broadest interpretation that includes within the Court's advisory jurisdiction any treaty concerning the protection of human rights in which one or more American States are Parties.[139] The Court itself favoured the latter interpretation as follows:

> The nature of the subject matter itself, however, *militates against a strict distinction between universalism and regionalism*. Mankind's universality and the universality of the rights and freedoms which are entitled to protection form the core of all international protective systems. In this context, it would be improper to make distinctions based on the regional or non-regional character of the international obligations assumed by States, and thus deny the existence of the common core of basic human rights standards.[140]

In sum, both regional courts, when invoking the living instrument doctrine of evolutionary interpretation, have abandoned the *closed* and *formal* regional paradigm and taken an *open-minded* stance seeking *substantively* more favourable protection at the universal level of human rights protection.

---

138 Hélène Tigroudja, 'The Inter-American Court of Human Rights and International Humanitarian Law' in Robert Kolb and Gloria Gaggioli (eds), *Research Handbook of Human Rights and Humanitarian Law* (Edward Elgar 2013) 466–479, 473–474 (emphasis in the original text).

139 *'Other Treaties' Subject to the Consultative Jurisdiction of the Court* (n 80) para 32.

140 Ibid para 40 (emphasis added).

(ii) Universal Consensus

In parallel with the recent practice of connecting the regional Conventions in light of universal standards, human rights courts have sought an *emerging consensus*, rather than that among States Parties, as the legitimate source of evolutionary interpretation.[141] In *Demir and Baykara*, the ECtHR placed emphasis on emerging consensus and *common ground in modern societies* beyond the European region:

> The consensus emerging from *specialised international instruments* and from the practice of Contracting States may constitute a relevant consideration for the Court when it interprets the provisions of the Convention in specific cases. In more concrete terms, the Court clarified that 'it is not necessary for the respondent State to have ratified the entire collection of instruments that are applicable in respect of the precise subject matter of the case concerned. It will be sufficient for the Court that the *relevant international instruments* denote a continuous evolution in the norms and principles applied in international law or in the domestic law of the majority of member States of the Council of Europe and show, in a precise area, that there is *common ground in modern societies*'.[142]

As Burgorgue-Larsen points out, '[t]he "common ground" that the Court referred in [this] paragraph [...] of its judgment was unquestionably universal in scope'.[143] Indeed, the Court made a caveat against the respondent's claim, stating that 'in searching for *common ground among the norms of international law* it has never distinguished between sources of law according to whether or not they have been signed or ratified by the respondent State'.[144]

Another significant instance being placed in the same stream is the evolution of case law concerning the rights of sexual minorities. In the first stage *Rees v the United Kingdom*, the ECtHR could find little 'common

---

141 For the criticisms and problems of this approach, see Shai Dothan, *International Judicial Review: When Should International Courts Intervene?* (Cambridge University Press 2020) 41–60.

142 *Demir and Baykara* (n 117) para 86 (emphasis added).

143 Laurence Burgorgue-Larsen, 'Interpreting the European Convention: What Can the African Human Rights System Learn from the Case Law of the European Court of Human Rights on the Interpretation of the European Convention?' (2012) 5 *Inter-American and European Human Rights Journal* 90–123, 100.

144 *Demir and Baykara* (n 117) para. 78 (emphasis added).

ground between the Contracting States in this area', and therefore, it granted a national margin of appreciation.[145] In the subsequent *Sheffield and Horsham* case, the Court similarly concluded that there was neither a 'generally shared approach among the Contracting States' nor a 'common European approach', notwithstanding a survey by the human rights NGO Liberty that demonstrated 'an unmistakably clear trend in the member States of the Council of Europe towards giving full legal recognition to gender re-assignment'.[146] The momentum to reverse these decisions came from the *Christine Goodwin v the United Kingdom* judgement, in which the Strasbourg Court, relying on an updated survey by Liberty that indicated 'a continuing international trend towards legal recognition',[147] prioritised universal consensus over European consensus:

> The Court accordingly attaches less importance to *the lack of evidence of a common European approach* to the resolution of the legal and practical problems posed, than to *the clear and uncontested evidence of a continuing international trend* in favour not only of increased social acceptance of transsexuals but of legal recognition of the new sexual identity of post-operative transsexuals.[148]

George Letsas did not overlook the shift from regional consensus to universal consensus: 'the new Court has moved away from placing decisive weight on the absence of consensus amongst Contracting States and from treating it as the ultimate limit on how far it can evolve the meaning and scope of Convention rights'.[149] The newly transformed Strasbourg Court,

---

145 *Rees v the United Kingdom*, ECtHR (Plenary), App. No. 9532/81, Judgment on Mertis of 17 October 1986, para 37.

146 *Sheffield and Horsham v the United Kingdom*, ECtHR (Grand Chamber), App Nos 22985/93 and 23390/94, Judgment on Merits of 30 July 1998, paras. 35, 58.

147 For the role of NGOs in building consensus, Laura Van den Eynde, 'The Consensus Argument in NGOs' *Amicus Curiae* Briefs Defending Minorities Through A Creatively Used Majoritarian Argument' in Panos Kapotas and Vassilis P Tzevelekos (eds), *Building Consensus on European Consensus: Judicial Interpretation of Human Rights in Europe and Beyond* (Cambridge University Press 2019) 96–119.

148 *Christine Goodwin v the United Kingdom*, ECtHR (Grand Chamber), App No 28957/95, Judgment on Merits and Just Satisfaction 11 July 2002, para 85 (emphasis added).

149 George Letsas, 'The ECHR as a Living Instrument: Its Meaning and Legitimacy' in Andreas Føllesdal, Birgit Peters and Geir Ulfstein (eds), *Constituting Europe: The European Court of Human Rights in a National, European and Global Context* (Cambridge University Press 2013) 106–141, 122 (emphasis in the original text).

in his view, 'treats the ECHR as a living instrument by looking for *common values* and *emerging consensus* in international law'.[150]

A more universality-oriented interpretative practice may be found in the IACtHR jurisprudence. In *Juridical Condition and Human Rights of the Child*, the Court equated consensus of States Parties with *opinio juris communis*, which has been utilised as a term indicating the subject element of customary international law:

> The Convention on the Rights of the Child has been ratified by almost all the member States of the Organization of American States. The large number of ratifications shows *a broad international consensus* (*opinio iuris comunis*) in favor of the principles and institutions set forth in that instrument, which reflects current development of this matter. It should be highlighted that the various States of the hemisphere have adopted provisions in their legislation, both constitutional and regular, regarding the matter at hand; the Committee on the Rights of the Child has repeatedly referred to these provisions.[151]

Opinio juris communis means here 'the expression of the *universal juridical conscience* through the observance, by most of the members of the international community, of a determined practice because it is obligatory'.[152] Antonio Augusto Cançado Trindade, a proponent of these concepts who presided over the San José Court at that time and currently is a World Court judge, regards universal juridical conscience as the material source of international law functions, beyond the formal sources anchored by state consent, for 'an in-depth examination of the legal foundations, and, ultimately, of the validity [or *substratum*] itself, of the norms of International Law'.[153] According to his Hague Academy lecture, juridical conscience may be practically observed 'in the elaboration of adopted texts of international treaties, in the proceedings before international tribunals and in international case law, and in the works of international legal doctrine'.[154]

---

150 Ibid.

151 *Juridical Condition and Human Rights of the Child*, IACtHR, Series A No17, Advisory Opinion OC-17/02 of 28 August 2002, para 29. See also, Georg Nolte, *Treaties and Subsequent Practice* (Oxford University Press 2013) 274.

152 *Baena-Ricardo Others v Panama*, IACtHR, Series C No 104, Judgment on Preliminary Objections of 28 November 2003, para 102.

153 Antonio Augusto Cançado Trindade, *International Law for Humankind: Towards a New Jus Gentium* (Brill 2010) 139.

154 Ibid.

Atala Riffo and Daughters v Chile serves as a typical example in which the sexual orientation of persons was recognised as a category protected under Article 1(1) of the ACHR despite the absence of regional consensus. In this case, while the Chilean Supreme Court ruled that there was a lack of consensus regarding sexual orientation as a prohibited category for discrimination, the IACtHR did not consider the alleged lack of consensus as a valid argument to deny or restrict these individuals' human rights or to perpetuate and reproduce the historical and structural discrimination that these minorities have suffered.[155] At the same time, the Inter-American judges rejected the closed interpretative approach, sticking to the formal framework of the ACHR:

> The fact that this is a controversial issue in some sectors and countries, and that it is not necessarily a matter of consensus, cannot lead this Court to abstain from issuing a decision, since in doing so it must refer solely and exclusively to the stipulations of the international obligations arising from a sovereign decision by the States to adhere to the American Convention.[156]

The San José Court adopted the dynamic interpretation of Article 1(1) of the ACHR by what should be called juridical conscience extensively evidenced by the universal and regional practices beyond the will of individual states.[157] The subsequent cases followed the Inter-American 'consistent jurisprudence that the presumed lack of consensus within some countries regarding full respect for the rights of sexual minorities cannot be considered a valid argument to deny or restrict their human rights or to reproduce and perpetuate the historical and structural discrimination that such minorities have suffered'.[158] This universalist approach was furthermore recalled in the 2017 Advisory Opinion concerning gender identity, and equality and non-discrimination with regard to same-sex couples.[159]

---

155 *Atala Riffo and Daughters v Chile*, IACtHR, Series C No 239, Judgment of Merits, Reparations and Costs of 24 February 2012, para 92.

156 Ibid.

157 Ibid paras 83–93.

158 *Duque v Colombia*, IACtHR, Series C No 310, Judgment on Preliminary Objections, Merits, Reparations and Costs of 26 February 2016, para 123.

159 *Gender Identity, and Equality and Non-discrimination with Regard to Same-sex Couples, State Obligations in Relation to Change of Name, Gender Identity, and Rights Deriving from a Relationship between Same-sex Couples*, IACtHR, Series A No 24, Advisory Opinion OC-24/17 of 24 November 2017, para 219.

In sum, in line with the dynamic interpretation of regional conventions in light of universal standards, its legitimacy source has been gradually shifted from regional consensus to universal consensus. Consequently, individual states can no longer block the establishment of consensus between States Parties. Nor can they discourage universal consensus built through material sources that reflect juridical conscience. The foregoing analysis cannot immediately abolish traditional state-centrism and voluntarism, both of which have been closely intertwined with international legal positivism.[160] However, as Francisco Pascual Vives rightly noted, the recent interpretative practices of human rights courts certainly produce a *sensible erosión* of the principle of sovereign equality.[161]

2. *Pro Homine Principle's International Functions for Conventionality Control*

A. Unified Interpretation of Conventionality Control Parameters

(i) Unification through Interpretative Rules

The recent interpretative practices examined above thoroughly indicate the *pro homine* approach seeking the most favourable way to persons in regional and universal experiences. Raising regional standards in accordance with more favourable universal criteria contribute to the *unity* of international human rights law by constructing a *constitutionalist* hierarchy between norms. The tendency of *constitutionalisation* of international law has been advocated to provide an answer to the so-called *fragmentation* phenomena in international law resulting from increased specialisation. The vocabularies of constitutionalisation and fragmentation suggest 'a vision of unity that the earlier international law vocabulary, with its insistence on sovereignty and independence, could never provide'.[162] Paraphrasing it with postmodern philosophers Gilles Deleuze and Félix Guattari, in-

160 For the correlation among the three positions, Jean d'Aspremont, *Formalism and the Sources of International Law: A Theory of the Ascertainment of Legal Rules* (Oxford University Press 2011) 21–24.

161 Francisco Pascual Vives, 'Consenso e interpretación evolutiva de lots tratados regionales de derechos humanos' (2014) 66 *Revista Española de Derecho Internacional* 113–153, 129–134.

162 Jan Klabbers, 'International Legal Positivism and Constitutionalism', in Jean d'Aspremont and Jörg Kammerhofer (eds), *International Legal Positivism in a Post-Modern World* (Cambridge University Press 2014) 264–290, 266.

ternational lawyers who problematise fragmentation in a constitutional sense presuppose the 'arborescent' unity of international law as a system and struggle to control the 'rhizomatic' network of human consciousness leading to the appearance of new institutions, new regimes and new disciplines.[163] As identified by Sahib Singh, the 2006 ILC report titled *Fragmentation of International Law*, issued under the initiative of Martti Koskenniemi, reflects *plausible constitutionalism*: it is both a *positivist* statement and a description of international law as a system, and an *ethical* project of resistance to the current state of affairs in international law.[164]

The integralist ambition towards the unity of international law was implied in the 2010 *Ahmadou Sadio Diallo* judgement on the merits. The ICJ made the following statement in assessing the alleged violation of Article 13 of the ICCPR and Article 12(4) of the African Charter:

> Although the Court is in no way obliged, in the exercise of its judicial functions, to model its interpretation of the Covenant on that of the Committee, it believes that it should ascribe great weight to the interpretation adopted by this independent body that was established specifically to supervise the application of that treaty. The point here is to achieve the *necessary clarity* and the *essential consistency* of international law, as well as *legal security*, to which both the individuals with guaranteed rights and the States obliged to comply with treaty obligations are entitled.[165]

Subsequently, the World Court for the first time in its history expressly took into account the contribution of the jurisprudence of the ECtHR and IACtHR to achieve 'their common mission – the realization of international justice – in a spirit of respectful dialogue, learning from each other'.[166] It thus follows that the ICJ seemed to perform a 'quasi-constitutional role in the international order by identifying those elements which ensure the

---

163 David Koller, '... and New York and The Hague and Tokyo and Geneva and Nuremberg and...: The Geographies of International Law' (2012) 23 *European Journal of International Law* 97–119, 114.

164 Sahib Singh, 'The Potential of International Law: Fragmentation and Ethics' (2011) 24 *Leiden Journal of International Law* 23–43, 38.

165 *Ahmadou Sadio Diallo (Republic of Guinea v. Democratic Republic of the Congo,* Merits, Judgment, ICJ Reports 2010, para 66 (emphasis added).

166 Separate opinion of Judge Cançado Trindade, *ibid*, paras 232–245. See also, Sir Nigel Rodley, 'The International Court of Justice and Human Rights Treaty Bodies' in James A Green and Christopher PM Waters (eds), *Adjudicating International Human Rights: Essays in Honour of Sandy Ghandhi* (Martinus Nijhoff Publishers 2014) 12–33, 20–22.

unity and coherence of the international legal system'.[167] As expressed in the ILC's Conclusion 13 titled *Subsequent Agreements and Subsequent Practice in Relation to Interpretation of Treaties*, '[a] pronouncement of an expert treaty body may give rise to, or refer to, a subsequent agreement or subsequent practice by parties under article 31, paragraph 3, or subsequent practice under article 32'.[168]

In the context of regional human rights protection, as indicated in the previous section, universal standards are taken into account in dynamically interpreting regional conventions to ensure the unity of international law.[169] Given that the Strasbourg jurisprudence interprets the ECHR by resorting to public international law including universal human rights instruments, Adamantia Rachovista observes a positive potential for combating the fragmentation of international law: that the ECtHR interprets the ECHR by taking a great variety of relevant international law norms into account, suggests, in principle, that the Court employs a policy of embedding the ECHR into international law and, hence, avoids taking any kind of isolationist or fragmented approach towards international law.[170] Similarly, Lucas Lixinski points out that the San José Court, by acting in the way it does, performs a service that favours the 'defragmentation' of international law, while not unauthorisedly expanding its mandate, and therefore, promotes the unity of international law, while preserving its own institutional constraints.[171]

As a justification for such regional interpretative practices, the present volume rather focuses on the *pro homine* principle reflected in the so-called more favourable provisions (Article 53 of the ECHR and Article 29(b) of the ACHR). Their main function is to prohibit an interpretation that restricts the existing human rights standards established by other international and national legal instruments. As these provisions prohibit the

---

167 Oriol Casanovas y La Rosa, *Unity and Pluralism in Public International Law* (Martinus Nijhoff The Hague 2001) 246–247.

168 Report of the International Law Commission (n 98) 106–116.

169 Anne van Aaken 'Defragmentation of Public International Law through Interpretation: A Methodological Proposal' (2009) 16 *Indiana Journal of Global Legal Studies* 483–512, 487.

170 Adamantia Rachovitsa, 'Fragmentation of International Law Revisited: Insights, Good Practices and Lessons to be Learned from the Case Law of the European Court of Human Rights' (2015) 28 *Leiden Journal of International Law* 863–885, 878.

171 Lucas Lixinski, 'Treaty Interpretation by the Inter-American Court of Human Rights: Expansionism at the Service of the Unity of International Law' (2010) 21 *European Journal of International Law* 585–604, 604.

restriction of *external* criteria by the Conventions, Article 17 of the ECHR and Article 29(a) of the ACHR prevent the limitation of *internal* standards by other Convention rights 'to a greater extent than is provided for' therein. A large number of universal and regional human rights instruments include such 'more favourable' clauses, such as Article 5(2) of the ICCPR and the ICESCR, and Article 53 of the CFREU.[172] These 'more favourable' provisions are also found in other branches of international law,[173] including international environmental law,[174] international humanitarian law,[175] international labour law[176]and international cultural heritage law.[177]

(ii) Unification by Prioritising Most Favourable Standards

One aspect of such 'more favourable' provisions is the standard unification by determining the relative, not absolute, priority between legal norms. In practice, 'more favourable' clauses are often utilised for aggregating regional and universal human rights criteria. This is evident in 'the Inter-American Court […] interpret[ing] Article 29 as the formal admittance by

172 See in general, Jean Dhommeaux, 'Hiérarchie et conflits en droit international des droits de l'homme' (2009) 4 *Annuaire international des droits de l'homme* 55–62. Other examples are the International Convention on the Elimination of All Forms of Racial Discrimination (Article 1(3)); the Convention on the Elimination of All Forms of Discrimination against Women (Article 23); the Convention against Torture and Other Cruel, Inhuman or Degrading Treatment (Article 1(2)); the Convention on Rights of the Child (Article 41); the International Convention for the Protection of All Persons from Enforced Disappearance (Article 37); the Convention on the Rights of Persons with Disabilities (Article 4(4)).

173 Sadat-Akhavi, *Methods of Resolving Conflicts between Treaties* (Brill 2004) 163–168.

174 For example, Article 11 of the Basel Convention on the Control of Transboundary Movements of Hazardous and their Disposal; Article 2(4) of the Cartagena Protocol on Biosafety to the Convention on Biological Diversity.

175 For example, Art 6(2) of the Geneva Convention (GC) I, GC II and GC III; Art 7(2) GC IV; Arts 34(1), 45 (3), 75(7)(b), (8) of Protocol Additional to GC (Protocol I). See also, Anne-Laurence Graf-Brugère, '*A lex favorabilis*? Resolving Norm Conflicts between Human Rights and Humanitarian Law' in Kolb and Gaggioli (n 138) 251–270, 258–260.

176 Art 19(8) of the Constitution of the International Labor Organization. See also, Nicolas Valticos and Gerald W von Potobsky, *International Labour Law*, 2nd ed (Kluwer 1995) 79.

177 Art 21 of the Convention on the Protection of the Architectural Heritage of Europe.

States of such references to other International Rules' and consequently, 'as an authorization to enlarge the content of the rights protected by the Convention'.[178] In the 2014 *RMT v the United Kingdom* ruling, in which it was contested whether secondary action by the National Union falls within the scope of Article 11 of the ECHR, the Strasbourg Court likewise stipulated '[i]t would be inconsistent with this method for the Court to adopt in relation to Article 11 an interpretation of the scope of freedom of association of trade unions that is much narrower than that which prevails in international law'.[179] In this sense, 'more favourable' provisions are analogous to 'consistent interpretation' provisions, both of which enable an *open-minded* interpretation in light of external legal sources.[180]

Exploring the essence of 'more favourable' provisions, we find the so-called *pro homine* or *pro persona* principle that prioritises the most beneficial interpretation and application of norms for individuals. This principle has already been developed in domestic legal systems, such as *in dubio pro reo*, *in dubio pro operario*, *favor debilis*, *favor libertatis* and *pro actionae*.[181] At the international level, the IACtHR explicitly recognises that Article 29 of the ACHR includes the *pro homine* principle, which serves not only for substantive rights but also for procedural regulations. For example, *Advisory Opinion OC-13/93* demonstrated that the decision of the IACHR on whether to submit the case to the Court in accordance with Article 51 of the ACHR 'is not discretionary, but rather must be based upon the alternative that would be *most favorable for the protection of the rights established in the Convention*'.[182] Because the Inter-American system adopts 'a true *actio popularis*' that permits any legally recognised non-governmental

---

178 Tigroudja (n 138) 471–472 (both quotations).

179 *The National Union of Rail, Maritime and Transport Workers (RMT) v. the United Kingdom*, ECtHR, App No 31045/10, Judgment on Merits and Just Satisfaction of 8 April 2014, para 76. See also, Concurring Opinion of Judge Wojtyczek, *Ibid* para. 3.

180 Burgorgue-Larsen (n 24) 443–452.

181 Ximena Medellín Urquiaga, *Principio pro persona* (Comisión de Derechos Humanos del Distrito Federal, Suprema Corte de Justicia de la Nación y Oficina en México del Alto Comisionado de las Naciones Unidas para los Derechos Humanos 2013) 16–17.

182 *Certain Attributes of the Inter-American Commission on Human Rights (Arts. 41, 42, 44, 46, 47, 50 and 51 of the American Convention on Human Rights)*, IACtHR, Advisory Opinion OC-13/93 of 16 July 1993, para 50 (emphasis added).

entity to lodge petitions with the commission (Article 44 of the ACHR),[183] such a procedural advancement based on the *pro homine* principle would operate in favour of juridical persons as well as natural persons.[184]

With regard to its validity beyond Latin America, HRC members Helen Keller and Fabián Salvioli referred to the *pro homine* principle in noting that '[i]nternational bodies have a responsibility to make sure that they do not end up adopting a decision that weakens standards already established in other jurisdictions'.[185] It should also be reminded here that 'more favourable' provisions allegedly embodying the *pro homine* principle are prescribed in almost all universal and regional human rights treaties. Taking these doctrinal and normative supports into account, it may be convincingly argued that the *pro homine* principle is enshrined as 'the backbone of the post–Second World War international law of human rights'.[186]

As the origin of the unifying function of 'more favourable' provisions, the *pro homine* principle also operates to elevate Convention criteria in terms of other international legal instruments. Connecting the 'living instrument' doctrine of evolutionary interpretation, the *pro homine* principle in fact dramatically raises the ACHR standards.[187] As previously examined in detail, the IACtHR indeed took an evolutionary approach to interpretation in *Atala Riffo* to include the sexual orientation of persons as the categories of 'any other social condition' protected from discrimination under Article 1(1) of the ACHR.[188] The same reasoning was repeated in *Norín Catrimán v. Chile* with regard to the ethnic origin of an individual, in terms of juridical conscience evinced by several international and domestic

183 Héctor Faúndez Ledesma, *The Inter-American System for the Protection of Human Rights: Institutional and Protection Aspects*, 1st ed in English, trans of 3rd ed in Spanish (Inter-American Institute of Human Rights 2007) 231.

184 Entitlement of Legal Entities to Hold Rights under the Inter-American Human Rights System (Interpretation and scope of Article 1(2), in relation to Articles 1(2), 8, 11(2), 13, 16, 21, 24, 25, 29, 30, 44, 46 and 62(3) of the American Convention on Human Rights, as well as of Article 8(1)(A) and (B) of the Protocol of San Salvador), IACtHR, Series A No 22, Advisory Opinion OC-22/16 of 26 February 2016, para 42.

185 Individual Opinion of Helen Keller and Fabián Salvioli, *Elgueta v. Chile*, HRC, Comm No 1536/2006, CCPR/C/96/D/1593/2006, Decision of 28 July 2009, para 11.

186 Valerio De Oliveira Mazzuoli and Dilton Ribeiro, 'The *Pro Homine* Principle as an Enshrined Feature of International Human Rights Law' (2016) 3 *Indonesian Journal of International & Comparative Law* 77–99, 78.

187 Medellín Urquiaga (n 181) 25.

188 *Atala Riffo and Daughters v Chile* (n 155) paras 83–93.

documents including soft law such as the 2007 United Nations Declaration on the Rights of Indigenous Peoples.[189] *Advisory Opinion OC-22/16* also endorses the unifying approach in determining the entitlement of legal entities, particularly trade unions, under Article 8 of the Protocol of San Salvador, to hold rights under the Inter-American human rights system. Emphasising the *pro persona* principle's role of not excluding or limiting the effect of other instruments, the IACtHR interpreted the provision in light of Article 45(c) of the OAS Charter, Article 10 of the Inter-American Democratic Charter and the ILO Declaration on Fundamental Principles and Rights at Work.[190]

B. Diversified Interpretation of Conventionality Control Parameters

(i) Diversification through Interpretative Rules

Despite the tendency of constitutionalisation, different bodies granted different powers may take the opposite direction to promote the *diversity* of international human rights law through reaching *fragmented* interpretations. We therefore need to pay attention to the adverse effect of the constitutionalisation of international law, namely, the *fragmentation* of international law. In the words of Jan Klabbers, '[f]ighting fragmentation by constitutionalism will, likewise, only result in deeper fragmentation, as the various competing regimes and organizations will be locked firmly in constitutional place – and in battle with each other'.[191] Gunther Teubner made a similar claim that 'in the discrepancy between globally established social subsystems and a politics stuck at inter-state level, the constitutional totality breaks apart and can then only be replaced by a form of *constitutional fragmentation*'.[192]

In this respect, we need to acknowledge that 'the development of international law through specialized mechanisms is seen sometimes as healthy

---

189 *Norín Catrimán and Others (Leaders, Members and Activist of the Mapuche Indigenous People) v Chile*, IACtHR, Series C No 279, Judgment on Merits, Reparations and Costs of 29 May 2014, paras 202–206.

190 *Entitlement of Legal Entities to Hold Rights under the Inter-American Human Rights System* (n 184) para 95.

191 Jan Klabbers, 'Constitutionalism Lite' (2004) 1 *International Organizations Law Review* 31–58, 53.

192 Gunther Teubner, *Constitutional Fragments: Societal Constitutionalism and Globalization* (Oxford University Press 2012) 51 (emphasis added).

pluralism ("diversification"), sometimes as perilous division ("fragmentation")'.[193] As a matter of fact, the proliferation of international courts and tribunals does not necessarily cause the negative phenomenon of fragmentation, but rather positively promotes 'creative diversity, the potential for cross-fertilisation of ideas, and a chance to see established categories, preferences and hierarchies challenged or revisited'.[194] With such a healthy aspect, the pluralist (or fragmenting) approach can complement the constitutionalist approach: 'If constitutionalisation is coupled with global legal pluralism or fragmentation it may support the proposition that constitutionalisation can occur at different paces within different sectors of international law'.[195]

The danger of fragmentation through interpretation would be more aggravated within the constitutional sectors that co-exist within different regional human rights systems. Gérard Cohen-Jonathan and Jean-François Flauss did not overlook this symptom appearing in the Strasbourg Court's interpretative practices: A sufficiently rationalised and controlled appeal to external sources of inspiration with a view to enriching Convention law can in fact have two unintended consequences. First, the European Court might contribute, despite appearances, to the fragmentation of international human rights law, to the extent that it would 'independently' interpret the external standard. Second, and most importantly, the fragmentation of international human rights law (which is unfortunately a reality) could, to the extent that the latter was purely and simply received, undermine the consistency of Convention rights.[196]

The theoretical risk was actually triggered by the ECtHR in the *Correia de Matos v. Portugal* case, which was identical to the individual communication brought by the applicant before the HRC.[197] In light of Article 31(3)(c) of the VCLT, the ECtHR confirmed that the Convention cannot be interpreted in a vacuum and should as far as possible be interpreted in alignment with other rules of international law concerning the inter-

---

193 Anne-Charlotte Martineau, 'The Rhetoric of Fragmentation: Fear and Faith in International Law' (2009) 22 *Leiden Journal of International Law* 1–28, 2.

194 Mario Prost, *The Concept of Unity in International Law* (Hart 2012) 11.

195 Aoife O'Donoghue, *Constitutionalism in Global Constitutionalisation* (Cambridge University Press 2014) 144.

196 Jean-François Flauss and Gérard Cohen-Jonathan, 'Cour européenne des droits de l'homme et droit international général' (2008) 54 *Annuaire français de droit international* 529–546, 533–534.

197 *Correia de Matos v Portugal*, HRC, Comm No 1123/2002, UN Doc CCPR/C/86/D/1123/2002, Views of 28 March 2006.

national protection of human rights.[198] Nonetheless, despite the almost identical character of the opinions, the Strasbourg judges denigrated the views from Geneva as 'not determinative' in that the interpretation of the same fundamental right by the Committee and by the Court may not always correspond.[199] The Court concluded that while there might be 'a tendency amongst the Contracting Parties to the Convention' to recognise the relevant right, there was no consensus as such, and therefore, afforded the State Party the margin of appreciation.[200] The majority opinion's overemphasis on the exceptional 'outlier' rather than the 'tendency' (thirty-one out of thirty-five member States), and its plea for the fragmentation of international law without engaging in a dialogue with the HRC were harshly criticised in the dissenting opinions.[201]

Another scenario of fragmentation between Strasbourg and Geneva concerns the prohibition on wearing the burqa in France. In the *SAS v France* judgement, the ECtHR supported the French law because individual freedom in religious practice should be sacrificed in order to protect 'the rights and freedoms of others', that is, the majority's rights, in terms of Article 9(2) of the ECHR. In leading to this conclusion, the Strasbourg judges supported the French government's position by holding that 'the impugned ban can be regarded as justified in its principle solely in so far as it seeks to guarantee the conditions of "living together [*vivre ensemble*]" deriving from the very *fraternité* culture'.[202] The partly dissenting opinion, however, doubted whether the general, abstract notion of living together directly falls under any of the rights and freedoms guaranteed within the Convention.[203] In the *Yaker* and *Hebbadi* cases, the Committee members in Geneva cast the same doubt, asserting that the concept of living together

---

198 *Correia de Matos v Portugal*, ECtHR (Grand Chamber), App no 56402/12, Judgment on Merits and Just Satisfaction of 4 April 2018, para 134.

199 Ibid para 137.

200 Ibid.

201 Joint Dissenting Opinion of Judges Tsotsoria, Motoc and Mits, para 18; Dissenting opinion of Judge Pinto de Albuquerque joined by Judge Sajó, para 17.

202 *SAS v France*, ECtHR (Grand Chamber), App No 43835/11, Judgment on Merits and Just Satisfaction of 1 July 2014. See also, *Dakir v Belgium*, ECtHR, App No 4619/12, Judgment on Merits and Just Satisfaction of, paras 121–122; *Belcacemi v Belgium*, ECtHR, App No 37798/13, Judgment on Merits and Just Satisfaction of 11 July 2017. See also, Ilias Trispiotis, 'Two Interpretations of "Living Together" in European Human Rights Law' (2016) 75 *Cambridge Law Journal* 580–607.

203 Partly Dissenting Opinion of Judges Angelika Nußberger and Helena Jäderblom in *SAS v France* (n 202) paras 3–12.

is 'very vague and abstract', and therefore, cannot provide the basis for permissible restrictions.[204]

The risk of fragmentation, however, should not be unnecessarily exaggerated. In its first advisory opinion concerning the scope of 'other treaties' subject to its advisory jurisdiction, as has been noted above, the IACtHR rejected the narrowest interpretation that only those treaties adopted within the framework or under the auspices of the Inter-American system are deemed to be within its advisory scope.[205] The Court instead, by endorsing the broadest interpretation that its advisory jurisdiction extends to any treaty concerning the protection of human rights in which one or more American States are Parties, discouraged the overreaction against the fragmenting trend of international law:

> The Court believes that it is here dealing with one of those arguments which proves too much and which, moreover, is less compelling than it appears at first glance. It proves too much because the possibility of conflicting interpretations is a phenomenon common to all those legal systems that have certain courts which are not hierarchically integrated. Such courts have jurisdiction to apply and, consequently, interpret the same body of law. Here it is, therefore, not unusual to find that on certain occasions courts reach conflicting or at the very least different conclusions in interpreting the same rule of law.[206]

Such ambivalence between the unifying and diversifying approaches is certainly common in the practice of international adjudication. In the *Diallo* case cited above, Judges Kenneth Keith and Christopher Greenwood tackled the question of whether Article 13 of the ICCPR imposes a general substantive non-arbitrariness limit on the power of expulsion over and above the procedural guarantees which they contain.[207] Having closely examined the HRC interpretations, as opposed to the majority opinion, the two judges asserted that Article 13 does not impose a substantive 'arbitrariness' criterion but provides procedural protections.[208] As one observ-

---

204 *Yaker v France*, HRC, Comm No 2747/2016, UN Doc CCPR/C/123/D/2807/2016, View of 17 July 2018 UN Doc. CCPR/C/123/D/2747/2016, para 8.10; *Hebbadi v. France*, Communication No. 2807/2016, View of 17 July 2018, UN Doc CCPR/C/123/D/2807/2016, para 7.10.

205 *"Other Treaties" Subject to the Consultative Jurisdiction of the Court* (n 80) para 32.

206 Ibid para 50.

207 Joint Declaration of Judges Keith and Greenwood, *Ahmadou Sadio Diallo* (n 165) paras 3–13.

208 Ibid.

er commented, extending the meaning determined by the HRC 'would be wrong in principle as it would risk "fragmentation" in the interpretation'.[209]

(ii) Diversification by Prioritising Most Favourble Standards

Whereas we observed the constitutionalist function of 'more favourable' provisions in practice, their original purpose is to prohibit an interpretation that restricts the existing human rights standards established by other international and national legal instruments. This logic does not mean that treaty criteria and national standards are unified as a single right answer.[210] Rather, treaty criteria are 'essentially seen as a floor of protection' giving States Parties the freedom to set their own higher national standards than the treaty minimum standards.[211] As long as these 'more favourable' provisions are relied upon, conventionality control of domestic law is based on the pluralist *diversifying* approach.[212]

These 'more favourable' clauses are of particular significance with regard to certain treaty mechanisms, such as derogation and reservation, by which States Parties may escape from the full application of treaty provisions. Typically, Articles 5(2) of the ICCPR and the ICESCR provide a safeguard against derogation measures which restrict the existing rights in States Parties 'on the pretext that the present [treaty] does not recognize such rights or that it recognizes them to a lesser extent'. In *Advisory Opinion OC-8/87* concerning *habeas corpus* in emergency situations, the IACtHR interpreted the derogation clause (Article 27(2) of the ACHR) in light of 'the need to prevent a conclusion that could give rise to the suppression of "the enjoyment or exercise of the rights and freedoms recognized in this Convention or to restrict them to a greater extent than is provided for therein" (Article 29(a))'.[213] In the case law on the reservation of the death

---

209 Sandy Ghandhi, 'Human Rights and the International Court of Justice: The Ahmadou Sadio Diallo Case' (2011) 11 *Human Rights Law Review* 527–555, 545.

210 Robert Spano, 'Universality or Diversity of Human Rights? Strasbourg in the Age of Subsidiarity' (2014) 14 *Human Rights Law Review* 487–502, 493.

211 Federico Fabbrini, *Fundamental Rights in Europe: Challenges and Transformations in Comparative Perspective* (Oxford University Press 2014) 35–44.

212 Andrew Legg, *The Margin of Appreciation in International Human Rights Law: Deference and Proportionality* (Oxford University Press 2012) 58 and 112.

213 *Habeas Corpus in Emergency Situations (Arts 27(2), 25(1) and 7(6) ACHR)*, IACtHR, Series A No 7, Advisory Opinion of 30 January 1987, para 18.

penalty, the San José Court also held that 'the application of Article 29(a) compels the conclusion that a reservation may not be interpreted so as to limit the enjoyment and exercise of the rights and liberties recognized in the Convention to a greater extent than is provided for in the reservation itself'.[214]

With the *diversifying* aspect, 'more favourable' provisions promote the heterarchy, or at least deny the formal hierarchy, between regional and universal decision-making. In the above-cited *RMT v the United Kingdom* judgement, although the Strasbourg Court declined to adopt 'a much narrower than that which prevails in international law', it carefully discerned that the negative assessments made in the more general terms by the relevant monitoring bodies of the ILO and the ESC were 'not of such persuasive weight for determining' the case-specific evaluation under Article 11 of the ECHR.[215] In the last paragraph laying out its reasoning, the Strasbourg judges offered a caveat that it has no competence to assess the respondent State's compliance with the relevant standards of the ILO or the ESC, 'the latter containing a more specific and exacting norm regarding industrial action'.[216]

As a pluralist account of Article 29(b) of the ACHR, the IACtHR stated in *Pacheco Tineo Family* that 'by using the sources, principles and criteria of international refugee law as a special normative applicable to situations concerning the determination of the refugee status of a person and their corresponding rights in a way that is complementary to the provisions of the Convention, *the Court is not assuming a ranking [jerarquización] between norms*'.[217] The same approach was adopted in *The Disappeared from the Palace of Justice* in rejecting the Respondent's preliminary objection alleging the lack of the Court's material competence due to the need to apply international humanitarian law: '[B]y using international humanitarian law as a norm of interpretation that complements the Convention, *the Court is not ranking [jerarquización] the different laws*, because the applicabil-

214 *Restrictions to the Death Penalty (Arts 4(2) and 4(4) American Convention on Human Rights)*, IACtHR, Series A No 8, Advisory Opinion of 8 September 1983, para 66; *Constantine and Ohters v Trinidad and Tobago*, IACtHR, Judgment on Preliminary Objections of 1 September 2001, para 66.

215 RMT (n 179) para 98.

216 Ibid para 106.

217 *The Pacheco Tineo Family* (n 115) para 143 (emphasis added).

ity and relevance of international humanitarian law in situations of armed conflict is not in doubt'.[218]

Reflecting the pluralist diversifying approach of 'more favourable' clauses, the *pro homine* principle prohibits the restrictive interpretation to the detriment of existing human rights standards. In fact, the IACtHR recognised in *Advisory Opinion OC-5/85* the *pro homine* principle to forbid the external restriction of ACHR rights:

> Hence, if in the same situation both the American Convention and another international treaty are applicable, *the rule most favourable to the individual* must prevail. Considering that the Convention itself establishes that its provisions should not have a restrictive effect on the enjoyment of the rights guaranteed in other international instruments, it makes even less sense to invoke restrictions contained in those other international instruments, but which are not found in the Convention, to limit the exercise of the rights and freedoms that the latter recognizes.[219]

In *Advisory Opinion OC-21/14* concerning children's rights in the context of migration, the IACtHR invoked the *pro homine* principle reflected in Article 29(b) as regards the principle of *non-refoulement* as follows:

> [T]he principle of non-refoulement is an integral part of these different branches of international law in which it has been developed and codified. However, in each of these contexts, the content of the principle of non-*refoulement* has a particular sphere of application *ratione personae* and *materiae*, and specific correlative obligations, which must be understood to have a complementary nature in the terms of Article 29 of the American Convention and the pro persona principle. Overall, this entails making the most favorable interpretation for the effective enjoyment and exercise of the fundamental rights and freedoms by

---

218 *Rodríguez Vera and others (the Disappeared from the Palace of Justice) v Colombia*, IACtHR, Series C No 287, Judgment on Preliminary Objections, Merits, Reparations and Costs of 14 November 2014, para 39 (emphasis added); *Vásquez Durand and Others v Ecuador*, Series C No. 332, Judgment on Preliminary Objections, Merits, Reparations and Costs 15 of February 2017, para 31.

219 *Compulsory Membership in an Association Prescribed by Law for the Practice of Journalism (Arts. 13 and 29 American Convention on Human Rights)*, IACtHR, Series A No 5, Advisory Opinion of 13 November 1985, para 52 (emphasis added).

> applying the norm that accords the greatest protection to the human being.[220]

In this context, the *pro homine* principle, by requiring the Inter-American judges to select the *substance* most favourable to *individuals* among the *openly* interacted sources, contributed not only to the *unity of* the principle of *non-refoulement* enshrined in 'different branches of international law' but also to its pluralistic diversity of 'a particular sphere of application *ratione personae* and *materiae*, and specific correlative obligations'.

Another example is *Advisory Opinion OC-25/18* regarding the institution of asylum and human rights under the Inter-American system, in which the IACtHR was asked by Ecuador to give an authoritative interpretation on the right to seek and receive asylum 'in a foreign territory' under Article 22(7) of the American Convention. The answer was given in favour of 'the will of the States' to exclude the concept of diplomatic asylum on the understanding that it constitutes a State prerogative.[221] In concluding, while recognising the applicability of the *pro homine* principle, the Court took a conservative position as follows:

> However, the application of this [*pro homine*] principle cannot displace the use of the other methods of interpretation, nor can it ignore the results achieved as a result of them, since all of them must be understood as a whole. Otherwise, the unrestricted application of the *pro homine* principle would lead to the delegitimisation of the interpreter's actions. Therefore, based on the analysis of the preceding paragraphs, for this Court, both from the literal interpretation of Article 22(7) of the Convention and from the interpretation of its context, in particular the conditions established in the Latin American conventions that clearly define the meaning of the terms 'in foreign territory', it is clear that the purpose of the configuration of the right to seek and receive asylum is the protection of persons in foreign territory who have been forced to flee for certain reasons, which translates into the protection of territorial asylum. This is because it is not possible to assimilate

220 *Rights and Guarantees of Children in the Context of Migration and/or in Need of International Protection*, IACtHR, Series A No 21, Advisory Opinion OC-21/14 of 19 August 2014, para 234.

221 *The Institution of Asylum, and Its Recognition as a Human Right under the Inter-American System of Protection (interpretation and scope of Arts 5, 22(7) and 22(8) in Relation to Art 1(1) of the American Convention on Human Rights)*, IACtHR, Series A No. 25, Advisory Opinion OC-25/18 of 3 May 2018, para 153.

> legations to foreign territory. This interpretation is confirmed by the preparatory work of the American Declaration, [...].[222]

This pronouncement demonstrates that the *pro homine* principle does not only function for constitutional unification but also admits the existence of other interpretative methods to create an environment in which interpreters may flexibly adopt the best solution depending on the problems and contexts in question.

222 Ibid 149.

Chapter 2
International Distribution of Conventionality Control Powers

The second aspect of the constitutionalisation of international adjudication is that human rights courts perform judicial review of national acts against the yardstick of convention parameters. It should be reminded here that the subsidiarity principle presumes that the *primary* responsibilities are incumbent on States Parties and that treaty mechanisms are essentially *subsidiary* to domestic systems.[223] As the primary guardians of human rights, States Parties are required to perform general obligations to respect and ensure treaty rights and to align their domestic law and practice in line with treaty criteria.[224] As a literal meaning, subsidiarity governing the allocation of public authority in systems of multilevel governance shows a preference for functions at the lowest level of governance.[225] Moreover, subsidiarity inversely reallocates authority to the higher level if, and to the extent that, the higher level is better placed to fulfil the task in question.[226] In other words, subsidiarity includes both the *negative* aspect of limiting the competence of higher entities in favour of lower ones, and the *positive* aspect of permitting the higher authority to interfere with the lower authority.[227]

Regarding the competence allocation between human rights courts and States Parties in conventionality control, Judge Eduardo Ferrer MacGregor presented a particularly remarkable opinion in *Cabrera Garcia and Montiel Flores v. Mexico*:

---

223 Carozza (n 2) 56–68.

224 Ioannis Panoussis, 'L'obligation générale de protection des droits de l'homme dans la jurisprudence des organes internationaux' (2007) 70 *Revue trimestrielle des droits de l'homme* 427–461, 447–452.

225 Isabel Feichtner, 'Subsidiarity' in Rüdiger Wolfrum (ed), *Max Planck Encyclopedia of Public International Law* (Oxford University Press), updated in 2007, para 1.

226 Andreas L Paulus, 'Subsidiarity, Fragmentation and Democracy: Towards the Demise of General International Law?' in Tomer Broude and Yuval Shany (eds), *The Shifting Allocation of Authority in International Law: Considering Sovereignty, Supremacy and Subsidiarity: Essays in Honour of Professor Ruth Lapidoth* (Hart 2008) 193–213, 197.

227 Ken Endo, 'The Principle of Subsidiarity: From Johannes Althusius to Jacques Delors' (1994) 46 *Hokudai Hogaku Ronsyu* 2064–1965, 2054–2052.

> [T]he 'concentrated control of conformity with the Convention' has been developed by the IACtHR since its very first judgements, submitting the actions and norms of the State, in each particular case, to an examination of said conformity. That 'concentrated control' was carried out, fundamentally, by the IACtHR. Now, it has been transformed into a 'diffused control of conformity with the Convention' by extending said 'control' to all the domestic judges as a requirement for action within the domestic forum, although the IACtHR retains its power as 'last interpreter of the American Convention' when the effective protection of human rights in the domestic forum is not achieved.[228]

At first glance, his view appears to indicate a complete transformation from the *centralised* model to the *decentralised* model of conventionality control. However, a careful reading of the last point illuminates the context-based variability between *centralisation* and *decentralisation* of conventionality control powers, depending on the effectiveness of human rights protection at the domestic level. Put differently, this is a reference to the coexistence of the *centralisation* and *decentralisation* models of authority allocation among human rights courts and national organs in accordance with the achievement level of conventionality control.

Based on this assumption, this present study demonstrates the dual pattern of power allocation (centralisation and diffusion) for conventionality control in light of subsidiarity. In particular, this book focuses on subsidiarity in providing national discretion for choosing remedial measures, namely *remedial subsidiarity*.[229] The chapter starts by reviewing the principle of subsidiarity that allocates judicial powers either to States Parties, especially domestic courts (Section 1-A), or regional courts (Section 1-B) depending on the level of human rights protection that is achieved. Given such a general observation, it then advocates the *hybrid* model of conventionality control under the principle of subsidiarity: *concentrated* conventionality control by human rights courts under *positive* subsidiarity (Section 2-A) and *diffused* conventionality control by national authorities under *negative* subsidiarity (Section 2-B).[230]

---

228 Concurring Opinion of Judge *ad hoc* MacGregor Poisot, *Cabrera Garcia and Montiel Flores* (n 35) para 22.

229 Neuman (n 1) 371–374.

230 Outside the context of subsidiarity, human rights courts, as ultimate defenders of regional systems underpinned by human rights and democracy, have decisively faced human rights violations caused by undemocratic "abuse of pow-

1. Relationship between Regional and Domestic Courts

A. Distributing Powers for Domestic Courts

(i) Negative Subsidiarity for Allocating Powers to Domestic Courts

The subsidiarity principle is incorporated into the Convention provisions that assume collaboration between States Parties that have primary jurisdiction, and human rights courts that possess complementary competences. In other words, the subsidiary principle represents both the *negative* concept prioritising the Conventions' national implementation and the *positive* concept of permitting international control. As Ken Endo cautiously noted, '[t]hough only the *negative* sense of subsidiarity is quite often circulated, and [...] its *positive* concept is of secondary importance at least in its origin, *both concepts* should not be neglected'.[231] The negative aspect of subsidiarity is defined as 'the *limitation* of competences of the "higher" organization in relation to the "lower" entity'.[232] Replacing the definition in the Convention contexts, the negative concept requires human rights courts to show deference to States Parties. Under *negative subsidiarity*, non-performance of international judicial control by human rights courts serves to 'reinforce the legitimacy of the sovereign's actions by suggesting that the sovereign is respecting the social compact'.[233]

The collective guarantee of human rights rests on the principle of *subsidiarity*, one of the structural principles of international human rights law, according to which sovereign States retain the primary responsibilities to respect and to ensure to all individuals within their jurisdiction the rights recognised in the relevant treaties. Paragraph 2 of the ACHR preamble originally provides subsidiarity: 'The American states signatory to the present Convention, [...] recognizing that the essential rights of man are not derived from one's being a national of a certain state, but are

---

ers" in States Parties. See, Yota Negishi, 'Conventionality Control of Domestic 'Abuse of Power' Influencing Human Rights and Democracy' (2016) XXVI *Italian Yearbook of International Law* 243–264.

231 Endo (n 227) 2053 (emphasis added).

232 Ibid 2054–2053 (emphasis in original text).

233 Karen Alter, 'The Multiple Roles of International Courts and Tribunals: Enforcement, Dispute Resolution, Constitutional and Administrative Review' in Jeffrey L Dunoff and Mark A Pollack (eds), *Interdisciplinary Perspectives on International Law and International Relations: The State of the Art* (Cambridge University Press 2012) 345–370, 353–354.

based upon attributes of the human personality, and that they therefore justify international protection in the form of a convention reinforcing or complementing the protection provided by the domestic law of the American states'. As a more recently adopted document, the ECHR Protocol No. 15 adds in Article 1 the following new statement at the end of the preamble to the Convention: 'Affirming that the High Contracting Parties, in accordance with the principle of subsidiarity, have the primary responsibility to secure the rights and freedoms defined in this Convention and the Protocols thereto, and that in doing so they enjoy a margin of appreciation, subject to the supervisory jurisdiction of the European Court of Human Rights established by this Convention'.

Rights to domestic remedies are also the cornerstone of the Convention systems based on the subsidiarity principle (Article 13 ECHR of the and Article 25 of the ACHR).[234] The rules on the exhaustion of domestic remedies are the counterparts of rights to domestic remedies (Article 35(1) of the ECHR and Article 46(1) of the ACHR). In line with generally recognised principles of international law on state responsibility, these rules presume that applicants exhaust local remedies before having recourse to international instances. These provisions also reflect the principle of subsidiarity because they allow States Parties the opportunity to remedy human rights violations in the first instance within their domestic legal orders and, thereby, protect them from unwarranted international proceedings.[235] In the sense that international instances aim to provide appropriate redress that domestic remedies fall short of meeting, the remedial powers of human rights courts are rooted in the subsidiarity principle (Article 41 of the ECHR and Article 63(1) of the ACHR).[236] According to IACtHR jurisprudence, the broad terms in Article 63(1) codify a customary law of state responsibility, namely the *Chorzów* principle of reparation.[237] There-

234 Concurring opinion of Judge Diego García-Sayán, *Cepeda Vargas v Colombia*, IACtHR, Series C, No. 213, Judgment on Preliminary Objections, Merits, Reparations and Costs of 26 May 2010, para 8; *Kudła v Poland*, ECtHR, App No 30210/96, Judgment on Merits and Just Satisfaction of 26 October 2000, para 152.

235 *Velásquez-Rodríguez v Honduras* (n 9) para 61; *Kudła v Poland* ibid para 152.

236 Concurring Opinion of Judge García-Sayán, *Cepeda Vargas* (n 234) para 14; Mark E Villiger, 'The Principle of Subsidiarity in the European Convention on Human Rights' in Marcelo G Kohen (ed), *Promoting Justice, Human Rights and Conflict Resolution through International Law: Liber Amicorum Lucius Caflisch* (Martinus Nijhoff 2007) 623–637, 631–633.

237 *Aloeboetoe and Others v Suriname*, IACtHR, Series C No 15, Judgment on Reparations and Costs of 10 September 1993, para 43.

fore, the Court indirectly interprets and applies the customary rule even when it directly interprets and applies this provision.[238] In contrast, the ECtHR has conferred a limited remedial power under Article 41, which is a *lex specialis* modifying one aspect of the general law on state responsibility that leaves other aspects applicable.[239]

Given the premise that national implementation is prioritised over international control, general obligations under human rights treaties incumbent on States Parties are classified into two categories. The first category is the *obligation to respect* the treaty rights and freedoms and *to ensure* their exercise (Article 2(1) of the ICCPR; Article 1 of the ECHR; Article 1(1) of the ACHR). Under these provisions, States Parties are required to uphold not only negative obligations to respect the rights and freedoms specified in the Conventions but also positive obligations to ensure their enjoyment.[240] To complement the case-by-case mandate, the second category more comprehensively imposes on States Parties the *obligation to harmonise* domestic legal systems with Convention standards (Article 2(2) of the ICCPR; Article 2 of the ACHR).[241] Although the ECHR does not have a provision concerning this second obligation, the ECtHR has developed its jurisprudence in Article 1 to include the second category of general obligations to harmonise domestic legal systems in line with the Convention.[242] According to the formal wordings of relevant provisions, the second obligation to harmonise is complementary to the first obligation to respect and ensure.[243]

---

238 Lucius Caflisch and Antonio Augusto Cançado Trindade, 'Les conventions américaine et européenne des Droits de l'Homme et le droit international général' (2004) 108 *Revue générale de droit international public* 5–62, 40.

239 Commentary to ARSIWA (n 16) Art 32, para 2; Art 55, para 3.

240 *Velásquez-Rodríguez* (n 9) para 166; *Ireland v the United Kingdom* (n 80) para 239.

241 Riccardo Pisillo-Mazzeschi, 'Responsabilité de l'État pour violation des obligations positives relatives aux droits de l'homme' (2009) Recoueil des cours 177–506, 311–389. See also, *Exchange of Greek and Turkish Populations*, PCIJ, Series B No 10, Advisory Opinion of 21 February 1925, 20.

242 *Maestri v Italy*, ECtHR (Grand Chamber), App No 39748/98, Judgment on Merits and Just Satisfaction of 17 February 2004, para 47 (stating that 'it follows from the Convention, and from Article 1 in particular, that in ratifying the Convention the Contracting States undertake to ensure that their domestic legislation is compatible with it').

243 For example, Article 2 of the ACHR put a condtion that '[w]here the exercise of any of the rights or freedoms referred to in Article 1 is not already ensured by legislative or other provisions, [...]'.

As evidence of negative remedial subsidiarity, human rights courts initially adopted the *cost-centred* approach rather than the *victim-centred* approach.[244] In fact, the IACtHR in the first decade of its history denied the alleged violation of Article 25 of the ACHR without seriously considering whether domestic remedies were effective.[245] The procedural requirement of exhaustion of domestic remedies under Article 46(1)(a) 'allows the State to resolve the problem under its internal law before being confronted with an international proceeding' and was designed for the 'benefit of the State'.[246] During the same period, the San José Court focused on monetary 'fair compensation' enshrined in Article 63(1) of the ACHR for injuries suffered by victims.[247] In a similar way, the ECtHR categorically determined that the safeguards of Article 6(1) of the ECHR (right to a fair trial), implying the full protection of a judicial procedure, had been stricter as a *lex specialis* than those of Article 13.[248] The Strasbourg Court also relied on pecuniary compensation and declaratory relief as 'just satisfaction' stipulated in Article 41 of the ECHR.[249]

Remedial subsidiarity is also implied in the execution or compliance with the judgements of human rights courts. In the ECHR context, States Parties abide by the Strasbourg Court's judgement (Article 46(1)), and it shall be transmitted to the CoM, which shall supervise its execution (Article 46(2)).[250] When the implementation of comprehensive and complex measures, possibly of a legislative and administrative character, involve

---

244 Thomas M Antkowiak, 'An Emerging Mandate for International Courts: Victim Centered Remedies and Restorative Justice' (2011) 47 Stanford Journal of Internationall Law 270–332, 288–292.

245 For example, *Caballero-Delgado and Santana v Colombia*, IACtHR, Series C No 22, Judgment on Merits of 8 December 1995, para 66 (the Court determined that Art. 25 was not violated 'inasmuch as the writ of habeas corpus filed on behalf of the victim).

246 *Velásquez-Rodríguez* (n 9) para 61.

247 Douglas Cassel, 'The Expanding Scope and Impact of Reparations Awarded by the Inter-American Court of Human Rights' in Koen De Feyter, Stephan Parmentier, Marc Bossuyt and Paul Lemmens (eds), *Out of the Ashes: Reparation for Victims of Gross and Systematic Human Rights Violations* (Intersentia 2005) 191–223, 194.

248 *Brualla Gómez de la Torre v Spain*, ECtHR, App No 155/1996/774/975, Judgment on Merits and Just Satisfaction of 19 December 1997, para 41.

249 Bernhardt (n 3) 245–246.

250 For a variety of actors in the supervision process, see Andrew Drzemczewski, 'The Parliamentary Assembly's Involvement in the Supervision of the Judgments of the Strasbourg Court' (2010) 28 *Netherlands Quarterly of Human Rights* 164-178; Lucja Miara and Victoria Prais, 'The Role of Civil Society in the Execu-

various authorities, the Strasbourg Court often refrains from exercising its judicial function when the political body is 'better placed and equipped' to address the judgement execution.[251] In contrast, the ACHR itself does not determine which organ of the Inter-American system has jurisdiction to monitor compliance with IACtHR binding judgements (Article 68(1) of the ACHR). Although Article 65 of the ACHR stipulates the report procedure for judgement compliance, there has been little discussion on this topic in the General Assembly of the Organization of American States because States Parties are reluctant to have their own human rights situations brought to light.[252] In other words, there has certainly been an 'institutional gap' between the political and judicial treaty organs for the supervising mechanism of judgement compliance.[253]

(ii) Granting Margin of Appreciation to Domestic Courts

Judicial control by international courts has a significant influence on the legislative, administrative and judicial acts of domestic authorities. It is unlikely that States Parties intend to transfer to international courts the authority to decide issues as closely related to state sovereignty such as criminal justice, and thus lose their power of self-government.[254] As long as the function beyond dispute settlement exercised by international courts wields significant influence over domestic legal orders, other legitimacy sources need to be explored to complement state consent and international

---

tion of Judgments of the European Court of Human Rights' (2012) 5 *European Human Rights Law Review* 528–537.

251 For example, *Burdov v Russia (No.2)*, ECtHR, App No. 33509/504, Judgment on Merits and Just Satisfaction of 15 January 2009, para 137.

252 Cecilia M Baillet, 'Measuring Compliance with the Inter-American Court of Human Rights: The Ongoing Challenge of Judicial Independence in Latin America' (2013) 31 *Nordic Journal of Human Rights* 31 (2013) 477–495, 478–480.

253 Magnus Jesko Langer and Elise Hansbury, 'Monitoring Compliance with the Decisions of Human Rights Courts: The Inter-American Particularism' in Laurence Boisson de Chazournes, Marcelo Gustavo Kohen, Jorge E Viñuales (eds), *Diplomatic and Judicial Means of Dispute Settlement* (Martinus Nijhoff 2013) 213–245, 230–236.

254 Ezequiel Malarino, 'Judicial Activism, Punitivism and Supranationalisation: Illiberal and Antidemocratic Tendencies of the Inter- American Court of Human Rights' (2012) 12 *International Criminal Law Review* 665–695, 685.

legality as the bases of the judicial function of international courts.[255] As a matter of fact, the ICJ decisions in consular assistance cases left to the national discretion to choose measures, has been respected in granting remedies.[256] In the *LaGrand* judgement, the Hague judges clarified that the remedial obligation incumbent upon the Respondent 'can be carried out in various ways' and that '[t]he choice of means must be left to the United State'.[257] In a later ruling in *Avena*, the World Court reiterated that 'the concrete modalities for such review and reconsideration should be primarily left to the United States'.[258]

To legitimise the judicial control of national acts by human rights courts, the margin of appreciation doctrine has been developed as a corollary of the subsidiarity principle. Margin of appreciation refers to 'a degree of flexibility in the operation of the law' and calls for 'a certain deference towards the principal actors of society'.[259] In relation to international adjudication, the margin of appreciation doctrine, like the standard of review, functions as a means for determining the degree of deference to states in the performance of international obligations.[260] The ECtHR is the principal contributor to the margin of appreciation doctrine, by which it is defined as 'the breadth of deference the Strasbourg organs will allow to national legislative, executive and judicial bodies before they will disallow a national derogation from the Convention, or before they will find a restriction of a substantive Convention right incompatible with a State Party's obligations under the Convention'.[261] As this definition shows, the ECtHR has finessed the doctrine mainly with respect to Articles 8–11

---

255 Armin von Bogdandy and Ingo Venzke, 'On the Functions of International Courts: An Appraisal in Light of Their Burgeoning Public Authority' (2013) *Leiden Journal of International Law* 49–72, 50.

256 Yuval Shany, 'Toward a General Margin of Appreciation Doctrine in International Law?' (2005) 16 *European Journal of International Law* 907–940, 935–936.

257 *LaCrand (Germany v United States of America)*, Judgment of 27 June 2001, ICJ Reports 2001, 466, para 125.

258 *Avena and Other Mexican Nationals (Mexico v United States of America)*, Judgment, ICJ Reports 2004, 12, para 131.

259 Jean-Pierre Cot, 'Margin of Appreciation' in Wolfrum (n 225) updated in 2007, para 1.

260 See in general Lukasz Gruszczynski and Wouter Werner (eds), *Deference in International Courts and Tribunals: Standard of Review and Margin of Appreciation* (Oxford University Press 2014).

261 Howard Charles Yourow, 'The Margin of Appreciation Doctrine in the Dynamics of European Human Rights Jurisprudence' (1987) 3 *Connecticut Journal of International Law* 111–159, 118.

(personal sphere rights), Article 1 of the First Protocol (right to property), Article 14 (the prohibition of discrimination), and Article 15 (derogation) under the ECHR.[262] The European *consensus*, as discussed in the previous chapter, has been pursued by the Strasbourg Court to determine 'the wider the margins the court is prepared to grant to the national institutions'.[263]

In contrast, the IACtHR has approached the margin of appreciation doctrine in a limited number of cases. Behind the IACtHR's static jurisprudence on this doctrine, there has been frontal opposition, as represented by former president Cançado Trindade, who stated that no domestic discretion should be allowed with regard to traditional types of grave violations in the Americas, such as forced disappearances, extrajudicial killings or torture.[264] As we already confirmed in the previous chapter, the same logic may be applied to the Court's reluctance to search for regional *consensus* as the criterion for determining the degree of national discretion.[265]

Legitimacy sources from subsidiarity and the margin of appreciation doctrine can be elucidated through the constitutional principle of *separation of powers beyond the State*.[266] According to the characterisation by Mattias Kumm, the principle of subsidiarity provides the *jurisdictional* legitimacy that compensates international legality as the formal legitimacy of international law.[267] As a jurisdictional legitimacy factor, subsidiarity serves in two opposite directions: *negatively* working 'to assess, guide and constrain transnational legal practice', and *positively* working to 'strengthen rather than weaken the comparative legitimacy of international law over national law'.[268] As its corollary, the margin of appreciation doctrine is also described as a 'natural product' of the separation of powers between

262 Yutaka Arai-Takahashi, The Margin of Appreciation Doctrine and the Principle of Proportionality in the Jurisprudence of the ECHR (Intersentia 2002) 5–8.

263 Eyal Benvenisti, 'Margin of Appreciation, Consensus, and Universal Standards' (1999) 31 *New York Journal of International Law and Policy* 834–854, 851.

264 Pablo Contreras, 'National Discretion and International Deference in the Restriction of Human Rights: A Comparison between the Jurisprudence of the European and the Inter-American Court of Human Rights' (2012) 11 *Northwestern Journal of International Human Rights* 28–82, 61–67.

265 Neuman (n 112)107.

266 Christoph Möllers, *The Three Branches: A Comparative Model of Separation of Powers* (Oxford University Press 2015) Chap 4.

267 Matthias Kumm, 'The Legitimacy of International Law: A Constitutionalist Framework of Analysis' (2004) 15 *European Journal of International Law* 907–931, 920–924.

268 Ibid.

States Parties and human rights courts.[269] In terms of the separation of powers, the subsidiarity principle and the margin of appreciation doctrine are based on an argument from *institutional competence*, which emphasises 'a *chronological* or *procedural* priority of domestic control over international control'.[270] The institutional aspect emphasises the criteria of relative *efficiency* and *effectiveness* to determine 'which can better maximize results while minimizing costs in the pursuit of a given shared objective'.[271]

Another source that legitimatises subsidiarity-based conventionality control is the constitutional principle of *democracy*, which is described as one of the central cornerstones in the ACHR and ECHR preambles and provisions. Even within domestic legal systems, judicial review might undermine democratic values because unelected judges performed the task (the counter-majoritarian difficulty).[272] This problem can be more worrisome when decision-making is left to international tribunals which are beyond national control.[273] Although there is no necessary correlation among decentralisation, democracy and respect for human rights, any decentralisation permits greater community and individual participation in self-government, favouring small political units with substantial autonomy.[274] Thus, by allocating authority for the benefit of States Parties as the lower entities, the principle of subsidiarity also functions in 'setting out the conditions under which and the manner in which international courts should decide a case, following the purpose to protect, safeguard and promote individual and collective self-determination'.[275]

In terms of democratic legitimacy, subsidiarity involves not only the institutional aspect but also another aspect that 'requires an assessment of

269 Herbert Petzold, 'The Convention and the Principle of Subsidiarity' in Ronald St J MacDonald, Franz Matscher and Herbert Petzold (eds), *The European System for the Protection of Human Rights* (Martinus Nijhoff 1993) 41–62, 49.

270 Goerge Letsas, 'Two Concepts of the Margin of Appreciation' (2006) *Oxford Journal of Legal Studies* 705–732, 721 (emphasis in the original text).

271 Andreas von Staden, 'The Democratic Legitimacy of Judicial Review beyond the State: Normative Subsidiarity and Judicial Standards of Review' (2012) 10 *International Journal of Constittuional Law* 1023–1049, 1034–1038.

272 Alexander M Bickel, *The Least Dangerous Branch: The Supreme Court at the Bar of Politics*, 2nd ed (Yale University Press 1986) 16.

273 Ulfstein (n 26) 147.

274 Dinah Shelton, 'Subsidiarity and Human Rights Law' (2006) 27 *Human Rights Law Journal* 4–11, 7–11.

275 Simon Hentrei, 'Generalising the Principle of Complementarity: Framing International Judicial Authority' (2013) 4 *Transnational Legal Theory* 419–435, 426 (carefully distinguishing complementarity and subsidiarity).

the *relative normative appropriateness* of taking decisions at the lower or the higher level of political organization'.[276] To borrow the words of Letsas, 'national authorities are not only the first ones to deal with complaints regarding the Convention rights and provide remedies, but also the ones who have either *more legitimacy* or are *better placed* than an international body to decide on human rights issues'.[277] Based on the normative concept, the application of a national margin of appreciation suggests that a human rights court 'lacks democratic accountability so that it ought to defer to national or local legitimacy' in light of negative subsidiarity.[278] Conversely, conventionality control by human rights courts may be legitimised under positive subsidiarity to the extent that States Parties are no longer *better placed* to decide the human rights issues at stake.[279]

B. Distributing Powers to Regional Courts

(i) Positive Subsidiarity for Allocating Powers to Regional Courts

The positive aspect of subsidiarity, in contrast to its negative one, is defined as 'the *possibility* or even the *obligation* of interventions from the higher organization'.[280] Put differently, 'should the Member States not successfully guarantee minimum protection – harming human rights and human dignity – then an appeal could be made on positive subsidiarity'.[281] The positive concept of subsidiarity may be found in other fields of international law. A literal example is the ICC's *positive complementarity*, which could help 'the Court regulate a "margin of appreciation" afforded to national governments in determining which accountability mechanisms

---

276 Von Staden (n 271) 1034–1038 (emphasis in the original text).

277 Letsas (n 270), 720–721 (emphasis added).

278 Yutaka Arai-Takahashi, 'Disharmony in the Process of Harmonisation? – The Analytical Account of the Strasbourg Court's Variable Geometry of Decision-Making Policy Based on the Margin of Appreciation Doctrine' in Mads Andenas and Camilla Baasch Andersen (eds), *Theory and Practice of Harmonization* (Edward Elgar 2011) 95–114, 104–106.

279 Regarding the 'better placed' arguments, Janneke Gerards, 'Pluralism, Deference and the Margin of Appreciation Doctrine' (2011) 17 *European Law Journal* 80–120, 110–111.

280 Endo (n 227) 2054–2053 (emphasis in original text).

281 Didier Fouarge, *Poverty and Subsidiarity in Europe: Minimum Protection from an Economic Perspective* (Edward Elgar 2004) 30.

are most appropriate within their particular context'.[282] In a broader context, the *responsibility to protect* doctrine similarly includes the positive aspect of 'the subsidiary responsibility of the international community for guaranteeing human security when the territorial state fails in its duty to protect'.[283]

The positive aspect in the margin of appreciation can also be observed in ICJ jurisprudence. In the previously mentioned consular cases *LaGrand* and *Avena*, the Hague judges underlined that 'freedom in the choice of means for such review and reconsideration is not without qualification [but] has to be carried out "by taking account of the violations of the rights set forth in the Convention"'.[284] The World Court caught another opportunity to elaborate this point in the third consular conflict between India and Pakistan in the *Jadhav* ruling: 'a special emphasis must be placed on the need for the review and reconsideration to be effective' by 'ensur[ing] that full weight is given to the effect of the violation of the rights set forth in Article 36, paragraph 1, of the Convention and guarantee that the violation and the possible prejudice caused by the violation are fully examined'.[285]

Apart from the context of remedial obligation, the margin of appreciation doctrine for judicial review was implicitly developed in the *Whaling* case.[286] The ICJ acknowledged that Article VIII of the Whaling Convention 'gives discretion to a State party to the International Convention for the Regulation of Whaling to reject the request for a special permit or to specify the conditions under which a permit will be granted'.[287] The Court established conditions, however, that the question of whether the killing, taking and treating of whales 'for purposes of' scientific research under Article VIII 'cannot depend simply on that State's perception', and therefore, shall be assessed by 'examining whether, in the use of lethal

---

282 William W Burke-White, 'Proactive Complementarity: The International Criminal Court and National Courts in the Rome System of International Justice' (2008) 49 Harvard International Law Journal 53–108, 75.

283 Peters (n 48) 536–537.

284 LaGrand (n 17) para 125; Avena (n 17) para 131.

285 *Jadhav (India v Pakistan)*, Judgment, ICJ Reports 2019, 418, para 139. See also, Victor Kattan, 'Jadhav Case (India v. Pakistan)' (2020) 114 *American Journal of International Law* 281–287.

286 Enzo Cannizzaro, 'Proportionality and Margin of Appreciation in the Whaling Case: Reconciling Antithetical Doctrines?' (2017) 27 *European Journal of International Law* 1061–1069.

287 *Whaling in the Antarctic (Australia v Japan: New Zealand intervening)*, Judgment, ICJ Reports 2014, para 61.

methods, the programme's design and implementation are reasonable in relation to achieving its stated objectives'.[288]

(ii) Restricting Margin of Appreciation by Regional Courts

The principle of subsidiarity turns to the positive side to combat systemic human rights violations caused by domestic legal deficiencies. Traditionally, the ECtHR has maintained the declaratory nature of judgements and allowed States Parties broad discretion in choosing appropriate means for judgements execution. In comparison with the IACtHR activism, the Strasbourg Court's approach has been evaluated as *delegative* compliance.[289] However, the situation has recently changed because human rights violations have occurred repeatedly and under similar circumstances due to malfunctions within domestic legal systems, mainly within the new member states of the CoE from Central and Eastern Europe.[290] In some instances, the Strasbourg Court has concretely specified the remedial measures if, by its very nature, the violation did not leave any real choice as to the measures required to remedy it.[291]

The epoch-making decision is *Kudła v. Poland*, in which the ECtHR revised its own case law judgement concerning the excessive length of proceedings so that Article 13 of the ECHR could be viewed independently of the examination of Article 6. In this context, the Strasbourg Court emphasised that '[t]he growing frequency with which violations in this regard are being found has recently led the Court to draw attention to "the important

288 Ibid para 67.

289 Darren Hawkins and Wade Jacoby, 'Partial Compliance: A Comparison of the European and Inter-American Courts of Human Rights' (2010) 6 *Journal of International Law & International Relations* 35–85, 43–55.

290 Ed Bates, *The Evolution of the European Convention on Human Rights: From its Inception to the Creation of a Permanent Court of Human Rights* (Oxford University Press 2010) 485–486.

291 Valerio Colandrea, 'On the Power of the European Court of Human Rights to Order Specific Non-Monetary Measures: Some Remarks in Light of the *Assanidze, Broniowski* and *Sejdovic* Cases' (2007) 7 *Human Rights Law Review* 396–411, 408–410; Alastair Mowbray, 'An Examination of the European Court of Human Rights' Indication of Remedial Measures' (2017) 17 *Human Rights Law Review* 451–478; Veronika FikFak, 'Non-pecuniary Damages before the European Court of Human Rights: Forget the Victim: It's All about the State' (2020) 33 *Leiden Journal of International Law* 335–369.

danger" that exists for the rule of law within national legal orders'.[292] Subsequently, based on the principle of subsidiarity embedded in Articles 1, 13 and 35, the Court issued a warning that individual complaints 'in the Court's opinion more appropriately, have to be addressed in the first place within the national legal system'.[293] As a conclusion, it found that the means available to the applicant in Polish law did not meet the standard of effectiveness for the purpose of Article 13.[294]

As regards the admissibility test, new criteria were introduced under Article 35(3)(b) of the ECHR with the entry into force of its Protocol No 14 on 1 June 2010, which allows the Court to declare inadmissible any individual application, according to this new provision, if it is considered that 'the applicant has not suffered a significant disadvantage'. The significance-focused criteria were 'necessary in view of the ever-increasing caseload of the Court' against the background of repeated human rights violations.[295] Additionally, the protocol also inserted a safeguard clause that an individual application may be admissible if 'respect for human rights as defined in the Convention and the Protocols thereto requires an examination of the application on the merits'. The 'respect for human rights' safeguard can be invoked, according to the Strasbourg jurisprudence, 'where a case raises questions of a *general* character affecting the observance of the Convention, for instance whether there is a need to clarify the States' obligation under the Convention or to induce the respondent State to resolve a *structural deficiency*'.[296] To the extent that neither 'significant disadvantage' nor 'respect for human rights' is clearly defined, the new mechanism of admissibility will allow the ECtHR to 'be free to use wide discretion in application of this criterion so that it might be relaxed in order to do justice' beyond individual cases.[297]

These judgements and institutions imply that subsidiarity nowadays works for both directions to the restriction of and to the enforcement of

---

292 *Kudła v Poland* (n 234) paras 146–149.

293 Ibid paras 154–155.

294 Ibid paras 150–160.

295 Explanatory Report to Protocol No. 14 to the Convention for the Protection of Human Rights and Fundamental Freedoms, amending the control system of the Convention, para 78.

296 *Savelyev v Russia*, ECtHR, App No 42982, Decision of 21 May 2019, para 33 [emphasis added].

297 Fiona de Londras and Kanstantsin Dzehtsiarou, *Great Debates on the European Convention on Human Rights* (Macmillan International Higher Education, 2018) 61–62.

the control by the human rights court, as a function of the evaluation of the effectiveness of national remedial systems concerning the Convention rights.[298] In the latter *positive* enforcement, the ECHR provisions reflecting subsidiarity are exploited 'to reshape national legal systems to the likelihood that state officials will remedy human rights violations at home'.[299] In this process, *positive* subsidiarity can justify the Court's becoming 'more prescriptive in defining remedial measures' when States Parties fail to fully secure Convention rights at the national level.[300]

In comparison to the European practice, the IACtHR has more dramatically developed its case law on *reparaciones transformadoras* to great effect in order to reconstruct domestic legal measures that are in line with the ACHR.[301] Because the San José Court specifies concrete remedial courses of action against the respondent States, its approach has been described as *checklist* compliance, as if saying: 'Complete this list of remedies, and tell us when it's finished. We will then check what you have done'.[302] These reparations are also characterised as *dissuasive* measures in the sense that '[s]uch rulings are oriented toward the future and are not strictly concerned with injured party'.[303]

In the 1997 merits judgement of *Castillo-Páez v. Peru*, as a pre-emptive example, the IACtHR decided for the first time the violation of Article 25 of the ACHR, in relation to Article 1(1), to the detriment of both the vic-

---

298 Kaoru Obata, 'The Emerging Principle of Functional Complementarity for Coordination Among National and International Jurisdictions: Intellectual Hegemony And Heterogeneous World' in Takao Suami, Anne Peters, Mattias Kumm and Dimitri Vanoverbeke (eds.), *Global Constitutionalism from European and East Asian Perspectives* (Cambridge University Press 2018) 451–469, 455.

299 Laurence R Helfer, 'Redesigning the European Court of Human Rights: Embeddedness as a Deep Structural Principle of the European Human Rights Regime' (2008) 19 *European Journal of International Law* 125–159, 146.

300 Philip Leach, 'No Longer Offering Fine Mantras to a Parched Child? The European Court's Developing Approach to Remedies' in Føllesdal and Others (n 149) 142–180, 178.

301 Rodrigo Uprimny Yepes y María Paula Saffon, 'Reparaciones transformadoras, justicia distributiva y profundización democrática' in Catalina Díaz Gómez, Nelson Camilo Sánchez, Rodrigo Uprimny Yepes (eds), *Reparar en Colombia: los dilemas en contextos de conflicto, pobreza y exclusión* (Centro Internacional para la Justicia Transicional y Centro de Estudios de Derecho, Justicia y Sociedad 2009) 31–70.

302 Hawkins and Jacob (n 289) 43–55.

303 Judith Schönsteiner, 'Dissuasive Measures and the 'Society as a Whole': A Working Theory of Reparations in the Inter-American Court of Human Rights' (2007) 23 *American University International Lwe Review* 127–164, 139–159.

tim and his next of kin due to the ineffectiveness of the remedy of *habeas corpus*.[304] In the 1998 reparation judgement, the Court combined Articles 25 and Article 8 (the right to a fair trial), the close link of which imposes on the respondent state 'a duty to investigate the human rights violations and prosecute those responsible and thus avoid impunity'.[305] In conclusion, noting the special nature of the violation of the right to judicial protection, the Court decided to integrate the obligations of investigation and punishment of those responsible into reparation measures.[306] As Judge Ferrer MacGregor characterised it, the rights to judicial protection and a fair trial possess 'an integrative dimension of the sources of law (domestic and of the Convention) that serve as the basis for guaranteeing' domestic remedies.[307] It thus follows that these provisions function not only to provide effective relief to victims but also to control the compatibility of domestic legal systems with Convention standards.[308]

The effectiveness of domestic remedies has been increasingly significant in examining the way they have been exhausted as a criterion of admissibility. Historically, dictatorship remained endemic in the political life of Latin American States, and violence continued to be the principal vehicle for the attainment of political power in many States.[309] Against the background of these chaotic environments, Latin American States abused the admissibility criteria under Article 46(1) to escape from international jurisdiction that might be unfavourable to them, by claiming the formal existence of domestic remedies for the victims.[310] This situation had already been anticipated, however, even in the drafting stage of the Convention, as Article 46(2) thereof stipulates a number of exceptions to the requirement of exhaustion of domestic remedies. Inter-American jurisprudence has also consolidated the view that the remedies to be exhausted at the domestic level by victims must be *adecuados y efectivos*.[311]

304 *Castillo-Páez v Peru*, IACtHR, Series C, No. 34, Judgment on Merits of 3 November 1997, para 43.

305 Ibid paras 69–70.

306 Ibid.

307 Concurring Opinion of Judge Eduardo Ferrer MacGregor Poisot, *Liakat Ali Alibux v Surinam*, IACtHR, Series C No 276, Judgment on Preliminary Objections, Merits, Reparations and Costs of 30 January 2014, para 73.

308 Ibid paras 69–94.

309 Cabranes (n 6) 1175–1176.

310 Burgorgue-Larsen (n 8) 138.

311 Ibid 138–143; Liliana Tojo y Pilar Elizalde, 'Artículos 44–47: Competencia de la Comisión Interamericana de Derechos Humanos' in Christian Steiner and

In a nutshell, it may be argued that the *negative* aspect of 'subsidiarity play[s] a fairly small role in the IACtHR's remedial practice'.[312] Instead, its *positive* aspect restricts the national margin of appreciation for choosing appropriate remedial means. In practice, the Competence Judgement of *Baena-Ricardo* elucidated that Article 63(1) of the ACHR 'grants the Inter-American Court a wide margin of judicial discretion to determine the measures that all the consequences of the violation to be repaired'.[313] Given this broad remedial power, as the Inter-American judges themselves admit, '[i]f [national] mechanisms do not satisfy criteria of *objectivity*, *reasonableness* and *effectiveness* to make adequate reparation for the violations of rights recognized in the Convention that have been declared by this Court, it is for the Court, in exercise of its subsidiary and complementary competence, to order the pertinent reparations'.[314]

2. *International Centralisation and Decentralisation of Conventionality Control Powers*

A. Centralising Conventionality Control Powers to Regional Courts

(i) Prescribing Remedies for Systemic Violations

Against the background of systemic human rights violations, especially in Central and Eastern Europe, the ECtHR has increasingly engaged in supervising compliance with its own judgements under Article 46 of the European Convention.[315] In the 2004 *Broniowsk v Poland* ruling, the European Court further departed from its moderate stance and elaborated the so-called *pilot-judgement procedure* to prescribe general measures.[316] In the application of Article 46 of the ECHR, the Strasbourg Court observed

---

Patricia Uribe (eds), *Convención Americana sobre Derechos Humanos: Comentarios* (Konrad Adenauer Stiftung 2014) 765–784, 778–781.

312 *Neuman* (n 1) 373.

313 *Baena-Ricardo and Others* (n 152) para 64.

314 *Cepeda Vargas* (n 234) para 246 (emphasis added).

315 Lize R Glas, 'The European Court of Human Rights supervising the execution of its judgments' (2019) 37 *Netherlands Quarterly of Human Rights* 228–244.

316 Lech Garlicki, 'Broniowski and After: On the Dual Nature of 'Pilot Judgments' in Lucius Caflisch, Johan Callewaert, Roderick Liddell, Paul Mahoney and Mark Villiger (eds), *Liber Amicorum Luzius Wildhaber: Human Rights: Strasbourg Views* (N P Engel 2007) 177–192, 182–186.

a widespread problem resulting from a malfunction in Polish legislation and administrative practice affecting, and remaining capable of affecting, a large number of persons.[317] Based on Articles 1 and 13 of the ECHR incorporating the principle of subsidiarity, the Court finally expressed that general measures at a national level were undoubtedly called for in execution of the present judgement.[318]

The pilot-judgement procedure of *Burdov v Russia (No 2)* is also worth noting, in which the ECtHR clearly demanded legislative reform of the respondent state. With regard to the violation of Article 6 of the ECHR, the Court noted that the implementation of necessary measures 'raises a number of complex legal and practical issues which go, in principle, beyond the Court's judicial function'.[319] However, the Court differentiated the violation of Article 13 from that of Article 6 and asserted that '[i]t appears highly unlikely in the light of the Court's conclusions that such an effective remedy can be set up without changing the domestic legislation on certain specific points'.[320]

It is notable in this context that the ECtHR has become aggressive in effectively implementing its own judgements. The new mechanism of infringement proceedings introduced under Article 46(4) was introduced through Protocol No 14, based on which the Court is required to make a definitive legal assessment of the question of compliance by taking into consideration all aspects of the procedure before the Committee of Ministers. The only opportunity for mobilising this tool thus far is the *Ilgar Mammadov v Azerbaijan* case, in which the failure of compliance with the 2014 principal judgement was determined in the 2019 infringement procedure judgement.[321] Another occasion in which the Strasbourg Court substantively intervened in the execution of its own judgements through the pilot-judgement procedure was the 2014 judgement on just satisfaction in *Cyprus v Turkey*. To deal with systemic human rights violations caused by the dysfunction of domestic legal systems, the ruling was 'the first time in the Court's history that the Court has made a specific judicial statement as to the import and effect of one of its judgments in the

317 *Broniowski v Poland*, ECtHR (Grand Chamber), App No 31443/96, Judgment on Merits of 22 June 2004, para 189.

318 Ibid paras 191–192.

319 *Burdov (No.2)* (n 251) para 137.

320 Ibid paras 138–139.

321 *Ilgar Mammadov v Azerbaijan*, ECtHR (Grand Chamber), App No 15172/13, Judgment on Article 46(4) of 29 May 2019.

context of execution'.[322] Facing the non-execution of the 2001 principal judgement by the Respondent state under the CoM's political supervision, the Court emphasised that Turkey is still formally bound by the relevant terms of the principal judgement and reaffirmed that the 2005 *Demopoulos* inadmissibility decision did not intend to dispose of the question of Turkey's compliance with the principal judgement.[323] According to the concurring opinion of nine judges, '[t]he present judgment heralds a new era in the enforcement of human rights upheld by the Court and marks an important step in ensuring respect for the rule of law in Europe'.[324]

As the Strasbourg Court invokes Articles 1, 13, 35 and 46 of the ECHR, all of which reflect the principle of subsidiarity, the pilot-judgement procedure involving changes in national legislation fit with the idea of positive subsidiarity.[325] Laurence Helfer has developed the doctrine of *embeddedness*, according to which '[s]trategically embedding the ECtHR in national legal systems provides such solutions where the justifications for [negative] subsidiarity are lacking'.[326] The embeddedness doctrine, in his view, 'authorizes the ECtHR to adopt a more interventionist stance' or 'a more assertive (but hopefully temporary) supervisory role' in order to 'enhance the ability of domestic actors to prevent or remedy violations of international rules "at home"'.[327] Essentially, 'embeddedness is a deep structural principle of the European Convention, one that provides an essential counterpoint to the deep structural principle of subsidiarity'.[328]

Inter-American jurisprudence on transformative reparations has furthermore been radicalised to intervene into domestic spheres. A representative example is the reparation judgement of *Bámaca-Velásquez v. Guatemala*, in which the IACtHR proceeded to order guaranteeing of non-repetition to *la sociedad como un todo* (the society as a whole). Remarkably, the Court developed the *right to the truth*, which stems from the combination of Arti-

322 Ibid, Joint Concurring Opinion of Judges Zupančič, Gyulumyan, David Thór Björgvinsson, Nicolaou, Sajó, Lazarova Trajkovska, Power-Forde, Vučinić and Pinto de Albuquerque, para 1.

323 *Cyprus v Turkey*, Judgment on Just Satisfaction (n 116) para 63.

324 Ibid Joint Concurring Opinion of Judges Zupančič, Gyulumyan, Davíd Thór Björgvinsson, Nicolaou, Sajó, Lazarova Trajkovska, Power-Forde, Vučinić and Pinto de Albuquerque, para 1.

325 Eva Brems, 'Positive Subsidiarity and Its Implications for the Margin of Appreciation Doctrine' (2019) 37 *Netherlands Quarterly of Human Rights* 210–227.

326 Helfer (n 299) 130.

327 Ibid 149 (parenthesis in the original text).

328 Ibid 130.

cles 8 and 25 of the ACHR.[329] According to its reasoning, the opportunity for the victim's next of kin to know the truth was a means of reparation and therefore an expectation by the state to satisfy the victim's next of kin and the society as a whole.[330] Based on the collective aspect of the right to the truth, the Court explained that the reparations that had to be made by Guatemala necessarily included not only effective investigation of the facts and punishment of all those responsible but also dissemination of their results to the *society as a whole*.[331] In accordance with Article 1(1) of the ACHR, the respondent state was mandated to take all necessary steps to 'ensure that these grave violations do not occur'.[332]

As previously explained in the Introduction to the monograph, the doctrine of conventionality control emerged from the essential connection between primary (obligation to *harmonise*) and secondary norms (future-oriented, preventative *restoration*). In the major *Almonacid-Arellano v. Chile* ruling, concerning the amnesty law under the Pinochet regime, the IACtHR expressed for the first time in its jurisprudence the necessity of conventionality control of legislative actions. During the merits stage, the Court concluded that Article 2 of the ACHR had been violated because the amnesty law was 'manifestly incompatible with the wording and the spirit of the American Convention, and undoubtedly affect[ed] rights embodied in such Convention'. Subsequently, the Court ordered the state to 'ensure that [the amnesty law] does not continue to hinder the investigation, prosecution and, as appropriate, punishment of those responsible for similar violations perpetrated in Chile'.[333] The Court's aim becomes apparent when looking at its explanation in the judgement compliance procedure that 'the most appropriate way to [correct the root causes of violations] is through a legislative amendment'.[334]

Positive subsidiarity in the Inter-American jurispurdence is well explicated in Ariel Dulitzky's *integration principle.* As the case law analysed above demonstrates, the San José Court 'seeks to embed the American Convention in national legal systems in order to provide solutions where justi-

329 *Bámaca-Velásquez v Guatemala*, IACtHR, Series C No 70, Judgment on Merits of 25 November 2000, paras 199–202.

330 *Bámaca-Velásquez v Guatemala*, IACtHR, Series C No. 91, Judgment on Reparations and Costs of 22 February 2002, paras 76–77.

331 Ibid para 73.

332 Ibid para 77.

333 *Almonacid-Arellano and Others*, Judgment (n 21) paras 144–145.

334 *Almonacid-Arellano and Others v Chile*, IACtHR, Monitoring Compliance with Judgment, Order of 18 November 2010, para 20.

fications for [negative] subsidiarity fail'.[335] According to the integration model, '[b]y requiring domestic judges in each of their cases to examine the compatibility of state actions or omissions and the compatibility of the national legal framework with the Convention, the Inter-American instrument becomes an integral part of domestic legal systems at the highest possible level'.[336] At the same time, '[b]y grounding the conventionality control in a partnership between the Court and local tribunals, the integration principle embraces the foundations of the subsidiarity principle'.[337]

The IACtHR's prescription for remedies for systemic violations depends on the use of self-control to comply with its own judgements.[338] In contrast to the CoE framework, as noted above, the ACHR does not determine which organ of the Inter-American system has the jurisdiction to monitor compliance with the IACtHR binding judgements. Against this background, in *Baena-Ricardo et al v Panama*, the IACtHR recognised for the first time its competence in monitoring compliance with its own judgements.[339] However, the San José Court has been plagued with a low compliance rate, especially with regard to judgements demanding legislative and administrative reforms that are addressed to political bodies.[340] In the recent resolution in *Apitz-Barbera*, the IACtHR indeed invoked the concept of *garantía colectiva* to confirm 'the task of the OAS General Assembly, in the case of manifest non-compliance with a judgment delivered by the Inter-American Court by one of the States, is precisely that of protecting the practical effects of the American Convention and preventing inter-American justice from becoming illusory by being at the discretion of the internal decisions of a State'.[341]

As an interim conclusion, the jurisprudence of both human rights courts shows that the *positive* concept of subsidiarity *concentrates* the com-

335 Dulitzky (n 24) 54.

336 Ibid.

337 Ibid 81.

338 Pablo Saavedra Alessandri, 'The Role of the Inter-American Court of Human Rights in Monitoring Compliance with Judgments' (2020) 12 *Journal of Human Rights Practice* 178–184.

339 *Baena-Ricardo and Others* (n 152) paras 84–104.

340 For an excellent empirical analysis on compliance rate of the jugments of human rights courts, see in general Courtney Hillebrecht, *Domestic Politics and International Human Rights Tribunals: The Problem of Compliance* (Cambridge University Press 2014).

341 *Apitz-Barbera and Others ('First Court of Administrative Cisputes') v Venezuela*, IACtHR, Monitoring Compliance with Judgment, Order of 23November 2012, para 47.

petence in favour of human rights courts to prescribe specific reparations. The essential connection between those provisions that embody subsidiarity accordingly enables human rights courts to control the compliance of domestic legal systems against the yardstick of the Conventions.

(ii) Identifying Organs Responsible for Systemic Violations

It should not be underestimated that, when prescribing general remedial measures, human rights courts penetrate into the state to open a line of interaction with state organs. The IACtHR orders requiring investigation and punishment ordered are expected to be implemented by the public ministry and judiciary even though they are formally directed to the state as a whole.[342] In pilot-judgement procedures, the ECtHR similarly considered judgements of domestic courts and created momentum for a productive dialogue with counterparts inside the state.[343] These developments seem to be equivalent to *piercing the State's veil* that has ever decoupled national organs within the state from international actors.

The state has traditionally been regarded as an indivisible entity possessing its own separate personality.[344] This understanding stems from an *external* perspective that has been deeply ingrained in international law, which assumes 'a national constitutional order as a monolithic, undivided and undifferentiated, block of political and legal power, irrespective of the particularities of internal constitutional arrangements and constitutionalism more broadly'.[345] Nevertheless, as Rosalyn Higgins points out, 'compliance with the findings of international tribunals is made the more difficult exactly because while "the state" carries the international obligation to comply, the necessary action to achieve that must internally be performed by organs of state'.[346] Against this difficulty, Higgins then proposed 'the need to look behind the monolithic face of "the state", when dealing

---

342 Alexandra Huneeus, 'Courts Resisting Courts: Lessons from the Inter-American Court's Struggle to Enforce Human Rights' (2011) 44 *Cornell International Law Journal* 493–533, 521–525.

343 Lech Garlicki, Cooperation of Courts: The Role of Supranational Jurisdictions in Europe' (2008) 6 *International Journal of Constitutional Law* 509–530, 512–522.

344 Fitzmaurice (n 39) 77.

345 David Haljan, *Separating Powers: International Law before National Courts* (Springer 2013) 14.

346 Rosalyn Higgins, 'The Concept of 'The State': Variable Geometry and Dualist Perceptions' in Laurence Boisson de Chazournes and Vera Gowlland-Debbas

with issues of compliance, and the attendant problems of dualist systems (both for those states themselves and for international tribunals)'.[347] In other words, to ensure compliance with their own decisions, international courts should break down their orders within the lines of the separation of powers inside the state.[348]

Given this intricate problem, some international courts have ventured to pierce the veil of the state, which has completely decoupled the relationship between international courts and the national organs within it.[349] As has already been noted above, the ICJ recently addressed the judiciary's role because it has been presented with regard to certain cases concerning the administration of domestic justice.[350] Such a penetration into the state by international courts cannot immediately change the powers of state organs within domestic legal orders.[351] However, such a possible step from *black box theory* to *state organ obligation* can enhance compliance by specifying and urging the state organs to take responsibility for implementing judgements.[352] The potential to pierce the state's veil would be particularly significant for the IACtHR and ECtHR, whose judgement compliance rates have been relatively troubled.

The practice of piercing the state's veil can be found explicitly in the *control de convencionalidad* doctrine, which has been developed by the IACtHR since *Almonacid-Arellano*. In this judgement, the Court found a violation of Article 2 of the ACHR due to 'formally keeping within its legislative *corpus* a Decree Law which is contrary to the wording and the spirit of the Convention' and ordered reparation measures virtually aimed

(eds), *The International Legal System in Quest of Equity and Universality* (Martinus Nijhoff 2001) 547–561, 547.

347 Ibid 561.

348 Huneeus (n 342) 521–525.

349 Jean Matringe, 'L'exécution par le juge étatique des décisions judiciares internationales' (2013) 117 *Revue Générale de Droit International Public* 555–578, 561–567.

350 Vladen S Vereshchetin, 'On the Expanding Reach of the Rulings of the International Court of Justice' in Pierre-Marie Dupuy, Bardo Fassbender, Malcolm N Shaw and Karl-Peter Sommermann (eds), *Völkerrecht als Wertordnung: für Christian Tomuschat* (N P Engel 2006) 621–633, 624.

351 André Nollkaemper, 'Conversations among Courts: Domestic and International Adjudicators' in Cesare P R Romano, Karen Alter and Yuval Shany (eds), *The Oxford Handbook of International Adjudication* (Oxford University Press 2014) 523–549, 531.

352 Ward Ferdinandusse, 'Out of the Black-Box? The International Obligation of State Organs' (2003) 29 *Brooklyn Journal of International Law* 45–127, 109–120.

at political sectors.[353] Moreover, the Court also emphasised the original mission of domestic courts under the general obligations under the Convention and ordered corresponding reparations directed at the judiciary.[354] In this context, the Court stated that '*the Judiciary* must exercise a sort of "conventionality control" between the domestic legal provisions which are applied to specific cases and the ACHR. To perform this task, *the Judiciary* has to take into account not only the treaty, but also the interpretation thereof made by the Inter-American Court, which is the ultimate interpreter of the American Convention'.[355]

The reparation measure addressed to the judiciary was close to (judicial) *restitutio in integrum* in comparison with the above-mentioned reparation measure aimed at the legislature, which was a part of guarantees of non-repetition.[356] Oswald Ruiz-Chiriboga accurately categorised the distinctive roles of the legislature and the judiciary as follows: 1) the State must modify, derogate or otherwise annul or amend the municipal law that breached the Convention, and 2) *in the meantime* it should not apply that law to the case that was brought before the Court and all other similar cases. While the first reparation should be performed by the legislature, the second reparation is in the hands of the judiciary. Consequently, the judiciary must implement a 'narrow conventionality control', where the only discretion it has is to ascertain which cases fall into the same category as the one considered by the IACtHR; the judiciary has no discretion at all in the case decided by the IACtHR.[357]

In the case of 'narrow conventionality control', the judiciary would build a vertical relationship between the San José Court and domestic courts with little appreciation for the latter.[358] As a matter of fact, in the *Dismissed Congressional Employees v Peru*, the IACtHR expressly required domestic courts to 'exercise not only a control of constitutionality, but also of "conventionality" *ex officio* between domestic norms and the American

---

353 *Almonacid-Arellano and Others*, Judgment (n 21) paras 115–122.
354 Ibid paras 123–125, 145–157.
355 Ibid paras 123–125 (emphasis added).
356 Ibid para 144.
357 Oswaldo Ruiz-Chiriboga, 'The Conventionality Control: Examples of (Un)Successful Experiences in Latin America' (2010) 3 *Inter-American and European Human Rights Journal* 200–219, 205 (emphasis in the original text).
358 Humberto Nogueira Alcalá, 'El control de convencionalidad y el diálogo interjurisdiccional entre tribunales nacionales y Corte Interamericana de Derechos Humanos' (2013) 19 *Revista de Derecho Constitucional Europeo* 221–270, 247.

Convention'.[359] Moreover, in *Cabrera Garcia and Montiel Flores v Mexico*, the Court rejected the respondent state's preliminary objection that 'the national tribunals have exercised an *ex officio* "conventionality control" between the domestic rules and the American Convention', and proceeded to the merits stage to 'determine whether the conventionality control alleged by the State involved a respect for the State's international obligations in the light of this Tribunal's case law and under the applicable international law'.[360] In the same judgement, the Court also imposed conventionality control not simply on the judiciary but also on 'the judges and organs linked to the administration of justice *at all levels*'.[361]

Regarding these proactive interventions into domestic forums, the IACtHR in the *Santo Domingo Massacre* case for the first time expressed the connection between *control de convencionalidad* and subsidiarity (complementarity):

> [A] *dynamic and complementary* control of the States' treaty-based obligations to respect and ensure human rights has been established between the domestic authorities (who have the primary obligation) and the international instance (*complementarily*), so that their decision criteria can be established and harmonized.[362]

It follows then that subsidiarity, specifically its positive aspect, enables the San José Court to designate the particular national organs responsible for controlling the compliance of national legal systems with the ACHR, to the extent that the alleged conventionality control by States Parties falls short of the pertinent criteria.

A similar, but more moderate, practice of piercing the state's veil is demonstrated in the ECtHR case law. Examples include *Dimitrov and Hamanov v Bulgaria* and *Finger v Bulgaria*, which concerned the excessive length of proceedings and the lack of domestic remedy. In applying the pilot-judgement procedure to these cases, the Strasbourg Court differentiated the violation of Article 13 from that of Article 6 under the ECHR, and affirmed that 'the introduction of effective domestic remedies in this domain would be particularly important in view of the subsidiarity princi-

359 *The Dismissed Congressional Employees* (n 49) para 128.

360 *Cabrera Garcia and Montiel Flores* (n 35) para 21.

361 Ibid para 225 (emphasis added).

362 *The Santo Domingo Massacre v Colombia*, IACtHR, Series C No 259, Judgment on Preliminary Objections, Merits and Reparations of 30 November 2012, paras 142–143.

ple'.[363] Consequently, the Court found it appropriate to provide guidance to the respondent state 'in order to assist them in the performance of their duty under Article 46 § 1 of the Convention'.[364] To assist in the provision of redress for past proceedings delays, the Court provided detailed guidance for the Bulgarian judiciary.[365]

The ECtHR's power 'to assist the authorities in finding the appropriate solutions' for the structural violation of Article 13 of the ECHR was further developed in *Ananyev v Russia* regarding inhumane treatment in prisons. Given the logistical and legally complicated problems of violating Article 3 (prohibition of torture), the Court found that any *substantive mandate* in this area would go beyond its judicial function while still voicing its concerns and indicating possible ways to address the existing deficiencies.[366] By way of contrast, it was noted that the need for effective domestic remedies for violations of Article 13 was more pressing because the circumstance of large numbers of people affected by the violations being compelled to seek relief through time-consuming international litigation before the court is at odds with the principle of subsidiarity.[367] Stressing the special character of the violation of Article 13, the Strasbourg Court delivered a substantive mandate requiring 'clear and specific changes in the domestic legal systems that would allow all people in the applicants' position to complain about alleged violations'.[368] To facilitate national authorities in finding appropriate solutions, the Court then considered preventative and compensatory remedies, emphasising the work of the prosecutor's office and the domestic courts.[369] In the later decision of *Shmelev and Others*, the Court declared the individual applications inadmissible, as those applicants had not exhausted domestic remedies through the 2019 Compensation Act, which affords them an opportunity

363 *Dimitrov and Hamanov v Bulgaria*, ECtHR, App. No. 48059/06 and 2708/09, Judgment on Merits and Just Satisfaction of 10 May 2011, para 122.

364 Ibid para. 123. See also, *Neshkov and Other v Bulgaria*, ECtHR, App Nos 36925/10 and Other, Judgment on Just Satisfaction of 27 January 2015, para 280; *Varga and Others v Hungary*, ECtHR, App Nos 14097/12 and Others, Judgment on Merits and Just Satisfaction of 10 March 2015, para 108.

365 *Dimitrov and Hamanov* (n 363) para 128.

366 *Ananyev and Others v Russia*, ECtHR, App No 42525/07 and 60800/08, Judgment on Merits and Just Satisfaction of 10 January 2012, para 212.

367 Ibid para. 211.

368 Ibid paras 212–213.

369 Ibid paras 214–231.

to obtain compensatory redress domestically.[370] Moreover, the ECtHR resolutely retained its centralised power in dictating that 'the Court's ultimate supervisory jurisdiction remains in respect of any complaints lodged by the applicants who, in conformity with the principle of subsidiarity, have exhausted available avenues of redress'.[371]

In essence, another interim conclusion can be derived from the jurisprudence of human rights courts: *positive* subsidiarity *centralises* the competence towards human rights courts to discover underlying structural problems, indicate particular measures for rectifying those problems and, if necessary, pierce the veil of the state to designate the liable state organs. The subsidiarity principle therefore supports 'a revised system of states whose sovereignty is limited and conditional on whether the state actually does respect and promote individuals' well-being – perhaps enjoying a certain margin of appreciation'.[372]

B. Decentralising Conventionality Control Powers to Domestic Courts

(i) Margin of Appreciation in Conventionality Control

In developing the *control de convencionalidad* doctrine, the IACtHR has recognised a certain margin of appreciation for realising conventionality control at the national level. This attitude became apparent when the Court explained in *Liakat Ali Alibux v Surinam* that 'the American Convention does not impose a specific model for the regulation of issues of constitutionality and control for conformity with the Convention'.[373] According to the IACtHR jurisprudence, States Parties retain the freedom to allocate the authority for conventionality control among national organs. Even at an early stage, the judiciary has been allowed to exercise conventionality control 'evidently in the context of their respective spheres of competence and the corresponding procedural regulations'.[374] In addition, the San José

370 *Shmelev and Others v Russia*, ECtHR, App Nos 41743/17 and Others, Decision of 17 March 2020, para 137.

371 Ibid, para 128. This formula has already appeared in *Demopoulos and Others v Turkey*, ECtHR (Grand Chamber), App Nos 46113/99 and Others, Decision of 1 March 2010, para 128.

372 Andreas Føllesdal, 'The Principle of Subsidiarity as a Constitutional Principle in International Law' (2013) 2 *Global Constitutionalism* 37–62, 60.

373 *Liakat Ali Alibux* (n 307) para 124.

374 *The Dismissed Congressional Employees v Peru* (n 49) para 128.

Court has clarified that conventionality control is delegated to '*all bodies of the State*, including its judges and other mechanisms related to the administration of justice at all levels'.[375] Compared with the original simple term *the judiciary*, this statement shed light on the range of organs responsible for conventionality control to include both judicial and political sectors.

As regards the compatibility between conventionality control and margin of appreciation, we can gain inspiration again from Judge MacGregor's opinion in *Cabrera Garcia and Montiel Flores v. Mexico*:

> [The control de convencionalidad doctrine] does not aim to establish which body has the final word, but to encourage creative jurisprudential dialogue, responsible and committed to the effectiveness of fundamental rights. National judges will now become the first Inter-American judges. It is they who bear the greatest responsibility to harmonize national legislation within the Inter-American parameters. The IACtHR should monitor this and be fully aware of the standards that will be constructed through the use of its jurisprudence, considering also the 'national discretion' [*margen de apreciación nacional*] that nation-States have to interpret the Inter-American *corpus juris*.[376]

In making a comment on these passages, Andrew Legg asserts that, while the conventionality control doctrine is supportive of the 'standard-unifying' approach to the role of Tribunals, it is clear that this doctrine is likewise compatible with the doctrine of margin of appreciation.[377]

The more diffused nature of conventionality control may be discovered in ECtHR jurisprudence, even in pilot-judgement procedures in which national discretion is regulated to a great extent. For instance, in *Greens and M T v the United Kingdom*, the ECtHR emphasised the wide margin of appreciation clarified in the *Hirst* judgement with regard to 'organising and running electoral systems and a wealth of differences, inter alia, in historical development, cultural diversity and political thought within Europe which it is for each Contracting State to mould into their own democratic vision'.[378] Therefore, the Court held that 'it is for the Government,

---

375 *Gelman v Uruguay*, IACtHR, Monitoring Compliance with Judgment, Order of 20 March 2013, para 66 (emphasis added).

376 Eduardo Ferrer Mac-Gregor, 'Interpretación conforme y control difuso de convencionalidad: El nuevo paradigma para el juez mexicano' (2011) 9 *Estudioos Constitucionales* 531–622, 620.

377 Legg (n 212) 112.

378 *Hirst v the United Kingdom (No 2)*, ECtHR (Grand Chamber), App No 74025/01, Judgment on Merits and Just Satisfaction of 6 October 2005, para 61.

following appropriate consultation, to decide in the first instance how to achieve compliance with Article 3 of Protocol No 1 when introducing legislative proposals'.[379]

(ii) Deference to Domestic Margin of Appreciation

Negative subsidiarity restricts an international review by human rights courts if national authorities have already achieved appropriate control in the domestic realm. When the IACtHR clarified for the first time the connection between *control de convencionalidad* and subsidiarity in *The Santo Domingo Massacre v Colombia* case, it also articulated that '[t]he State's responsibility under the Convention can only be required at the international level after the State has had the opportunity to declare the violation and to repair the damage caused by its own means'.[380] If domestic courts award reparations based on 'objective and reasonable' criteria, the Inter-American Court declines to order additional reparations.[381] In *Operation Genesis v Colombia*, concerning a case related to transitional justice in which a massive scale of reparations was required for numerous victims, the IACtHR recognised that 'the principle of complementarity of international law [...] has been taken into account by the Court in other cases to acknowledge the compensation granted at the domestic level and to abstain from ordering reparations in this regard, when this is pertinent'.[382]

In recent jurisprudence, the Inter-American judges have remarkably refrained from determining State responsibility, especially when domestic judges appropriately exercised control of conventionality. In *Andrade Salmón v Bolivia*, the IACtHR appreciated that the alleged violation ceased because the State effectively guaranteed the victim's right to personal freedom through the judgements of the Plurinational Constitutional Court, which in turn constituted '*oportuno y adecuado control de convencionalidad*'.[383]The San José Court accepted preliminary objections to admissibility by the State Party in *Amrhein et al v Costa Rica* because the national

379 *Greens and M T v the United Kingdom*, ECtHR, App Nos 60041/08 and 60054/08, Judgment on Merits and Just Satisfaction of 23 November 2010, para 114.

380 *The Santo Domingo Massacre v Colombia* (n 362) para 142.

381 *ROdríguez Vera and others* (n 218) para 595.

382 *The Afro-descendant Communities v Colombia* (n 133) para 474.

383 *Andrade Salmón v Bolivia*, IACtHR, Series C No 330, Judgment on Merits, Reparations and Costs of 1 December 2016, para 100.

authorities, including the Constitutional Chamber of the Supreme Court, provided 'sufficient measures' and 'adequate responses' to the alleged violations.[384] The *Rosadio Villavicencio v Peru* judgement, by referring to the subsidiarity principle, did not find the State Party responsible for the alleged violation of Article 8 of the ACHR due to the decisions of the criminal jurisdiction of the Supreme Court.[385] The negative aspect of subsidiarity in conventionality control was also evident in *Colindres Schonenberg v El Salvador*, in which the San José Court did not find the State Party responsible because the Court appreciated the decisions of the Constitutional Chamber of the Supreme Court.[386]

The national margin of appreciation has also been broadly redistributed when national authorities have realised conventionality control by providing appropriate reparations. The ECtHR pointed out this possibility in *Scordino v Italy (No 1)*, stating that '[w]here a State has taken a significant step by introducing a compensatory remedy, the Court must leave a wider margin of appreciation to the State to allow it to organise the remedy in a manner consistent with its own legal system and traditions and consonant with the standard of living in the country concerned'.[387] In the case of *Hiernaux v. Belgium*, the Court found no violation of Article 13 in light of Article 6(1), as the compensatory remedy allowed a complaint about the length of the criminal proceedings, including during the judicial investigation or at the committal stage.[388]

Pilot-judgement procedures for which conventionality control powers are once centralised to regional courts can be closed depending on the degree of compliance by States Parties. A re-decentralising, negative subsidiarity approach has been taken, for example, in the pilot judgements of

384 *Amrhein y otros v Costa Rica*, IACtHR, Serie C No 354, Judgment of Preliminary Objections, Merits, Reparations and Costs of 25 April 2018, paras 97–115.

385 *Rosadio Villavicencio v Peru*, IACtHR, Series C No 388, Judgment of Preliminary Objections, Merits, Reparations and Costs of 14 October 2019, para 167–169.

386 *Colindres Schonenberg v El Salvador*, IACtHR, Series C No. 373, Judgment of Merits, Reparations and Costs of 4 February 2019, paras 75–80.

387 *Scordino v Italy (No 1)*, ECtHR (Grand Chamber), App No 36813/97, Judgment on Merits and Just Satisfaction of 29 March 2006, para 189.

388 *Hiernaux v Bel*gium, ECtHR, App No 28022/15, Judgment on Merits and Just Satisfaction of 24 January 2017, paras 59–62.

Hutten-Czapska v Poland[389] and *Sujagic v Bosnia Herzegovina*.[390] A remarkable success story is the *Kurić and Others v Slovenia* case concerning the so-called erased group of former nationals of the Socialist Federal Republic of Yugoslavia. After holding a pilot-judgement procedure on the merits in 2012, the Strasbourg Court indicated in its judgement on just satisfaction in 2014 that 'according to the principle of *subsidiarity* and the margin of appreciation which goes with it, the amounts of compensation awarded at a national level to other adversely affected persons in the context of general measures under Article 46 of the Convention are at the discretion of the respondent State, provided that they are compatible with the Court's judgment ordering those measures'.[391] In the later decision in *Anastasov and Others*, the Strasbourg judges were satisfied that the system introduced by the respondent government offered to other affected 'erased' persons reasonable prospects of receiving compensation for the damage caused by the systemic violation of their Convention rights.[392] In other words, '[b]y proposing a solution for many individual cases arising from the same structural problem at the domestic level, the respondent State thus gave effect to the *subsidiarity* principle, which underpins the Convention system'.[393] Therefore, the Court decided to close the pilot-judgement procedure initiated in *Kurić et al*, considering it no longer justified.[394]

In the same vein, the ECtHR started declaring the inadmissibility of new applications in accordance with Article 35(1) of the ECHR, reflecting the subsidiarity principle, if national authorities are successful at introducing appropriate general measures in response to pilot-judgement procedures.[395] This approach has been adopted in (semi-)pilot-judgement proce-

389 *Hutten-Czapska v Poland*, ECtHR (Grand Chamber), App No 35014/97, Judgment on Merits and Just Satisfaction of 19 June 2006; *The Assocation of Real Property Owners in Łódź v Poland*, ECtHR, App No 3485/02, Decision of 8 March 2011.

390 *Sujagic v Bosnia Herzegovina*, ECtHR, App No 27912/02, Judgment on Merits and Just Satisfaction of 3 November 2009; *Zadrić v Bosnia and Herzegovina*, ECtHR, App No 18804/04, Decision of 16 November 2010.

391 *Kurić and Others v Slovenia*, ECtHR (Grand Chamber), App No 26828/06, Judgment on Just Satisfaction of 12 March 2014, para 141 [emphasis added].

392 *Anastasov and Others* v *Slovenia*, ECtHR, App No 65020/13, Decision of 10 October 2016, para 88.

393 Ibid, para 99 [emphasis added].

394 Ibid, para 103.

395 As to the judicial role in judgments execution, Giorgio Malinverni, 'La compétence de la Cour pour surveiller l'exécution de ses propres arrêts' in Dean Spielmann, Marialena Tsirti, Panayotis Voyatzis (eds), *La Convention européenne*

dures concerning the structural violations of right to property protection (*Broniowski v Poland* (2004),[396] *Xenides-Arestis v Turkey* (2005),[397] and *Maria Atanasiu and Others v Romania* (2010)[398]); prolonged non-enforcement of court decisions (*Burdov v Russia (No 2)* (2009)[399] and *Olaru and Others v the Republic of Moldova* (2009)[400]); excessive length of proceedings (*Rumpf v Germany* (2010),[401] *Vassilios Athanasiou and Others v Greece* (2010),[402] *Dimitrov and Hamanov v Bulgaria* and *Finger v Bulgaria* (2011),[403] and *Ümmühan Kaplan v Turkey* (2012)[404]); and, inhuman and/or degrading conditions of detention (*Torreggiani and Others v Italy* (2013)[405]).

---

des droits de l'homme, un instrument vivant : Mélanges en l'honneur de Chirstos L. Rozakis (Bruylant 2011) 361–375.

396 *Broniowski v Poland* (n 317); *Wolkenberg and Others v Poland*, ECtHR, App No 50003/99, Decision of 4 December 2007.

397 *Xenides-Arestis v Turkey*, ECtHR, App No 46347/99, Judgment on Merits of 22 December 2005; *Demopoulos and Others v Turkey* (n 371).

398 *Maria Atanasiu and Others v Romania*, ECtHR, App Nos 30767/05 33800/06, Judgment on Merits and Just Satisfaction of 12 October 2010; *Preda and Others v Romania*, ECtHR, App Nos 9584/0 and Others, Judgment on Merits and Just Satisfaction of 29 April 2014.

399 *Burdov v Russia* (n 251); *Nagovitsyn and Nalgiyev v Russia*, ECtHR, App Nos 27451/09 and 60650/09, Decision of 23 September 2010. In the subsequent judgment, however, the Court found the violation of Art 13 of the ECHR again on the matter. See, for example, *Ilyushkin and Others v Russia*, ECtHR, App. Nos. 5734/08 and Others, Judgment on Merits and Just Satisfaction of 17 April 2012.

400 *Olaru and Others v the Republic of Moldova*, ECtHR, App Nos 476/07, 22539/05, 17911/08 and 13136/07, Judgment on Merits of 28 July 2009; *Balan v the Republic of Moldova*, ECtHR, App No 44746/08, Decision of 24 January 2012.

401 *Rumpf v Germany*, ECtHR, App No 46344/06, Judgment on Merits and Just Satisfaction of 2 September 2010; *Taron v Germany*, ECtHR, App No 53126/07, Decision of 29 May 2012.

402 *Vassilios Athanasiou and Others v Greece*, ECtHR, App No 50973/08, Judgment on Merits and Just Satisfaction of 21 December 2010; *Techniki Olympiaki A E v Greece*, ECtHR, App No 40547/10, Decision of 1 October 2013.

403 *Dimitrov and Hamanov v Bulgaria*, App Nos 48059/06 and 2708/09, Judgment on Merits and Just Satisfaction of 10 May 2011; *Finger v Bulgaria*, App No 37346/05, Judgment on Merits and Just Satisfaction of 10 May 2011; *Valcheva and Abrashev v Bulgaria*, ECtHR, App Nos 6194/11 and 34887/11, Decision of 18 June 2013.

404 *Ümmühan Kaplan v Turkey*, ECtHR, App No 24240/07, Judgment on Merits and Just Satisfaction of 20 March 2012; *Müdür Turgut and Others v Turkey*, ECtHR, App No 4860/09, Decision of 26 March 2013.

405 *Torreggiani and Others v Italy*, ECtHR, App No 43517/09 and Others, Judgment on Merits and Just Satisfaction of 8 January 2013; *Stella and Others v Italy*, ECtHR, App Nos 49169/09 and Others, Decision of 16 September 2014.

Overall, the IACtHR and ECtHR case law proves that the subsidiarity principle not only endorses the centralisation of competences on the side of human rights courts but also illuminates the normative framework in which conventionality control is exercised in a 'pluralistic' manner.[406] *Diffused* conventionality control is supposed to be exercised principally by States Parties and complementarily by human rights courts. It contributes to 'convert[ing] the domestic judges into [...] the *first* and *true* guardian of the Convention[s]', thereby enhancing the primary roles of national organs.[407] Eventually, conventionality control by human rights courts must be regulated from the perspective of *negative* subsidiarity 'when domestic decision makers have resumed their *rightful* position as the Convention's *first-line* defenders'.[408] If the ultimate goal of revitalising domestic authorities is attained, the *negative* concept of subsidiarity *decentralises* competences in favour of States Parties, which were once concentrated towards human rights courts, entrusting conventionality control to the primary guardians of human rights.

406 Jonas Christoffersen, 'Individual and Constitutional Justice: Can the Power Balance of Adjudication be Reversed?' in Jonas Christoffersen and Mikael Rask Madsen (eds), *The European Court of Human Rights between Law and Politics* (Oxford University Press 2011) 181–203, 190. See also, Nico Krisch, *Beyond Constitutionalism: The Pluralist Structure of Postnational Law* (Oxford University Press 2010) Chap 4. It is suggestive that Greer and Wildhaber, who had advocated the ECtHR's constitutional justice, altered their position incorporating these pluralists' perspectives. Steven Greer and Luzius Wildhaber, 'Revisiting the Debate about "Constitutionalising" the European Court of Human Rights' (2012) 12 Human Rights Law Rreview 655–687, 684.

407 Mac-Gregor (n 376) 570 (emphasis added).

408 Helfer (n 299) 149 (emphasis added).

Part II
Internationalised Constitutional Adjudication

Chapter 1
Application of Conventionality Control Parameters

The first aspect of the internationalisation of constitutional adjudication is that domestic judges are required to exercise control over domestic law in accordance with not only national constitutions but also regional conventions. In the contemporary era, sovereign States have faced heavy pressure from the international community, and consequently, the absolute supremacy of the constitution is relativised through the 'internationalisation of constitution'.[409] Referring to Daniel Thürer's term *kosmopolitische Verfassungsentwicklungen*,[410] Anne Peters rightly captures the recent phenomenon of constitutional development where 'the international community, or at least its most powerful members, have been supervising regime changes and have induced, accompanied, steered, or even installed new state constitutions'.[411]

The applicability of international law within constitutional frameworks has been debated with great interest in theory and practice. On the international level, Article 27 of the VCLT stipulates the supremacy of internal law by prohibiting the invocation of domestic legal provisions as justification for the failure to uphold treaty provisions. Article 46(1) thereof furthermore hinders a State from invoking domestic circumstances as invalidating its consent to be bound by a treaty 'unless that violation was manifest and concerned a rule of its internal law of fundamental importance'. At the domestic level, as is implied in the 'fundamental importance' condition attached to the latter, the problems of whether international law is a part of national law and whether it is applicable before national courts

409 Wen-Chen Chang and Jiunn-Rong Yeh, 'Internationalization of Constitutional Law' in Michel Rosenfeld and A András Sajó (eds), *The Oxford Handbook of Comparative Constitutional Law* (Oxford University Press 2012) 1165–84, 1167–1169.

410 Daniel Thürer, 'Kosmopolitische Verfassungsentwicklungen' in Daniel Thürer (ed), *Kosmopolitisches Staatsrecht*, Vol 1 (Schulthess Zurich 2005) 3–39.

411 Anne Peters, 'Supremacy Lost: International Law Meets Domestic Constitutional Law' (2009) 3 *Vienna Online Journal of International Constitutional Law* 170–198, 173.

are constitutional in nature.[412] Therefore, the *supremacy of international law* over domestic law cannot duly answer the question of whether domestic courts can utilise human rights conventions in judicial review.

Moreover, human rights conventions and national constitutions share similar catalogues of rights and freedoms for the most part. An empirical study reveals that 'human rights treaties have a significant influence on the catalogue of human rights contained in national constitutions and, on the contrary, it follows from the very nature of human rights treaties that they are the result of reflected experience'.[413] Therefore, a judicial review involving fundamental rights would indicate the inevitable coexistence of conventionality control and constitutionality control. Quoting the IACtHR's expression of this, 'the constitutionality control necessarily implies the conventionality control, exercised in complementary manner'.[414] A conundrum thus arises when domestic courts find certain domestic provisions incompatible with a treaty and abstain from enforcing the treaty provisions. In this situation, no practical necessity would remain to re-evaluate these norms against the yardstick of the analogous catalogue of constitutional rights. Eventually, conventionality control would replace constitutionality control, and the latter's ultimate aim of ensuring the *supremacy of constitution* would also be undermined.

Against this background, national judges have tried to integrate human rights treaties into national constitutions to converge the parallel judicial control mechanisms. The present chapter first examines the battle for supremacy between regional conventions and national constitutions: incorporating regional conventions and regional courts' decisions into national constitutions, on the one hand (Section 1-A), and consubstantial and sovereigntist constitutional contestations against regional conventions, on the other hand (Section 1-B). To alleviate the tension between international and constitutional legal orders, it then unpacks the potential of the *pro homine* principle regarding two points: the *offensive* function as a *sword* to penetrate the border between the international and the national

412 James Crawford, *Brownlie's Principles of Public International Law*, 8th ed (Oxford University Press 2012) 55–59.

413 Eliska Wagnerova, 'The Direct Applicability of Human Rights Treaties' in Council of Europe (ed), *The Status of International Treaties on Human Rights* (2006) 111–128, 113.

414 *Gelman*, Order (n 375) para 88.

legal order (Section 2-A), and the *defensive* function as a *shield* to preserve constitutional principles and values (Section 2-B).[415]

1. Relationship between Regional Conventions and National Constitutions

A. Supremacy of Regional Conventions over National Constitutions

(i) Incorporating Regional Conventions through National Constitutions

Leaving aside the theoretical battle between dualism and monism, the doctrinal concept of *direct applicability* practically informs the relationship between international and constitutional law. Here it is worth recalling the well-worn *Danzig* formula: 'according to a well-established principle of international law, [...] an international agreement, cannot, as such, create direct rights and obligations for private individuals [b]ut it cannot be disputed that the very object of an international agreement, according to the intention of the Contracting Parties, may be the adoption by the Parties of some definite rules creating individual rights and obligations and enforceable by the national courts'.[416] As Yuji Iwasawa carefully categorised, the direct applicability (*Anwendbarkeit*) or 'self-executing' of international law in domestic law normally means 'susceptible of being applied without the need of further measures', which must be distinguished from its domestic legal force (*Geltung*).[417] The function of direct effect is formulated by André Nollkaemper into a duality: on the one hand, 'as a powerful *sword* that courts can use to pierce the boundary of the national legal order and protect individual rights where national law falls short';[418] on the other hand, direct effect serves as a *shield* to 'justify the non-application of international law by the courts, and thereby protect domestic political organs

---

415 The *pro homine* principle has the potential to be applied beyond the regions of Europe and Latin America. As a Japanese context, for example, Hajime Yamamoto and Yota Negishi, 'Japan' in Fulvio M Palombino (ed), *Duelling for Supremacy: International vs. National Fundamental Principles* (Cambridge University Press 2019) 210–233, 218–219.

416 *Jurisdiction of the Courts of Danzig* (Advisory Opinion), PCIJ Rep Series B No 15 (1928) 17–18.

417 Yuji Iwasawa, 'Domestic Application of International Law' (2016) 378 Recueil des Cours 9–261, 134–144.

418 André Nollkaemper, 'The Duality of Direct Effect of International Law' (2014) 25 *European Journal of International Law* 105–125, 112–115 (emphasis added).

and, more generally, domestic values, from review based on international law'.[419]

Alternatively, the internationalisation trend of national constitutions is accelerated by the mandate of *consistent interpretation*, according to which national authorities must construe legislation in conformity with international law.[420] In some countries, national constitutions incorporate an express provision that requires consistent interpretation. For example, the Constitutional Court of South Africa utilises Section 39(1)(b) of the constitution to 'consider international law as a tool to interpretation of the Bill of Rights'.[421] Similarly, Section 11(2)(c) of the Constitution of Malawi has required domestic courts in this country to 'have regard where applicable, to current norms of public international law and comparable foreign case law'.[422] Even lacking an evident constitutional provision, domestic courts often in practice gain inspiration for interpreting legislation from international law. A representative example is the *Charming Betsy* canon that was adopted by the US Supreme Court in a historical judgement in 1804.[423]

The specific contexts of regional human rights protection are also influenced by the *conventionalisation* trends of national constitutions and in more express manners. There indeed exists the 'progressive *rapprochement* between the European domestic orders with regard to the "position" of the ECHR in the national hierarchy of sources'.[424] The best example is found

---

419 Ibid 115–117.

420 Antonios Tzanakapoulos, 'Domestic Courts in International Law: The International Judicial Function of National Courts' (2011) 34 *Loyola of Los Angeles International and Comparative Law Review* 133–168, 157.

421 Sec 39(1)(b) Constitution of South Africa: When interpreting the Bill of Rights, a court, tribunal or forum [...]must consider international law. Constitutional Court of South Africa, Government of South Africa and ors v Grootboom, Appeal to Constitutional Court, [2000] ZACC 19, 2001 (1) SA 46, 2000 (11) BCLR 1169 (CC), 4 October 2000, paras 26–31 (ILDC 285 (ZA 2000) analysed by Waruguru Kaguongo).

422 Sec 11(2)(c): In interpreting the provisions of this Constitution a court of law shall [...] take full account of the provisions of Chapter III and Chapter IV. High Court of Malawi, Moyo v Attorney General, Constitutional Review, Constitutional Case No 12 of 2007, 26th August 2009, para 12 (ILDC 1370 (MW 2009) analysed by Mwiza Jo Nkhata).

423 *Murray v Charming Betsy*, 6 U.S. (2 Cranch) 64 (1804), 18.

424 Giuseppe Martinico, 'Is the European Convention Going to Be "Supreme"? A Comparative-Constitutional Overview of ECHR and EU Law before National Courts' (2012) 23 *European Journal of International Law* 401–424, 404 (emphasis in original text).

in Austria, where the ECHR has been granted constitutional rank and fully incorporated since 1964.[425] Due to its constitutional status, the Austrian Constitutional Court has the competence to review whether certain acts violate *Strasbourg* law and constitutional criteria.[426] Another example is provided by Article 94 of the Dutch Constitution, which is an open-minded provision for the international community which offers a legal basis for judges in the Netherlands to perform conventionality control of national statutes.[427]

A certain number of States Parties award the ECHR a supra-legislative status, that is, give it primacy over national legislation. For example, in Switzerland international law has priority over national law in situations in which they conflict.[428] In addition, Article 190 of the Federal Constitution is interpreted as a legal basis for the Federal Supreme Court to review the compatibility of a federal statute with constitutional and international law.[429] The Supreme Court has thus helped the ECHR become an essential element of the Swiss legal order 'by the equalization of the ECHR with the Constitution, at least on the procedural level, and by taking into account the conventional guarantees for the concretization of constitutional rights'.[430] As the guarantees under the ECHR and the Federal Constitution

---

425 Bundesverfafssungsgesetz vom 4. März, mit dem Bestimmungen des Bundesverfassungsfesetzes in der Fassung von 1929 über Staatsverträge abgeändert und ergänzt weden, 59/1964.

426 Philip Cede, 'Report on Austria and Germany' in Giuseppe Martinico and Oreste Pollicino (eds), *The National Judicial Treatment of the ECHR and EU Laws: A Comparative Constitutional Perspective* (Europa Law Publishing 2010) 55–80, 66; Daniela Thurnherr, 'The Reception Process in Austria and Switzerland' in Helen Keller and Alec Stone Sweet (eds), *A Europe of Rights: The Impact of the ECHR on National Legal Systems* (Oxford University Press 2008) 311–391, 326–328.

427 Gerhard van der Schyff, 'Constitutional Review by the Judiciary in the Netherlands' (2010) 11 *German Law Journal* 275–290, 279–281; Erika de Wet, 'The Reception Process in the Netherlands and Belgium' in Keller and Stone Sweet (n 28) 229–310, 240–241.

428 Daniel Thürer, 'Verfassungsrecht und Völkerrecht' in Daniel Thürer, Jean-François Aubert, Jörg Paul Müller (eds), *Verfassungsrecht der Schweiz* (Schulthess 2001) 179–206.

429 Thurnherr (n 426) 332–335.

430 Helen Keller, 'Reception of the European Convention for the Protection of Human Rights and Fundamental Freedoms (ECHR) in Poland and Switzerland' (2005) 65 *Zeitschrift für ausläandisches öffentliches Recht und Völkerrecht* 283–349, 307.

run parallel in many areas, there exists a type of *de facto* constitutional control with respect to federal statutes in case of their application.[431]

In Belgium, the Supreme Court of Appeal introduced in the 1971 *Franco-Suisse Le Ski* decision the monistic theory regarding the relationship between treaties and the Belgian Constitution.[432] Moreover, the Constitutional Court has implicitly confirmed its own authority to review the constitutionality of treaties, and therefore maintained its supremacy over treaties.[433] Against this background, there is a 'parallel system of control with ordinary jurisdictions (directly) reviewing the conformity with treaty provisions and the Constitutional Court reviewing the conformity with constitutional provisions'.[434] The Constitutional Court has also occasionally followed ECtHR jurisprudence, and therefore accepted that constitutional and treaty rights form 'an inseparable whole'.[435] A similar parallel judicial control can be found in the French legal system in which Article 55 of the Constitution explicitly recognises the supra-legal rank of treaties. Since the 1975 *IVG* judgement, the Constitutional Council has ruled that it has no jurisdiction to review the conformity of legal provisions in light of treaties.[436] Subsequently, the Court of Cassation and the Council of State performed the important task of judicial review *ex post* based on the ECHR, which had substantively complemented the constitutionality control *ex ante* assumed by the Constitutional Council.[437] Because these parallel systems can permit these ordinary courts to rely on the Strasbourg law rather than constitutional protection, the 2008 constitutional reform introduced the *Question prioritaire de constitutionnalité* (QPC) to ensure the priority of constitutional issues over Convention issues. Under the QPC procedure, if a party raises a constitutional question, the judge must exam-

431 Giovanni Biaggini, 'Switzerland' in Dawn Oliver and Carlo Fusaro (eds), *How Constitutions Change: A Comparative Study* (2011) 303–328, 322.

432 Cour de Cassation belge, *Fromagerie franco-suisse Le Ski. État Belge c SA*, arrêt du 27 mai 1971.

433 Matthias E Storme, 'The Struggle Concerning Interpretative Authority in the Context of Human Rights: The Belgian Experience' in Rainer Arnold (ed), *The Universalism of Human Rights* (Springer 2013) 223–235, 227–230.

434 De Wet (n 427) 251.

435 Cour Constitutionnelle belge, Arrêt n° 195/2009 du 3 décembre 2009, B. 7.

436 Conseil constitutionnel de la République Française, Décision n° 74–54 DC du 15 janvier 1975.

437 Didier Maus, 'Nouveux regards sur le contrôle de constitutionnalité par voie d'exception' in Dnys de Béchillon, Pierre Brunet, Véronique Champeil-Desplats and Éric Millard (eds), *L'architecture du droit : Mélanges en l'honneur de Michel Troper* (Economica 2006) 665–678, 675.

ine certain conditions, and if they are met, send the question to the Constitutional Council, not to the ordinary jurisdictions. The QPC mechanism does not isolate but rather reinforces the ECHR guarantees by inducing the Constitutional Council to pay attention to ECtHR jurisprudence.[438] In practice, the Constitutional Council seems to avoid diverging from the jurisprudence of the Strasbourg Court.[439]

The regionalisation of national constitutions has also been accelerated through so-called *consistent interpretation* clauses. Article 10(2) of the Spanish Constitution stipulates that '[t]he norms relative to basic rights and liberties which are recognized by the Constitution shall be interpreted in conformity with the Universal Declaration of Human Rights and the international treaties and agreements on those matters ratified by Spain'. Through this interpretative clause, the constitutional provisions of fundamental rights are considered incomplete, and open norms are subject to being specified or the content of human rights treaties may be placed there.[440] The ECHR thus rapidly became an important source of reference in the interpretation of the rights and freedoms recognised by the Constitution.[441] As a consequence, although the Constitutional Court maintains a monopoly on authentic interpretation of fundamental rights, it does not prevent ordinary judges from controlling conventionality of national acts by resolving the possible contradictions between constitutional and Strasbourg jurisprudence.[442] In the United Kingdom, the ECHR has become the source of statutory rights through the 1998 Human Rights Act

438 Frédéric Sudre, 'Question préjudicielle de constitutionnalité et Convention européenne des droits de l'homme' (2009) 3 *Revue du droit public et de la science politique en France et a l'etranger* 671–684, 672.

439 David Szymezak, 'Question prioritaire de constitutionnalité et Convention européenne des droits de l'homme : L'européanisation « heurtée » du Conseil constitutionnel français' (2012) 7 *Jus Politicum* 1–23, 11–14.

440 Patricia Cuenca Gómez, 'La incidncia del derecho interncional de los derechos humanos en el derecho interno: la interpretación del Artículo 10.2 de la Constitución española' (2012) 12 *Revista de Estudios Jurídicos* 1–24, 4.

441 Mercedes Candela Soriano, 'The Reception Process in Spain and Italy' in Keller and Stone Sweet (n 28) 393–450, 404.

442 María Isabel González Pascal, 'El CEDH como parte del Derecho Constitucional Europeo' in Queralt Jiménez (ed), *El Tribunal de Estrasburgo en el Espacio Judicial Europeo* (2013) 109–130, 124. For the conventionality control by ordinary jurisdiction, see Jimena Quesada, *Jurisdicción nacional y control de convencionalidad: A propósito del diálogo judicial global y de la tutela multinivel de derechos* (Aranzadi 2013) 119. See also Víctor Ferreres Comella, *Constitutional Courts and Democratic Values: A European Perspective* (Yale University Press 2009) 142 (arguing that it seems to be theoretically possible that ordinary judges can

(HRA). Regarding the interpretation of legislation, Section 3(1) of the HRA stipulates that '[s]o far as it is possible to do so, primary legislation and subordinate legislation must be read and given effect in a way which is compatible with the Convention rights'. Furthermore, against the background of the parliamentary supremacy that prohibits domestic judges from invalidating legislation, Section 4 (2) of the HRA provides that '[i]f the court is satisfied that the provision is incompatible with a Convention right, it may make a declaration of that incompatibility'. While the consistent interpretation under Section 3 serves as the 'prime remedial measure', the declaration of incompatibility under Section 4 functions as 'a measure of last resort' in order to realise conventionality control.[443] In the United Kingdom, where there are no entrenched constitutional rights and the Parliament is supreme, the HRA is gradually becoming a kind of constitutional statute.[444]

Even when formal provisions of consistent interpretation do not exist, the judiciary in practice interprets domestic law in conformity with human rights treaties, and thereby contributes to promoting their hierarchy within constitutional orders. For example, the German Constitutional Court expressed in the 2004 *Görgülü* decision that ECHR and ECtHR jurisprudence function as *Auslegungshilfen* (interpretative aid) for the Basic Law, even though it is not recognised as a direct parameter for constitutional review due to its domestic status as a federal statute.[445] Subsequently, the *Bundesverfassungsgericht* declared the unconstitutionality of legislation regarding preventive detention based on Strasbourg jurisprudence.[446] In the 2007 *Sentenze 'gemelle' № 348 e 349*, the Italian Constitutional Court expounded that ECHR provisions have the rank of *norme interposte*, according to which the constitutionality of domestic law must be

refuse to apply an unconventional statute but in practice this ability of ordinary courts has not given to a high level of judicial activism).

443 *Ghaidan v Mendoza* [2004] 3 WLR 113 paras 38–49 *per* Lord Steyn. See also, Aileen Kavanagh, *Constitutional Review under the UK Human Rights Act* (2009) at 19ff.

444 Samantha Besson, 'The Reception in Ireland and the United Kingdom' in Keller and Stone Sweet (n 28) 31–106, 55–56.

445 BVerfG, *Görgülü*, 2 BvR 1481/04, Entscheidung vom 14. Oktober 2004, at para. 32.

446 BVerfG, 2 BvR 2365/09, Entscheidung vom 4. Mai 2011. See also, Mads Andenas and Eirik Bjorge, '"Preventive Detention." No. 2 BvR 2365/09' (2011) 105 *American Journal of International Law* (2011) 768–774.

assessed.[447] Following the new formula, the *Corte costituzionale* determined the unconstitutionality of the legislation concerning the refund for unlawful expropriation and found that it was incompatible with the Convention yardstick.[448]

The ACHR has also been a driving force for 'the American internationalization of human rights'.[449] It is now accepted that the ACHR is directly applicable within the domestic legal orders of States Parties.[450] Furthermore, in the Latin American region, the phenomenon of 'the constitutionalization of human rights treaties from below' has been emerging where human rights conventions are incorporated into domestic legal orders with a constitutional rank.[451]

In some States Parties, conventionality control by domestic courts is facilitated by the incorporation of the ACHR into the constitutional hierarchy through constitutional clauses (e.g. Article 75(22) of the 1994 Constitution of Argentina).[452] As an example of a success story, the Supreme Court of Argentina declared in the *Simón Julio Héctor and others* case the unconstitutionality of amnesty law on the basis of conventionality control parameters, including the *Barrios Altos v. Peru* judgement of the IACtHR where Argentina was not the Respondent State.[453] Similarly, the 2010 Con-

---

447 Corte constituzionale italilana, Sentenze № 348 e 349 del 24 ottobre 2007, at Considerato in diritto para. 4.7 (№ 348) and para. 6.2 (№ 349). See also, Francesca Biondi Dal Monte and Filippo Fontanelli, 'The Decisions No. 348 and 349/2007 of the Italian Constitutional Court: The Efficacy of the European Convention in the Italian Legal System' (2008) 9 *German Law Journal* 889–932, 915–920.

448 Ibid.

449 Allan R Brewer-Carías, *Constitutional Protection of Human Rights in Latin America: A Comparative Study of Amparo Proceedings* (Cambridge University Press 2009) 27–60.

450 Héctor Gros Espiell, 'L'appplication du droit international dans le droit interne en amérique latine' in Studi di diritto internazionale in onore di Gaetano Arangio-Ruiz, Vol I (Editoriale Scientifica 2004) 529–549, 537.

451 Manuel Eduardo Góngora Mera, *Inter-American Judicial Constitutionalism: On the Constitutional Rank of Human Rights Treaties in Latin America through National and Inter-American Adjudication* (Inter-American Institute of Human Rights 2011) Chap II.

452 'The American Convention on Human Rights [...] in the full force of their provisions, they have *constitutional hierarchy*, do no repeal any section of the First Part of this Constitution and are to be understood as complementing the rights and guarantees recognized herein'.

453 Suprema Corte de Justicia de la Nación de Argentina, *Simón, Julio Héctor y otros*, Causa No 17.768, Sentencia de 17 de junio de 2005, paras 24–34.

stitution of the Dominican Republic manifestly recognises in Article 74(3) that '[t]he treaties, pacts and conventions concerning human rights, signed and ratified by the Dominican State, have constitutional hierarchy and are of direct and immediate application by the tribunals and other organs of the State'. On the basis of this constitutional provision, the Supreme Court formulated that the Dominican Republic 'has a constitutional system integrated by provisions of equal hierarchy that emanate from two essential normative sources: a) the national, formed by the Constitution and the local constitutional jurisprudence [...], and the international, composed of international treaties and conventions, the advisory opinions and decisions emanated from the Inter-American Court of Human Rights; normative sources that as a whole, [...] integrate the so-called block of constitutionality'.[454] The newly added Article 5(3) of the 1988 Constitution of Brazil (and the 2004 Amendment No. 45) stipulates that '[i]nternational human rights treaties and conventions which are approved in each House of the National Congress, in two rounds of voting, by three-fifths of the votes of the respective members shall be equivalent to constitutional amendments'. Based on this article, the Federal Supreme Court held that human rights treaties had acquired supra-legal status, remaining lower in rank than the Constitution yet higher than other laws.[455] However, it should be carefully observed that 'the court not only interpreted the infra-constitutional legislation to ensure it was compatible with the ACHR, but it also interpreted the Constitution itself based on this treaty'.[456] In Chile, Article 5(2) of the 1980 Constitution recognises that 'the sovereignty is limited by the respect for the essential rights emanating from human nature, recognised in the Constitution and international human rights treaties ratified by Chile that are in force'. In terms of this article, human rights treaties have hierarchical superiority over national law.[457] Furthermore, the Constitutional Court has employed human rights treaties, including the ACHR, as the

---

454 For example, Corte Suprema de Justicia de República Dominicana, Res Nº 1920–2003 de 13 de noviembre de 2003.

455 Supremo Tribunal Federal do Brasil, Recurso Extraordinário Nº 466,343, Julgamento do 3 de Dezembro de 2008.

456 Antonio Moreira Maués, 'Supra-Legality of International Human Rights Treaties and Constitutional Interpretation' (2013) 18 *SUR – International Journal on Human Rights* 205–223, 206–212.

457 José Ignacio Martínez Estay, 'The Impact of the Jurisprudence Inter-American Court of Human Rights on the Chilean Constitutional System' in Arnold (n 433) 63–79, 71–72.

parameter for constitutionality control of national acts.[458] The 1949 Constitution of Costa Rica simply provides in Article 7 that treaties in general 'shall have a higher authority than the laws'. Moreover, the Constitutional Chamber of the Supreme Court has established that 'once the instrument regarding Human Rights in force in Costa Rica not only has a similar value with the Constitution but also grant more rights or guarantees to the persons, they prevail over the Constitution'.[459] Similarly, Article 425 of the 2008 Constitution of Ecuador regulates '[t]he order of precedence for the application of the regulations' and assigns international treaties and conventions a supra-legal rank. The Constitutional Court went a step further by indicating that '[t]he block of constitutionality allows the interpretation of constitutional norms, but additionally, the human rights treaties guide the constitutional judges in identifying essential elements which define the irreplaceable physiognomy of the Constitution. In such a virtue, in order to resolve a juridical problem the Constitution is not the only one to be taken into consideration as other provisions and principles may have relevance to decide such issues'.[460] The 1983 Constitution of El Salvador also stipulates in Article 144 the supra-legal status of treaties in general. Moreover, in order to recapture the relationship between human rights treaties and the Constitution, the Constitutional Chamber of the Supreme Court articulated that 'the confluence between the Constitution and the international human rights law in the protection of the human rights, confirms that the relation between both definitely is *not of hierarchy*, but *of compatibility*, and therefore, the internal law, and the Constitutional law and the constitutional jurisdiction, must open the normative spaces for the international regulation on human rights'.[461] In the same vein, Article 18 of the 1982 Constitution of Honduras solely provides that 'in case of conflict between the treaty or convention, and the Law, the former shall prevail'. However, the Constitutional Chamber of the Supreme Court of Honduras expanded its meaning when stating that 'international treaties

458 Humberto Nogueira Alcalá, 'Diálogo interjurisdiccional, control de convencionalidad y jurispurdencia del Tribunal Constitucional en período 2006–2011' (2012) 10 *Estudios Constitucionales* 57–140, 103–126.

459 Sala Constitucional de la Corte Suprema de Justicia de Costa Rica, Exp 0421-S-90, Res N° 2313–95 de 9 mayo de 1995, considerando VI-VII.

460 Corte Constitucional del Ecuador, Sentencia 0001–09-SIS-CC, Caso 0003–08-IS [2009] consideraciones y fundamentos, Bloque de Consttucionalidad.

461 Sala de lo Constitucional de la Corte Suprema de Justicia de El Salvador, Sentencia 31–2004/34–2004/38–2004/6–2005/9–2005 de 6 de junio de 2008, considerando VI (emphasis in original text).

and conventions ratified by the State of Honduras are part of so-called block of constitutionality'.[462] Last, the 1967 Constitution of Uruguay does not clarify the rank of international treaties in the domestic legal order under Article 6. However, in the 2009 *Sabalsagaray Curuchet Blanca Stela* judgement, the Supreme Court declared the unconstitutionality of the Expiry Law because the legal consequences of this law with respect to the right to judicial protection were incompatible with the ACHR. In its reasoning, the Court explicitly stated that 'international human rights conventions are integrated into the Constitution by virtue of Article 72, dealing with inherent rights in human dignity that the international community recognises in such agreements'.[463] Subsequently, the IACtHR recognised in the 2011 *Gelman v Uruguay* judgement that the Supreme Court had 'exercised an appropriate control of conformity with the Convention in respect to the Expiry law'.[464]

Other domestic courts have constitutionalised the Convention through open interpretative clauses. This is epitomised by the 2009 Constitution of Bolivia which incorporates a human rights–oriented approach. Article 13(4) provides that '[t]he rights and duties consecrated in this Constitution shall be interpreted in accordance with the International Human Rights Treaties ratified by Bolivia'. Furthermore, Article 410 provides 'the block of constitutionality composed of the international Treaties and Conventions in the matter of Human Rights and the norms of Communitarian Law, which have been ratified by the country'. According to these provisions, the Constitutional Court 'as the organ in charge of the defence of human rights, the control of constitutionality, also realises between its labours, the control of conventionality, ensuring the compatibility of the internal normative system with the block of constitutionality formally integrated with the Bolivian judicial plexus'.[465] Likewise, the 1991 Con-

462 Sala de lo Constitucional de la Corte Suprema de Justicia de Honduras, Recurso de inconstitucionalidad (acumulado), Nos. 55 y 88, 13 de noviembre de 2007, Considerando 22.

463 *Sabalsagaray Curutchet, Blanca Stela. Denuncia de Excepción de Inconstitucionalidad*, Corte Suprema de Justicia de Uruguay, № 365 [2009] at Fondo para III.8.

464 *Gelman v Uruguay*, IACtHR, Series C No 221, Judgment on Merits and Reparations of 24 February 2011, para 239. However, the IACtHR recently determined that the decision of 22 February 2013 constituted an obstacle for the full compliance with the judgment. *Gelman*, Order (n 375) paras 65–90.

465 Tribunal Constitucional de Bolivia, Exp 2009–20768–42-AL, Sentencia 1907/2011-R de 7 de noviembre 2011, Fundamentos III.4. (De los crímenes de lesa humanidad y la CIDH; y, otras Cortes Control de convencionalidad).

stitution of Colombia gives special treatment to human rights treaties in Article 93 so that they 'have priority domestically'. The same article also requires that '[t]he rights and duties mentioned in this Charter will be interpreted in accordance with international treaties on human rights ratified by Colombia'. Based on this provision, the Constitutional Court has dynamically developed the doctrine of the block of constitutionality to include ACHR and IACtHR jurisprudence.[466] For example, the Court established that 'the block of constitutionality related to the freedom of expression has to be integrated by international norms, in particular the Pact of San José and the International Covenant on Civil and Political Rights, together with the interpretations which the Inter-American Commission on Human Rights, the Inter-American Court of Human Rights and the United Nations Human Rights Committee have presented on such texts'.[467] The 1993 Constitution of Peru does not determine the hierarchy of treaties over national law, but simply provides in Article 55 that they form a part of national law. However, fourth of the final and transitory provisions of the Constitution provides that '[r]ules concerning the rights and freedoms recognized by this Constitution are construed in accordance with the Universal Declaration of Human Rights and international treaties and agreements on those rights, which have been ratified by Peru'. Based on this provision, the Constitutional Court endorsed that 'our system of normative sources admits that human rights agreements serve to interpret the rights and freedoms recognized by the Constitution. Therefore, such agreements constitute the constitutionality parameter on the subject of rights and freedoms'.[468] In Mexico, the Constitution does not establish an explicit hierarchy between international treaties and domestic statutes under Article 133. However, through the 2011 Human Rights Amendment and the *Radilla Pacheco* judgement, the Supreme Court clarified the parameter for judicial control based on the Constitution and human rights

466 Sierra Porto, 'La Corte Constitucional colombiana frente al control de convencionalidad' in Edgar Corzo Sosa, Jorge Ulises Carmona Tinoco and Pablo Saavedra Alessandri (eds), *Impacto de las sentencias de la Corte Interamericana de Derechos Humanos* (Tirant lo Blanch México 2013) 427–447, 440–446.

467 Corte Constitucional de Colombia, Exp T-357702, Sentencia T-1319–01 de 7 de diciembre de 2001, Consideraciones y Fundamentos para 6 (Solución).

468 Tribunal Constitucional de Perú, Exp 0047–2004-AI/TC, Sentencia de 24 de abril de 2006, Fundamentos para 22. See in general, Natalia Torres Zúñiga, *El control de convencionalidad: Deber complementario del juez constitucional peruano y el juez interamericano (similitudes, deferencias y convergencias)* (Editorial Académica Española 2013) Chap 3.

treaties as follows: 'The parameter for analysing this type of control which all judges in the state must exercise is integrated as follows: All human rights set out in the Federal Constitution (based on Articles 1 and 133) as well as case law handed down by the Federal Judiciary; All human rights contained in international treaties to which Mexico is a party; Binding criteria of the Inter-American Court of Human Rights set out in rulings in cases in which Mexico was a party, guidelines contained in precedents and case law of the aforementioned Court where Mexico was not a party'.[469]

(ii) Regional Courts Decisions in National Constitutions

When talking about the effects of judgements of international courts, we are reminded of the words of Lord Denning in *Trendtex*: 'International Law knows no rule of *stare decisis*'.[470] Moreover, we can observe that international tribunals have heavily relied on their own precedents to determine rules. While formally limiting the effects of their decisions to the parties in concrete cases, human rights courts have developed jurisprudence in substance that generally extends towards themselves as well as States Parties. Put differently, the guardians of human rights hybridise the *civil law* tradition in treaty provisions and the *common law* tradition in practice. This task is recommended in the *Guidelines* of the ILA Committee on International Human Rights Law: 'All courts accordingly interpret domestic law in conformity with international human rights law. They take the pertinent judgments and decisions of courts and quasi-judicial bodies, also in those cases to which the state was not a party, fully into account and integrate them in their reasoning in good faith'.[471]

On the one hand, the *decisional* authority of their judgements (*res judicata*) obliges only the States Parties in concrete contentious cases (*inter partes*) to comply with the judgements (Article 46(1) o the ECHR and Article 68 of the ACHR). The *res judicata* effect does not allow States Parties to invoke domestic standards for failing to comply with their judgements in accordance with the supremacy of international law. On the other hand, the *jurisprudential* authority of their judgements (*res interpretata*) extends to

469 Suprema Corte de Justicia de la Nación de México, *Radilla-Pacheco v Estados Unidos Mexicanos*, Exp Varios 912/2010, 4, 5, 7, 11, 12 y 14 julio 2011, para 31.

470 *Trendtex Trading Corporation v Central of Bank of Nigeria* [1977] 1 QB 529.

471 *Guidelines* (n 50) para 9(a).

all States Parties beyond individual cases (*erga omnes*).[472] In practice, the ECtHR has repeatedly stated that '[t]he Court's judgments in fact serve not only to decide those cases brought before the Court but, more generally, to elucidate, safeguard and develop the rules instituted by the Convention, thereby contributing to the observance by the States of the engagements undertaken by them as Contracting Parties'.[473] In a similar way, the Strasbourg judges have been aware of their own role in 'determin[ing] issues on public-policy grounds in the common interest, thereby raising the general standards of protection of human rights and extending human rights jurisprudence throughout the community of Convention States'.[474] The IACtHR also explained in *Gelman* that it is necessary 'to exercise control of conformity with the Convention *ex officio*, taking into account the treaty itself and its interpretation by the Inter-American Court, [...] bearing in mind the treaty and, as appropriate, the jurisprudential precedents and guidelines of the Inter-American Court'.[475]

The *erga omnes* normativity of *res interpretata* does not only stem from the jurisprudence accumulated through contentious cases but also accumulates by means of non-contentious or adivisory opinions. The San José Court, which is granted advisory authority under Article 64 of the American Convention, clarified that conventionality control by State organs must be 'based also on the considerations of the Court in exercise of its non-contentious or advisory jurisdiction, which undeniably shares with its contentious jurisdiction the goal of the inter-American human rights

472 Samantha Besson, 'The *Erga Omnes* Effect of Judgments of the European Court of Human Rights: What's in a Name?' in Samantha Besson (ed), *La Cour européenne des droits de l'homme après le Protocole 14: Premier bilan et perspectives* (Schulthess 2011) 125–175, 164–168; Alfredo M Vítolo, 'Una novedosa categoría jurídica: el «querer ser». Acerca del pretendido carácter normativo erga omnes de la jurisprudencia de la Corte Interamericana de Derechos Humanos. Las dos caras del «control de convencionalidad»' (2013) 18 *Pensamiento Constitucional* 357–380, 373–374; Adam Bodnar, '*Res Interpretata*: Legal Effect of the European Court of Human Rights' Judgments for other States Than Those Which Were Party to the Proceedings' in Yves Haeck and Eva Brems (eds), *Human Rights and Civil Liberties in the 21st Century* (Springer 2014) 223–262; Christos Giannopoulos, 'The Reception by Domestic Courts of the *Res Interpretata* Effect of Jurisprudence of the European Court of Human Rights' (2019) *Human Rights Law Review* 537–559.

473 *Ireland v the United Kingdom* (n 80) para. 154.

474 *Karner v Austria*, (n 9) para 26. See also, Markus Fyrnys, 'Expanding Competences by Judicial Lawmaking: The Pilot Judgment Procedure of the European Court of Human Rights' (2011) 12 *German Law Journal* 1231–1259.

475 *Gelman*, Order (n 375) para 69.

system'.[476] The Strasbourg Court also granted advisory jurisdiction on the basis of Protocol No 16 to the ECHR.[477] As is noted in the Explanatory Report to the Protocol, 'there will be hardly any difference in legal force between an interpretation given to the Convention in an advisory opinion and an interpretation given in a judgment'.[478]

The binding nature of human rights judgements has not only a past-oriented *reparatory* aspect but also a future-oriented *preventative* aspect.[479] In the Advisory Opinion on *Gender Identity, and Equality and Non-discrimination with Regard to Same-Sex Couples*, the Inter-American Court dictated that its opinion 'contributes, especially in a *preventive* manner, to achieving the effective respect and guarantee of human rights' and 'can provide guidance when deciding matters relating to the respect and guarantee of human rights in the context of the protection of LGBTI persons, to *avoid possible human rights violations*'.[480] The *ex ante* preventative function of *res interpretata* was also implied for the ECtHR by the 2011 Izmir Declaration, in which the high-level conference characterised 'advisory opinions from the Court concerning the interpretation and application of the Convention that would help clarify the provisions of the Convention and the Court's case law, thus providing further guidance in order to assist States Parties in *avoiding future violations*'.[481] In the very first Advisory Opinion under Protocol No 16 in the *Mennesson* case, the Strasbourg Court itself recognised that its opinions' 'value also lies in providing the national courts with guidance on questions of principle relating to the Convention applicable in similar cases'.[482]

---

476 *Rights and Guarantees of Children in the Context of Migration and/or in Need of International Protection* (n 220) para 31.

477 Janneke Gerards, 'Advisory Opinion: European Court of Human Rights (ECtHR)' in Hélène Ruiz Fabri (ed), *Max Planck Encyclopedia of International Procedural Law* (Oxford University Press 2018).

478 Council of Europe, Explanatory Report to Protocol No 16, 5 June 2013.

479 Tribunal Constitucional de Perú, *Colegio de Abogados del Callao c. Congreso de la República*, Perú, Causa N° 00007–2007-PI-TC, Sentencia de 19 de Junio, 2007; ILDC 961 (PE 2007), reported by Salmón Gárate, E.

480 *Gender Identity, and Equality and Non-discrimination with Regard to Same-sex Couples* (n 159) para 171. For the advisory opinon's effects in the domestic sphere, see Jorge Contesse, 'Sexual Orientation and Gender Identity in Inter-American Human Rights Law' (2019) 44 *North Carolina Journal of International Law* 353–385 (emphasis added).

481 High Level Conference on the Future of the European Court of Human Rights, Izmir, Turkey 26 – 27 April 2011, Follow-up Plan, D(1) (emphasis added).

482 Advisory Opinion Concerning the Recognition in Domestic Law of a Legal Parent-child Relationship between a Child Born through a Gestational Surrogacy

The *erga omnes* effect of *res interpretata* is supported by the notion of the collective guarantee of human rights, which prioritises the judgements of regional courts as the central pillar of community-based mechanisms. The CoE Parliamentary Assembly's Resolution 1226 expresses that '[t]he principle of *solidarity* implies that the case law of the Court forms part of the Convention, thus extending the legally binding force of the Convention *erga omnes* (to all the other parties)'.[483] It follows from the European mechanism of collective enforcement that 'the states parties not only have to execute the judgments of the Court pronounced in cases to which they are party, but also have to take into consideration the possible implications which judgments pronounced in other cases may have for their own legal system and legal practice'.[484] In the Inter-American system, ex-judge Cançado Trindade explained that '[t]he exercise of *garantía colectiva* should not only be *reactive*, when the non-compliance with a judgment of the Court was produced, but also *proactive*, in the sense that all States Parties previously adopt positive measures of protection in accordance with the regulations of the American Convention'.[485] In the Advisory Opinion concerning the *Denunciation of the ACHR and the OAS Charter*, the San José Court opined that even the sovereign decision of denunciation cannot nullify the domestic effects of the Convention's norms which are interpreted as *parámetro preventivo* under the collective mechanism.[486]

The general effects of *res interpretata*, in contrast to the case-specific effects of *res judicata*, permit *margen interpretativo nacional* based on which national authorities can preliminarily realise more protective interpretations of domestic norms than the minimum standards of the courts' jurisprudence. According to Inter-American judge Ferrer MacGregor, re-

---

Arrangement Abroad and the Intended Mother, Advisory Opinion (Protocol 16) of 10 April 2019, para 26.

483 The Parliamentary Assembly of the CoE, Resolution 1226 (2000), Execution of judgments of the European Court of Human Rights, para 3.

484 Ibid.

485 Intervención del Presidente de la Corte Interamericana de Derechos Humanos, Juez Antonio Augusto Cançado Trindade, ante el Plenario de la Asamblea General de la Organización de los Estados Americanos, Barbados, 4 de junio de 2002, para 5 (emphasis added).

486 Denunciation of the American Convention on Human Rights and the Charter of the Organization of American States and the consequences for State human rights obligations (interpretation and scope of articles 1, 2, 27, 29, 30, 31, 32, 33 a 65 and 78 of the American Convention on Human Rights and 3(l), 17, 45, 53, 106 and 143 of the Charter of the Organization of American States), Series A No 26, Advisory Opinion OC-26/20 of 9 November 2020, paras 90–93.

gional courts' jurisprudence produces a 'relative' interpretative authority inasmuch as no other interpretation exists that grants greater effectiveness to the provision of the Convention in the domestic sphere.[487] Put conversely, the domestic authorities may expand the interpretative standard or even not apply Convention norms when another domestic or international norm exists that makes the right or freedom in question more effective in terms of Article 29 of the American Convention.[488] In the context of Europe, the Strasbourg Court has elaborated what Başak Çalı calls *nascent responsible courts* doctrine, 'allowing domestic courts a larger discretionary space with regard to making rights violation determinations, provided that domestic courts take ECtHR case law seriously'.[489] In practice, the recommendatory wording was adopted as regards *res interpretata* in the 2010 Interlaken Declaration ('calls upon')[490] and the 2012 Brighton Declaration ('enabling and encouraging').[491] This formula suggests 'certainly less than a requirement of strict adherence to ECtHR standards but *leaves room for divergent views of national judges*'.[492] However, such an enlarging of the margin of appreciation is but one side of the equation, and the ECtHR also draws negative inferences from the lack of due Convention diligence in this respect.[493]

487 Ibid, para 69.

488 Ibid.

489 Başak Çalı, 'From Flexible to Variable Standards of Judicial Review: The Responsible Domestic Courts Doctrine at the European Court of Human Rights', in Oddný Mjöll Arnardóttir and Antoine Buyse (eds), Shifting Centres of Gravity in Human Rights Protection: Rethinking Relations between the ECHR, EU, and National Legal Orders (Routledge 2016) 144–161.

490 High Level Conference on the Future of the European Court of Human Rights Interlaken Declaration 19 February 2010, Action Plan 4(c).

491 High Level Conference on the Future of the European Court of Human Rights Brighton Declaration 19–20 April 2012, 9(c)(iv).

492 Marten Breuer, 'Principled Resistance' to ECtHR Judgments: An Appraisal' in Marten Breuer (ed), *Principled Resistance to ECtHR Judgments: A New Paradigm?* (Springer 2019) 323–350, 338 [emphasis added].

493 Oddný Mjöll Arnardóttir, '*Res Interpretata*, *Erga Omnes* Effect and the Role of the Margin of Appreciation in Giving Domestic Effect to the Judgments of the European Court of Human Rights' (2017) 28 *European Journal of International Law* 819–843.

B. Supremacy of National Constitutions over Regional Conventions

(i) Consubstantial Constitutional Contestations against Regional Conventions

While accepting the increasing mandates from outside, sovereign states have resolutely reserved the ultimate power to limit the performance of international obligations that conflict with national fundamental principles and values.[494] The institutions involved in regional integration processes have abundant experience regarding this point. The Italian Constitutional Court devised the *controlimiti* doctrine in *Frontini* to restrict the absolute primacy of EU law in terms of national fundamental values.[495] Likewise, the German Constitutional Court elaborated the *Solange* doctrine to evaluate European Community acts against the yardstick of domestic basic rights.[496] In a series of *Lisbon* decisions, the *national identities* concept, incorporated into Article 4(2) of the Treaty on European Union, was employed by national constitutional courts 'as a synonym for constitutional core principles protected against the primacy of EU law'.[497]

Given that these constitutional limits have been invoked even in consolidated regional integration, it is unsurprising that similar practices are found in the more pluralistic context of international law.[498] According to the *Final Report of the ILA Study Group on Principles on the Engagement of Domestic Courts with International Law*, a constitutional contestation against international law may be positively evaluated as *consubstantial contestation* because it is based on 'norms which happen to exist both at the international and the domestic level, and provide for the same

494 André Nollkaemper, 'Rethinking the Supremacy of International Law' (2010) 65 *Zeitschrift für öffentliches Recht* 65–85, 67–71.

495 Corte costituzionale italiana, *Frontini v. Ministerio delle Finanze*, Sentenza № 183 del 27 dicembre 1973. See also, Vittoria Barsotti, Paolo G Carozza, Marta Cartabia and Andrea Simoncini, *Italian Constitutional Justice in Global Context* (Oxford University Press 2016), Chap 7.

496 BVerfG, *Solange I*, 2 BvL 52/71, Entscheidung vom 29. Mai 1974; BVerfG, *Solange II*, 2 BvR 197/83, Entscheidung vom 22. Oktober 1986.

497 Mattias Wendel, 'Lisbon Before the Courts: Comparative Perspectives' (2011) 7 *European Constitutional Law Review* 96–137, 131–136.

498 Fulvio M Palombino, 'Compliance with International Judgments: Between Supremacy of International Law and National Fundamental Principles' (2015) 75 *Heidelberg Journal of International Law* (2015) 503–529.

substantive regulation'.[499] Samantha Besson proposes, as a prominent theoretical approach, the *coordination-based* theory of legal authority, according to which the justification of legitimate authority is mostly found in the 'coordinating ability' of international law in circumstances of 'reasonable disagreement'.[500] Besson argues that the role of state consent is best understood and justified by reference to the circumstances of reasonable disagreement about and in international law, and hence to state democracy and equality.[501] In such reasonable disagreement cases, 'democratic state consent should work as an exception to the *prima facie* legitimate authority of international law'.[502]

As regards human rights norms that are *consubstantial* between international and constitutional law, the *Jurisdictional Immunities of the State (Germany v Italy)* case exposed the tension between international and constitutional adjudication. From the normative viewpoint of human rights protection, the ICJ ruling, which prioritised state immunity over individual victims, may be criticised on the grounds that it 'did not speak fairly for the whole society of the forum state, nor did the legal actions of the foreign state comply with the requirement of being fairly addressed to all those affected'.[503] In *Sentenza* 238/2014, the Italian Constitutional Court indeed declared the legislation for implementing the ICJ decision unconstitutional because it entailed the risk of sacrificing the judicial protection stipulated in Article 24 of the Italian constitution. Keeping in mind its *controlimiti* doctrine, the *Corte costituzionale* emphasised that the right is not only 'one of the supreme principles of our [Italian] constitutional order, intrinsically connected to the principle of democracy itself' but also 'one of the greatest principles of legal culture in democratic systems

499 The Final Report of the ILA Study Group on Principles on the Engagement of Domestic Courts with International Law, the 77th Conference of the International Law Association, held in Johannesburg, South Africa, 7–11 August 2016, para 30.

500 Samantha Bessson, 'The Authority of International Law: Lifting the State Veil' (2009) 31 *Sydney Law Review* 343–380, 352–355.

501 Samantha Bessson, 'State Consent and Disagreement in International Law-making: Dissolving the Paradox' (2016) 29 *Leiden Journal of International Law* 289–316, 300-302.

502 Ibid 307.

503 Benedict Kingsbury, 'International Law as Inter-Public Law', in Henry S Richardson and Melissa Williams (eds), *Nomos XLIX: Moral Universalism and Pluralism* (New York University Press 2009) 167–204, 182.

of our times'.[504] This critical message from Rome to the Hague enjoyed great acclaim because the *Consulta* fulfilled 'the creeping "educational" function that the Court felt entitled to perform vis-à-vis the international and UN legal orders (including the ICJ), by indicating a path that those orders should follow if they want to embrace a meaningful process of *democratization*'.[505]

As a comparable precedent to the Italian contestation, the US Supreme Court also engaged in a contestation to avoid compliance with the World Court ruling. Relying on the 'self-executing' (or direct effect) doctrine, the Supreme Court defended in *Medellín* that '[t]he *Avena* judgment creates an international law obligation on the part of the United States, but it is not automatically binding domestic law because none of the relevant treaty sources [...] creates binding federal law in the absence of implementing legislation, and no such legislation has been enacted'.[506] The ILA report categorised the American reaction against the World Court as a *local contestation* because the invocation of the 'self-executing' issue superficially seems to defend the peculiarly national 'procedural default' rule without a corresponding rule (in substance) in international law.[507] As Fulvio Palombino[508] and Anne Peters[509] determined, the Supreme Court more fundamentally vindicated constitutional principles, particularly federalism and the separation of powers, and therefore, implicitly engaged with international law by consubstantial contestation.

Consubstantial constitutional contestation against the absolute supremacy of international law has also occurred in the implementation of regional human rights conventions in various settings. In Europe, the ECHR's supremacy over national law has faced 'principled resistance' especially when the ECtHR lacks legitimacy over national authorities.[510] The German Constitutional Court in the *Görgülü* decision implied a momentum

504 Corte costituzionale italiana, Sentenza № 238 del 22 ottobre 2014 Considerato in diritto para 3.4.

505 Riccardo Pavoni, '*Simoncioni v. Germany*' (2015) 109 *American Journal of International Law* 400–406, 404 (emphasis added).

506 Medellín v Texas, 552 US 491 (2008).

507 The ILA Final Report (n 500) paras 25–26.

508 Palombino (n 499) 510.

509 Anne Peters, *Let Not Triepel Triumph – How To Make the Best Out of Sentenza No. 238 of the Italian Constitutional Court for a Global Legal Order*, EJIL: *talk!*, 22 December 2014, available at http://www.ejiltalk.org/let-not-triepel-triumph-how-to-make-the-best-out-of-sentenza-no-238-of-the-italian-constitutional-court-for-a-global-legal-order-part-i/ (last visited 28 February 2020).

510 See the articles included in Breuer (n 493).

of functional contestation. While admitting that the binding effect of statute and law under Article 20(d) of the Basic Law includes a duty to take into account ECHR standards, the *Bundesverfassungsgericht* made a caveat that '[b]oth a failure to consider [*fehlende Auseinandersetzung*] a decision of the ECHR and the "enforcement" of such a decision *in a schematic way*, in violation of prior-ranking law, may therefore violate fundamental rights in conjunction with the principle of the rule of law'.[511]

The claim that the *Völkerrechtsfreundlichkeit* (openness to international law) principle does not include the constitutional obligation of unconditional compliance with international law was militant in the 2015 judgement, where the German *Bundesverfassungsgericht* employed the constitutional principle of democracy to permit the legislature to revoke legal acts of previous legislatures.[512] This opaque idea was furthermore revitalised in the 2018 judgement concerning the constitutional right to strike that possibly conflicted with Article 11 of the ECHR.[513] Invoking the *Görgülü* formula, the Federal Constitutional Court maintained that '[i]t is therefore not contrary to the objective of openness to international law if the legislature does not observe international treaty law in exceptional cases, provided this is the only way to avert a violation of fundamental constitutional principles'.[514]

In the Americas, the situation in the *Fontevecchia and D'Amico* case is a more constitutionally nuanced example than those that are sovereignty oriented. This case is related to the civil sentence of the Supreme Court of Argentina imposing compensation for journalists who published articles on political scandals. The main cause of the conflict between national and international judges here was the possibility of revoking the Supreme Court's decision, issued 25 September 2001, with the *res judicata* effect. In the judgement on merits issued on 29 November 2011, the IACtHR, having determined the violation of the victims' freedom of expression, ordered as a reparation measure that 'the State must *dejar sin efecto* ['revoke' in the official English translation] the decision'.[515] This sensitive reparation order provoked a critical reaction from the Supreme Court in the judgement handed down on 14 February 2017. According to the Argentine

511 *Görgülü* (n 445) (emphasis added).

512 BVerfG, 2 BvL 1/12, Entscheidung vom 15. Dezember 2015, paras 53–54, 67.

513 Heiko Sauer, 'Principled Resistance to and Principled Compliance with ECtHR Judgments' in Breuer (n 493) 55–88, 63–64.

514 BVerfG, 2 BvR 1738/12 et al, Entscheidung vom vom 12. Juni 2018, para 133.

515 *Fontevecchia and D'Amico v Argentina*, IACtHR, Series C No 238, Judgment on Merits, Reparations and Costs of 29 November 2011, para. 105.

Supreme Court, the *dejar sin efecto* order suggested the substitution of its authority by the Inter-American Court, which was a clear transgression of constitutional principles. This position was reinforced with sovereignty-driven constitutional reasoning: 'The constituent has enshrined in Article 27 a sphere of sovereign reserve, delimited by the principles of public law established in the National Constitution, to which international treaties must be adjusted and with which must keep compliance'.[516]

The question raised in Buenos Aires was answered negatively in San José with an order on compliance issued on 18 October 2017. First, the Inter-American Court clarified that the meaning of its own wording *dejar sin efecto* is not synonymous with revoking as interpreted by the Argentine Supreme Court, but rather that 'the State should adopt "the judicial, administrative and other measures that may be necessary" to "render ineffective" such sentences'.[517] Next, the IACtHR mentioned the existence of other types of legal acts, different from such revocation, to comply with the ordered reparation measure, including some type of annotation that indicated the judgement in question was declared in violation of the American Convention by the Inter-American Court.[518] The Argentine judges sincerely welcomed this reflective clarification by the Inter-American judges in the decision issued on 5 December 2017. The Supreme Court admitted that the interpretation formulated by the Inter-American Court in October was completely consistent with its decision in February.[519] Therefore, the Buenos Aires judges resolved the issue by ordering the annotation, in line with the order by the San José judges, that 'the sentence [of 25 September 2001] was declared incompatible with the ACHR by the Inter-American Court'.[520] At the same time, however, *la Corte Suprema* rigidly maintained its position that the annotation sought by *la Corte Interamericana* does not violate the principles of public law established by Article 27 of the National Constitution.[521] This response from Argentina was positively evaluated

---

516 Corte Suprema de Justicia de la Nación de Argentina, Ministerio de Relaciones Exteriores y Culto s/ informe sentencia dictada en el caso 'Fontevecchia y D'Amico v Argentina' por la Corte Interamericana de Derechos Humanos, Sentencia de 14 de febrero de 2017, Considerando 16.

517 *Fontevecchia and D'Amico v Argentina*, IACtHR, Monitoring Compliance with Judgment, Order of 18 October 2017, para. 16.

518 Ibid paras 20–21.

519 Corte Suprema de Justicia de la Nación de Argentina, Resolución 4015/17 de 5 diciembre de 2017, Considerando para 2.

520 Ibid para 3.

521 Ibid para 4.

by the IACtHR in the order on compliance handed down on 11 March 2020, as 'a change in the position previously held by the Supreme Court of Justice of the Nation in this case, regarding the role that, within the scope of its powers, has to assume the internal court in the compliance or implementation of the Judgment of this case'.[522] Although the repeated dialogues seem a successful story in favour of compliance with the Inter-American judgement, it cannot be overlooked that the Supreme Court firmly maintained constitutional supremacy over international law in the domestic sphere.

(ii) Sovereigntist Constitutional Contestations against Regional Conventions

Constitutional contestations may take forms that are rather 'rebellious' against international law, mainly in the name of sovereignty. The notion of national or constitutional identity has the risk of being abuse in favour of sovereignty, which was allegedly realised within the European integration process. The Hungarian Constitutional Court in its ruling 22/2016 defended its competences to review EU legal acts if 'the sovereignty of Hungary' and 'its self-identity based on its historical constitution' as well as human dignity and another fundamental right can be presumed to be violated.[523] This sovereigntist constitutional identity claim is harshly criticised as 'national constitutional parochialism, an attempt to abandon the common European constitutional whole'.[524] The White Paper on the Reform of the Polish Judiciary took an interpretation that '[t]he European legal system is founded on the recognition of constitutional pluralism enshrined in Article 4 of the Treaty on European Union which also guarantees that each member state may shape its own judicial system in a sovereign manner'.[525] This mixture between sovereignty and national identity is another abusive example of constitutional pluralism by autocrats

---

522 *Fontevecchia and D'Amico v Argentina*, IACtHR, Monitoring Compliance with Judgment, Order of 11 March 2020, para 8.

523 Hungarian Constitutional Court, Decision 22/2016. (XII. 5.) AB of 30 November 2016, para 69.

524 Gábor Halmai, 'Abuse of Constitutional Identity. The Hungarian Constitutional Court on Interpretation of Article E (2) of the Fundamental Law' (2018) 43 *Review of Central and East European Law* 23–42, 42.

525 Poland, the Chancellery of the Prime Minister, the White Paper on the Reform of the Polish Judiciary, 7 March 2018, para 206.

and their captive courts.[526] In the context of Brexit, the Miller judgement opined that the withdrawal process under Article 50 of the TEU 'can and should be determined by Parliament not by the courts' under 'the fundamental principle of Parliamentary sovereignty'.[527] The ultimate fashion of exit triggered by the United Kingdom implies an atavism from a future-oriented post-sovereign arrangement predicated on constitutional pluralism to a classic dualist or Westphalian understanding of sovereignty.[528]

So-called nationalist/populist backlashes against international law and courts may likewise be observed worldwide.[529] In recent years several developing and emerging States expressed their distrust in the Investor-State Dispute Settlement, such as Bolivia, Ecuador, Nicaragua, Venezuela, South Africa, India and Indonesia.[530] The ICC currently faces resistance from Burundi, Gambia, Kenya, South Africa and the Philippines.[531] In Latin America, Venezuela under the administration of Hugo Chavez withdrew from the Andean Community, and Ecuador under the leadership of Rafael Correa launched mega-politics against the ATJ.[532] In Africa, the sub-regional courts such as the ECOWAS, the East African Court of Justice and

---

526 R Daniel Kelemen and Laurent Pech, 'The Uses and Abuses of Constitutional Pluralism: Undermining the Rule of Law in the Name of Constitutional Identity in Hungary and Poland' (2019) 21 *Cambridge Yearbook of European Legal Studies* 59–74.

527 *R(Miller) v Secretary of State for Exiting the European Union* [2017] UKSC 5, para 274.

528 Cormac Mac Amhlaigh, 'Back to a Sovereign Future?: Constitutional Pluralism after Brexit' (2019) 21 *Cambridge Yearbook of European Legal Studies* 41–58 (arguing that 'constitutional pluralism can and will remain relevant to EU/UK relations as well as within the EU, well into the future.').

529 Erik Voeten, 'Populism and Backlashes against International Courts' (2020) 18 Perspectives on Politics 407–422.

530 United Nations Conference on Trade and Development (UNCTAD), 'Denunciation of the ICSID Convention and BITs: Impact on Investor-State Claims' (2010) 2 *IIA Issues Note* 1–10.

531 Henry Lovat, 'International Criminal Tribunal Backlash' in Kevin Heller, Frédéric Mégret, Sarah Nouwen, Jens Ohlin, and Darryl Robinson (eds), *The Oxford Handbook of International Criminal Law* (Oxford University Press 2020) 601-625.

532 Karen J Alter and Laurence R Helfer, *Transplanting International Courts: The Law and Politics of the Andean Tribunal of Justice* (Oxford University Press 2017), 187; Salvatore Caserta, *International Courts in Latin America and the Caribbean: Foundations and Authority* (Oxford University Press 2020) 230–235.

the SADC Tribunal have encountered political contestation.[533] Rwanda, Tanzania, Benin and Côte d'Ivoire decided to withdraw the right of individuals and NGOs to submit complaints directly to the African Court on Human and Peoples' Rights under Article 34(6) of the Ouagadougou Protocol.[534]

Amongst various forms of contestation by European national authorities, Russia has posed the most serious challenge against the Strasbourg law.[535] In *Decision No. 21-П/2015*, setting aside the constitutionality issues of Federal Laws regarding ECHR ratification and international treaties, the Russian Constitutional Court generally reasoned that under Article 15(4) of the Constitution, the 'practical implementation [of the ECHR and the ECtHR jurisprudence] in the Russian legal system is only possible through recognition of the supremacy of the Constitution's legal force'.[536] To support this conclusion, the Constitutional Court clarified its attitude towards the Law of Treaties. First, by virtue of Articles 26 (*pacta sunt servanda*) and 31 (General Rule of Interpretation) of the VCLT, if the ECtHR interprets an ECHR provision in a way other than its normal meaning or contrary to the object and purpose of the Convention, the State Party has the right to refuse to follow the interpretation as exceeding the obligations voluntarily assumed by itself.[537] What the Russian Court particularly emphasised in this context is that Strasbourg Court judgements cannot be considered binding when they diverge from *jus cogens*, including the principle of sovereign equality and respect for the rights inherent in sovereignty as well

533 Karen J Alter, James T Gathii and Laurence R Helfer, 'Backlash against International Courts in West, East and Southern Africa: Causes and Consequences' (2016) 27 European Journal of International Law 293–328.

534 Amnesty International, *The State of African Regional Human Rights Bodies and Mechanisms 2019–2020*, 41–42.

535 Jeffrey Kahn, 'The Relationship between the European Court of Human Rights and the Constitutional Court of the Russian Federation: Conflicting Conceptions of Sovereignty in Strasbourg and St Petersburg' (2019) 30 *European Journal of International Law* 933–959; Lauri Mälksoo, 'Russia's Constitutional Court Defies the European Court of Human Rights: Constitutional Court of the Russian Federation Judgment of 14 July 2015, No 21-П/2015' (2016) 12 *European Constitutional Law Review* 377–395.

536 The Russian Constitutional Court, Decision No. 21-П/2015 of 14 July 2015. For English translation, see Smirnova, Russian Constitutional Court Affirms Russian Constitution's Supremacy over ECtHR Decisions, EJIL: *Talk!*, 15 July 2015, available at http://www.ejiltalk.org/russian-constitutional-court-affirms-russian-constitutions-supremacy-over-ecthr-decisions/ (last visited 5 April 2016).

537 Ibid para 3.

as the principle of non-interference in the internal affairs of States.[538] Second, according to Article 46(1) of the VCLT, the state retains to invoke the fact that its consent to be bound by a treaty has been expressed in violation of a provision of its internal law regarding competence to conclude treaties as invalidating its consent if that violation was manifest and concerned a rule of its internal law of fundamental importance.[539] Subsequently, legislation enacted on 14 December 2015 clearly granted the Russian Constitutional Court the power to declare 'impossible to implement' the decisions of a human rights body when they are inconsistent with the Constitution of the Russian Federation.

The *Конституционный Суд*'s new authority to justify non-compliance with international adjudication has in practice been exercised in three important instances. The first case is *Decision No. 12-П/2016* concerning the restriction of electoral rights of individuals sentenced to deprivation of liberty under Article 32(3) of the Constitution, which was identified as a violation of Article 3 of Protocol No. 1 to the ECHR (Right to Free Elections) by an ECtHR Chamber in *Anchugov and Gladkov*. The St Petersburg Court criticised the evolutionary interpretation of the Convention right by the Strasbourg Court, as regards which consensus has not yet emerged among States Parties.[540] The Russian court also paid attention to possible deviations from the principle of subsidiarity by the ECtHR itself, which can lead to 'a conflict with a constitutional legislator, whose powers are based on the principles of *State sovereignty*, supremacy and supreme legal force of the Constitution of the Russian Federation in the legal system of Russia'.[541] Recognising its primary role of reconciling a conflict between international and constitutional law, the Constitutional Court declared impossible the execution of the ECtHR *Anchugov and Gladkov* judgement, which in its view conflicted with Article 32(3) of the Constitution.[542]

The second occasion is *Decision No. 1-П/2017*, which is pertinent to the *Yukos* case where an ECtHR Chamber found the tax evasion criminal proceedings against a corporation to cause pecuniary damages in violation of Article 1 of ECHR Protocol No. 1 (Right to Property), which allegedly contradicted Article 57 of the Constitution that obliged everyone to

538 Ibid.

539 Ibid.

540 The Russian Constitutional Court, Decision No. 12-П/2016 of 19 April 2016, para 4.3.

541 Ibid para. 4.4 (emphasis added).

542 Ibid operative part para 1.

pay legally established taxes and dues. The Russian court reiterated that the tax offences committed by the OAO Neftyanaya Kompaniya Yukos would mean in essence not only suspension of the effect of Article 57 of the Constitution of the Russian Federation but also the violation of the principles of equality and justice embedded in the entire system of the Constitution.[543] Facing a normative conflict between international and constitutional norms, the St Petersburg Court once again rejected to execute the Strasbourg Court decision in light of the constitutional principles of equality and justice.[544]

The third instance is the opinion issued by the Constitutional Court on 16 March 2020 with respect to the draft constitutional amendments proposed by the president of the Russian Federation in January 2020. The proposed draft amendment to Article 79 of the Constitution added that 'Decisions of inter-state bodies adopted on the basis of provisions of international treaties of the Russian Federation, where construed in a manner *contrary to the Constitution* of the Russian Federation, shall not be subject to enforcement in the Russian Federation'. The proposed constitutional amendment, in asserting Russia's right to refuse to obey the decisions of international institutions if these were found not to comply with its constitution,[545] would in fact formalise several previous rulings which had also run counter to Article 15.[546] Notwithstanding this risk, the St Petersburg judges found that the draft amendment 'provisions, as follows directly from their wording, do not prescribe a repudiation by the Russian Federation of compliance with the international treaties themselves and of the honouring of its international obligations and, accordingly, are not contrary to Article 15(4) of the Russian Federation Constitution'.[547] The

543 The Russian Constitutional Court, Decision No 1-П/2017 of 19 January 2017, para 4.5.

544 Ibid operative part para 1.

545 In relation to this draft provision, the proposed draft amendment to Article 125 § 5 b) provides that the Constitutional Court of the Russian Federation 'shall, in accordance with the procedure stipulated by the federal constitutional law, resolve matters concerning the possibility of enforcing decisions of interstate bodies adopted on the basis of provisions of international treaties of the Russian Federation, where construed in a manner contrary to the Constitution of the Russian Federation'.

546 Elizabeth Teagu, 'Russia's Constitutional Reforms of 2020' (2020) 5 *Russian Politics* 301–328, 308–310.

547 The Russian Constitutional Court, Decision No 1-Z of 16 March 2020, para 3.3. See also, Venice Commission's unofficial translation, CDL-REF(2020)022, 30 April 2020.

Venice Commission showed its concern that the proposed amendments might enlarge the possibility that the Russian Constitutional Court could declare the non-execution of inter-state bodies' decisions, and risk 'the use of the notion "contrary to the Constitution", which is too broad a formula, broader than that of current Article 79'.[548]

In Latin America, ACHR and IACtHR decisions have been seriously assaulted by States Parties.[549] The ultimate form of backlash, the denunciation of the Convention, was triggered by Trinidad and Tobago in 1999 concerning individual petitions regarding the death penalty, and Venezuela in 2013 regarding complex political cases. Reflecting resistance from the executive branch, Peru under the Fujimori regime attempted to withdraw from IACtHR jurisdiction, which was however rejected by the Court. More recently, the Joint Declaration by Argentina, Brazil, Chile, Colombia and Paraguay represents another contestation that puts emphasis on the subsidiarity principle and the margin of appreciation before the inter-American system of human rights.[550]

Latin American contestations against the inter-American system may take judicial forms. Article 23 of the 1999 constitution of Venezuela also expressly stipulates that '[t]he treaties, pacts and conventions relating to human rights which have been executed and ratified by Venezuela have a constitutional rank, and prevail over internal legislation, insofar as they contain provisions concerning the enjoyment and exercise of such rights that are more favourable than those established by this Constitution and the laws of the Republic, and shall be immediately and directly applied by the courts and other organs of the Public Power'. In the *Rafael Chavero Gazdik* case involving a report published by the IACHR, the Supreme Court of Venezuela contended that the decisions of international courts

548 Opinion on the Draft Amendments to the Constitution (as Signed by the President of the Russian Federation on 14 March 2020) Related to the Execution in the Russian Federation of Decisions by the European Court of Human Rights, CDL-AD(2020)009, 18 June 2020.

549 Ximena Soley and Silvia Steininger, 'Parting Ways or Lashing Back? Withdrawals, Backlash and the Inter-American Court of Human Rights' (2018) 14 *International Journal of Law in Context* 237–257; Jorge Contesse, 'Resisting the Inter-American Human Rights System' (2018) 44 Yale Journal of International Law 179–237.

550 Melina Girardi Fachin & Bruna Nowak, *The Joint Declaration to the Inter-American System of Human Rights: Backlash or Contestation?* Int'l J. Const. L. Blog, Dec. 12, 2019, at: http://www.iconnectblog.com/2019/12/the-joint-declaration-to-the-inter-american-system-of-human-rights-backlash-or-contestation/.

should not be executed in a state if they contradict the national constitution.[551]

The Constitutional Tribunal of the Dominican Republic has also resisted the Inter-American judges, especially in cases of expelled Dominicans and Haitians.[552] In Judgement No. TC/0256/14, the *Tribunal Constitucional* declared that the 1999 presidential instrument without national congressional approval, by which the Dominican Republic accepted IACtHR jurisdiction, was unconstitutional.[553] To reach this conclusion, the constitutional judges relied on Article 46(1) of the VCLT to justify the invocation of 'the fact that its consent to be bound by a treaty has been expressed in violation of a provision of its internal law regarding competence to conclude treaties as invalidating its consent' as the instrument was 'in violation of our Constitution, supreme norm and foundation of the judicial order of the Dominican State'.[554] In particular, the instrument was alleged to 'harm national sovereignty, the principle of separation of powers, and the principle of non-intervention in the country's internal affairs'.[555] This sovereignty oriented logic is highly questionable, however, because the Tribunal did not deeply engage in discussion on the VCLT requirement under Article 46(2).[556]

2. *Pro Homine Principle's Domestic Functions for Conventionality Control*

The previous section showed that national judges have tried to integrate human rights treaties into national constitutions to converge the parallel judicial control mechanisms. This practice no longer appears to rest with the *closed* relationship between international and domestic law supported by the notion of *formal* supremacy. Rather, emphasis should be put on

551 Sala Constitucional del Tribunal Supremo de Justicia de Venezuela, Sentencia Nº 1942 de 13 noviembre 2003, at consideraciones para decidir I.

552 *Expelled Dominicans and Haitians v. Dominican Republic*, IACtHR, Series C No 282, Judgment on Preliminary Objections, Merits, Reparations and Costs of 28 August 2014.

553 Tribunal Constitucional de República Dominicana, Exp TC-01–2005–0013, Sentencia TC/0256/14 de 4 de noviembre de 2014.

554 Ibid, para 9.5 – 6.

555 Ibid, para 9.19.

556 Dinah Shelton and Alexandra Huneeus, '*In re* Direct Action of Unconstitutionality Initiated Against the Declaration of Acceptance of the Jurisdiction of the Inter-American Court of Human Rights' (2017) 109 *American Journal of International Law* 866–872, 869.

the *substantive* content, recognized through the *open* interaction between international and domestic sources, which are truly favorable to human beings (*pro homine*).

This section then analyses the *pro homine* principle's function of regulating the relationship between regional conventions and national constitutions. Apart from the role played by the *pro homine* principle in the relationship between regional conventions and other international legal sources (see Part I – Chapter 1), the present Part analyses the principle's concrete functions regarding the relationship between regional conventions and national constitutions. As a clue to comprehending the latter, the IACtHR made a valuable interpretation in *Advisory Opinion OC-18/03*:

> This Court notes that, since there are many legal instruments that regulate labor rights at the domestic and the international level, these regulations must be interpreted according to *the principle of the application of the norm that best protects the individual*, in this case, the worker. This is of great importance, because there is not always agreement either between the different norms or between the norms and their application, and this could prejudice the worker. Thus, *if a domestic practice or norm is more favorable to the worker than an international norm, domestic law should be applied*. To the contrary, *if an international instrument benefits the worker, granting him rights that are not guaranteed or recognized by the State, such rights should be respected and guaranteed to him*.[557]

According to this view, the *pro homine* principle may have two aspects: the *offensive* function as a *sword* to penetrate the border between international and national legal orders, and the *defensive* function as a *shield* to preserve constitutional principles and values.

A. Unified Application of Conventionality Control Parameters

(i) Sword Function for Regional Conventions against National Constitutions

In Latin America, the *pro homine* principle often engages in the offensive function of piercing the boundary of domestic legal orders to complement

557 *Juridical Condition and Human Rights of the Child*, IACtHR (n 151) para 156 (emphasis added).

constitutional fundamental rights with ACHR rights. In fact, recent constitutional reforms have tended to include *pro homine* provisions to combine national and international human rights: for example, the 2008 Constitution of Ecuador (Articles 424 and 426), the 2009 Constitution of Bolivia (Article 256), the 2010 Constitution of the Dominican Republic (Article 74(4)), and the 2011 Constitution of Mexico (Article 1). In addition to these formal clauses, a number of domestic courts in Latin America have materially relied on the *pro homine* principle to integrate international and constitutional human rights standards.[558] In this sense, just as Nollkaemper characterises the direct effect doctrine of international law, the *pro homine* principle may serve as a powerful *sword* piercing the boundary between the international and the constitutional legal order.[559]

First, domestic courts rely on the *pro homine* principle to prioritise ACHR rights over national constitutions if the former offers more ample protection to persons than the latter does. For example, the Bolivian Constitutional Court clearly articulated that 'based on the principle of favourability and *pro persona*, the Fundamental Law itself foresees the possible supra-constitutionality of some instruments of the International Law of the Human Rights, when its norms are *more favourable to the human being*'.[560] In a similar way, the Constitutional Chamber of the Supreme Court of Costa Rica confirmed that 'to such an extent that if [the International Instruments of Human Rights] recognise a right or offer *greater protection of a freedom* than the norm foreseen in the Constitution, they give priority over this one'.[561]

Second, the *pro homine* principle provides momentum to reconsider the overall relationship between the ACHR and national constitutions. For example, the Chilean Constitutional Court remarked that constitutional judges are required to apply the *pro homine* principle with the obligation of the state imposed by the constitution to be the 'servant of the human

558 In general, Mireya Castañeda, *El principio pro persona: experiencias y expectativas* (Comisión Nacional de los Derechos Humanos 2014)110–129, 191–239.

559 Nollkaemper (n 418) 112–115.

560 Tribunal Constitucional de Bolivia, Sentencia 1907/2011-R (n 465) Fundamentos III.4 (emphasis added).

561 Sala Constitucional de la Corte Suprema de Justicia de Costa Rica, Exp 08–012101–0007-CO, Res № 2008018884 de 19 deciembre 2008, Considerando III (emphasis added).

being' and to limit the exercise of the sovereignty in function.[562] Similarly, the Peruvian Constitutional Tribunal mentioned that the *pro homine* principle transforms 'the formal constitutional text' into 'the Constitution in the material sense' complemented by human rights treaties.[563] Notably, the Constitutional Chamber of the Supreme Court of El Salvador regards the relationship between the constitution and international human rights law not as *jerarquía* but as *compatibilidad* in terms of the *pro homine* principle.[564]

Third, the *pro homine* principle regulates the national acts of specific organs. As regards the executive, the Colombian Constitutional Court emphasised that the administrative practice on internally forced displacement 'must be in accordance with the *pro homine* principle and in any case not restrict the previously established standard in the norms of legal character and in the recommendations of international character'.[565] With respect to the judiciary, the Supreme Court of Argentina in *Cardozo* revoked the judgement of the Supreme Court of the Province of Buenos Aires, which 'avoided the pronouncement as to whether [...] the judge had chosen "that interpretation which was more respectful with the *pro homine* principle" within the framework of the duty to guarantee the right to the access that assists every person accused of crime'.[566]

As a controversial practice, the *pro homine* principle faces a challenge in Venezuela. According to the constitutional *pro homine* clause (Article 23), the Supreme Court at the stage of *Sentencia № 87/2000* compared the judicial guarantees under Article 8 ACHR and Article 49(1) of the Constitution, and concluded that the norm of the convention provision is more favourable to the exercise of such a right than the constitutional

562 Corte Suprema de Justicia de Chile, Sentencia 740–07-CDS de 18 abril 2008, at Considerando V (Las normas nacionales sobre regulación de la fertilidad y la duda razonable de afectación del derecho a la vida).

563 Tribunal Constitucional de Perú, Exp. 1417–2005-AA/TC, Sentencia de 8 julio 2005 Fundamentos para 9.

564 Sala de lo Constitucional de la Corte Suprema de Justicia de El Salvador, Sentencia 52–2003/56–2003/57–2003 de 1 abril 2004, Considerando V-3 (emphasis added).

565 Corte Constitucional de Colombia, Exp D-7473, Sentencia C-372/09 de 27 mayo 2009, 8 (Oficina en Colombia del Alto Comisionado de las Naciones Unidas para los Refugiados – ACNUR).

566 Suprema Corte de Justicia de la Nación de Argentina, Fallos 329:2265, Sentencia de 20 junio 2006, at Considerando para. 8.

one.[567] Nevertheless, since the *Rafael Chavero Gazdik* ruling cited above, the Constitutional Chamber has fiercely defended its own position as 'the maximum and last interpreter' of human rights treaties incorporated into the constitutional hierarchy.[568] The academic literature has harshly criticised the Tribunal's position on the grounds that '[b]y assuming the absolute monopoly of constitution interpretation, the Tribunal limited the general powers of all the other courts to resolve by means of judicial review on the matter and to directly apply and give prevalence to the American Convention regarding constitutional provisions'.[569]

The attitude of the Mexican Supreme Court also appears ambivalent. On the basis of the reformed constitutional *pro homine* provision (Article 1), the 2011 *Radilla Pacheco* judgement integrated the *parámetros de constitucionalidad y convencionalidad*, and transformed the judicial review system from a traditional (semi-)centralised version to a diffused version exercised by *all public authorities*.[570] In the *Contradicción de Tesis 293/2011*, however, the Supreme Court assertively defended that the Constitution has priority in cases where an express restriction is stipulated at the constitutional level.[571] It remains unclear whether this decision 'clearly undermines the *pro persona* principle, re-establishing old hierarchies' or 'still leaves room for interpretation, and thus a non-hierarchical, value-oriented deliberation on a case-by-case basis'.[572]

(ii) Relativising Absolute Protections of Constitutional Rights by Regional Conventions

Despite its potential to revise the supremacy of international law and constitution, the *pro homine* principle is not be a perfect panacea for govern-

567 Sala Constitucional del Tribunal Supremo de Justicia de Venezuela, Sentencia Nº 87 de 14 de marzo de 2000. See 81 *Revista de Derecho Público* (2000) 157.

568 Sala Constitucional del Tribunal Supremo de Justicia de Venezuela, Sentencia Nº 1942, *supra* note 28, at consideraciones para decidir I.

569 Brewer-Carías (n 449) 35–38.

570 *Radilla-Pacheco v Estados Unidos Mexicanos* (n 469) paras 23–36 (emphasis added).

571 *Contradicción de Tesis 293/2011*, SCJN de México, Sentencia de 3 septiembre de 2013, paras 64–65.

572 Alejandro Rodiles, 'The Law and Politics of the *Pro Persona* Principle in Latin America' in Helmut Philipp Aust and Georg Nolte (eds), *The Interpretation of International Law by Domestic Courts: Unity, Diversity, Convergence* (Oxford University Press 2015) 153–174, 170 (both quotations).

ing the relationship between conventionality control and constitutionality control. The thorniest issue arises in cases where different rights of several individuals contravene each other. A simple answer to the question of what is the most favourable to persons cannot be elicited from the principle. The final Part of this paper is therefore dedicated to reconsidering the principle's *raison d'être* in situations of conflicting rights.

The *pro homine* principle, which prioritises the most favourable protection to individuals, embraces a paradoxical problem. Alejandro Rodiles has criticised it, suggesting the *pro homine* principle may be labelled *intuitive* and *tautological* because 'it is the object and purpose of every human rights treaty to grant the broadest possible protection to each of the rights it contains, and that everything else would run counter to their very normative function'.[573] Experts contend that '[t]he limits of this principle become apparent when human rights of different individuals have to be balanced'.[574] The same problem is pointed out by Catherine Van de Heyning in her statement that 'it is not always clear what the best protection of fundamental rights is' and 'which court or which level, the national or [international], could decide what the best protection is'.[575]

Such limits, however, do not render the *pro homine* principle completely meaningless in cases of conflicting rights. This is corroborated by the *Artavia Murillo* case pertaining to alleged human rights violations resulting from the presumed general prohibition of the practice of *in vitro* fertilisation (IVF). Although IVF was authorised by the 1995 Executive Decree 24029-S in Costa Rica, it was declared unconstitutional by the Constitutional Chamber of the Supreme Court of Justice in Judgement No. 2000–02306 of 15 March 2000. The Chamber's decision allegedly constituted arbitrary interference in the right to private life and family in the name of the absolute protection of the right to life. As a response in the 2012 *in vitro Fertilisation* judgement, the IACtHR in fact relied on the *pro homine* principle to settle the conflict between the unborn child's rights and the mother's rights. In this context, the Inter-American judges rejected the Respondent's argument that 'its constitutional norms grant a greater protection to the right to life and, therefore, proceed to give this right

573 Helmut Philipp Aust, Alejandro Rodiles and Peter Staubach, 'Unity or Uniformity? Domestic Courts and Treaty Interpretation', 27 *Leiden Journal of International Law* (2014) 75–112, 97.

574 Ibid.

575 Catherine Van de Heyning, 'The Natural "Home" of Fundamental Rights Adjudication: Constitutional Challenges to the European Court of Human Rights' (2012) 31 *Yearbook of European Law* 128–161, 152.

absolute prevalence'.[576] This is because 'this approach denies the existence of rights that may be the object of disproportionate restrictions owing to the defence of the *absolute* protection of the right to life, which would be contrary to the protection of human rights, an aspect that constitutes the object and purpose of the treaty'.[577] To support its own position, the Court invoked the *pro homine* principle:

> [I]n application of the principle of *the most favourable interpretation*, the alleged 'broadest protection' in the domestic sphere cannot allow or justify the suppression of the enjoyment and exercise of the rights and freedoms recognized in the Convention or limit them to a greater extent than the Convention establishes.[578]

Following this statement, the IACtHR assessed the balance between these conflicting rights and concluded that there was 'an arbitrary and excessive interference in private and family life that makes this interference disproportionate'.[579] In this reasoning, the *pro homine* principle itself did not provide a direct answer for resolving the conflict of rights in question. The principle's role is rather found in the previous stage: it *relativises* the *absolute* protection of conflicting rights supported by the supremacy of the national constitution, and thereby creates an *open* circumstance for striking an appropriate balance *most favourable to persons* in terms of their *substance*.

The Costa Rican constitutional judges were again in favour of the right to life, in opposition to the Inter-American judges. To implement the reparation measure indicated by the IACtHR, the executive issued again Decree 39210-MP-S authorising IVF. It was however declared unconstitutional by the Constitutional Chamber judgement on 3 February 2016 for violating constitutional principles of *reserva de ley* and democracy. More concretely, the following constitutional reason was given:

> Compliance with the judgment of the IACHR [...] implies a reconfiguration of the level and scope of the right to life, as well as the definition of a new embryo protection status, in order to perform a new weighting of the protection of the other rights involved, [...], which, by virtue of the principle of *reserva de ley*, which governs in the

576

577 Ibid.

578 Ibid. (emphasis added).

579 Ibid paras 260–263.

> matter of fundamental rights, can only be done by means of a formal law promulgated by the Legislative Assembly.[580]

This case represented a confrontation between constitutional and Inter-American judges. In an order on compliance issued on 26 February 2016, the IACtHR valued positively the efforts made by the executive to annul the IVF prohibition, while it considered the negative attitude of the Constitutional Chamber just two weeks earlier as an obstacle to implementing the judgement.[581] It is remarkable in this context that the dissenting opinion of Judge Vio Grossi clearly mentions 'el margen de apreciación del Estado', which is recognised for implementing the obligations under international law.[582] As the last message from the Inter-American Court, its Order was issued in 2019, which verified that the state had complied fully with the judgement because Executive Decree No. 39210-MP-S of 11 September 2015 for authorising the assisted reproduction technique of *in vitro* fertilisation and embryo transfer remained in force.[583] It was also positively evaluated that Costa Rica had introduced in 2016 two decrees to ensure the proper implementation of the practice of the IVF in the country.[584] The Inter-American Court found that, with these three decrees, the state had not only regulated those aspects it considered necessary for the implementation of IVF in both public and private health establishments, but had also established a system of inspection and control by the Ministry of Health to periodically monitor all the public and private health clinics that carry out this assisted reproduction technique, as ordered by this Court.[585]

---

580 Sala Constitucional de la Corte Suprema de Justicia de Costa Rica, Exp 15–013929–0007, Sentencia Nº 01692/2016 de 3 febrero 2016, Considerando IV.

581 *Artavia Murillo and Others (In Vitro Fertilization) v Costa Rica*, IACtHR, Monitoring Compliance with Judgments, Order of 26 February 2016, paras 17–19.

582 Individual Dissenting Opinion of Judge Eduardo Vio Grossi, ibid para 25.

583 *Artavia Murillo and Others (In Vitro Fertilization) and Case of Gómez Murillo and Others v Costa Rica*, Monitoring Compliance with Judgments. Order of the Inter-American Court of Human Rights of 22 November 2019, para 17.

584 Ibid para 18.

585 Ibid para 22.

B. Diversified Application of Conventionality Control Parameters

(i) Shield Function for National Constitutions against Regional Conventions

In comparison to the Latin American experiences, the *pro homine* principle has not been explicitly referred to in the Strasbourg Court jurisprudence and by European national courts.[586] From their practices, however, we may extract some important functions of Article 53 of the ECHR, a similar 'more favourable' provision to Article 29(b) of the ACHR, and albeit indirectly, induce those of the *pro homine* principle. The following points, taken as a whole, show that Article 53 of the ECHR, which supposedly embraces the *pro homine* principle, plays a defensive role in safeguarding constitutional values from judicial control based on the Strasbourg law. In this situation, the *pro homine* principle in turn works as a *shield* to prioritise national legal sources over international ones and thereby protects constitutional principles and values.

First, as is the case with the 2005 *Okyay v. Turkey* judgement, national judges invoke Article 53 of the ECHR to emphasise its literal safeguarding function and to maintain existing national standards against the Convention standards.[587] As a representative example, the German Constitutional Court asserted the condition in the *Görgülü* decision that ECHR and ECtHR jurisprudence serve as interpretative guidelines for the Basic Law 'provided that this does not lead to a restriction or reduction of protection of the individual's fundamental rights under the Basic Law – and this the Convention itself does not desire'.[588] Similarly, the Italian Constitutional Court mentioned Article 53 of the ECHR to confirm that 'the need to comply with international law obligations can never constitute grounds for a reduction in protection compared to that available under internal

586 Article 20(2) of the 1991 Constitution of Romania incorporate a 'more favorable' clause. See also, Levent Gonenc and Selin Esen, 'The Problem of the Application of Less Protective International Agreements in Domestic Legal Systems: Article 90 of the Turkish Constitution' (2007) 8 *European Journal of Law Reform* 485–500, 492–497.

587 *Okyay and Others v. Turkey*, ECtHR, App No. 36220/97, Judgment on Merits and Just Satisfaction of 12 July 2005, paras 61–68 (finding the applicability of Article 6 ECHR on the grounds that 'the concept of a "civil right" under Article 6 § 1 cannot be construed as limiting an enforceable right in domestic law within the meaning of Article 53 of the Convention').

588 *Görgülü* (n 445) para 32.

law'.[589] Moreover, the Spanish Constitutional Court referred to Article 53 of the ECHR in *Declaración 1/2004*, elaborating the Spanish version of the *controlimiti* doctrine. In this context, Article 53 of the ECHR and a similar provision, Article II-113 of the Treaty establishing a Constitution for Europe (corresponding to Article 53 of the CFREU), were invoked to emphasise that 'the CFREU is conceived, in whatsoever case, as a guarantee of minimums on which the content of each right and freedom may be developed up to the density of content assured in each case by internal legislation'.[590]

Second, in line with the *E.B. v. France* judgement by the ECtHR,[591] national judicial authorities rely on Article 53 of the ECHR to progressively fix higher national standards than the Convention standards.[592] For example, in the *159/2004* decision, the Belgian Constitutional Court stated that it was free to go further than the Strasbourg Court regarding the right to same-sex marriage under Article 12 of the ECHR, referring to Article 53 of the ECHR and Article 5(2) of the ICCPR.[593] The Supreme Court of Norway took a similar approach with regard to the right to present evidence from child witnesses in court, which is found in both Norwegian due process guarantees and the ECHR. According to an explanation from Justice Øie, 'it is therefore not reasonable to consider the right to the questioning of children as anchored in the Convention, as interpreted by the Strasbourg Court, alone; it has rather been established in the interplay between Norwegian law and international human rights'.[594]

---

589 Corte constituzionale italilana, Sentenza № 317 del 3 novembre 2007 Considerato in diritto para 7.

590 Tribunal Constitucional español, Declaración 1 de 13 diciembre 2004 Fundamentos jurídicos para. 6.

591 *E B v France*, ECtHR, App no 43546/02, Judgment on Merits and Just Satisfaction of 22 January 2008, para 49. In the judgment, the Court indicated the possibility under Article 53 ECHR that 'a State is free to be "generous", that is, to do more than the Convention require it to do – but once it decided to take that step, the State should not discriminate.' See Rick Lawson, 'Beyond the Call of Duty? Domestic Courts and the Standards of the European Court of Human Rights', in Henk Snijders and Stefan Vogenauer (eds), *Content and Meaning of National Law in the Context of Transnational Law* (Sellier European Law Publishers 2010) 21–38, 25.

592 Mads Andenas and Eirik Bjorge, 'National Implementation of ECHR Rights' in Føllesdal and Others (n 149) 181–262, 205–206.

593 Cour constitutionnelle belge, Arrêt n° 159/2004 du 20 octobre 2004, paras 6.1 – 6.4.

594 Norges Høyesterett, HR-2011–00182-A, 26. januar 2011. For the English translation, Mads Andenas and Eirik Bjorge, 'The Norwegian Court Applies the ECHR

A problematic approach is that some States Parties have adopted the *mirror* principle to uncritically accept Strasbourg jurisprudence. In the 2004 *Ullah* ruling, Lord Bingham famously formulated the mirror principle, according to which the court must keep pace with evolving Strasbourg jurisprudence 'no more, but certainly no less'.[595] In the *NJ 2002/278* judgement, the Supreme Court of the Netherlands already elaborated the Dutch mirror principle under Article 53 of the ECHR by stating that the incompatibility between domestic law and the ECHR 'cannot be assumed solely on the basis of an interpretation by the national – Dutch – courts [...] which leads to a more extensive protection than may be assumed on the grounds of the jurisdiction of the ECHR'.[596] The mirror principle not only evinces respect for ECtHR case law as the authoritative ECHR interpretation but also minimises the risk of a decision of the national court being the subject of an application to the Strasbourg Court.[597] Particularly, due to this principle, domestic courts may 'leave important political and value choices to be made by the Legislature' by strictly mirroring international jurisprudence.[598] Notwithstanding these advantages, the mirror principle may prevent national judges from developing their own native approach to ECHR interpretation.[599] This consequence would defeat the purpose of Article 53 of the ECHR (and Section 11 of the 1998 Human Rights Act) on the basis of which a more generous approach than the Strasbourg Court is permitted.[600] Because on numerous occasions national standards

---

by Building upon Its Underlying Principles' (2013) 19 *European Public Law* 241–248.

595 *R (on the application of Ullah) v Special Adjudicator* [2004] UKHL 26, [2004] 2 AC 323, para 20.

596 Hoge Raad der Nederlanden, NJ 2002/278, 10 augustus 2001, para 3.9. For the English translation, Nick S Efthymiou and Joke C de Wit, 'The Role of Dutch Courts in the Protection of Fundamental Rights', (2013) 9 *Utrecht Law Review* 75–88, 78–79.

597 Rt Hon Lady Justice Arden DBE, 'Peaceful or Problematic? The Relationship between National Supreme Courts and Supranational Courts in Europe' (2010) 29 *Yearbook of European Law* 3–20, 14.

598 Janneke Gerards and Joseph Fleuren, 'The Netherlands' in Janneke Gerards and Joseph Fleuren (eds), *Implementation of the European Convention on Human Rights and of the Judgments of the ECtHR in National Case-Law: A Comparative Analysis* (Intersentia 2014) 217–260, 245–246.

599 Jeffery Jowell, *The Changing Constitution* (Oxford University Press 2015) 88.

600 Richard Clayton, 'Should the English Courts under the HRA Mirror the Strasbourg Case Law?', in Katja S Ziegler, Elizabeth Wicks and Loveday Hodson (eds), *The UK and European Human Rights: A Strained Relationship?* (Hart 2015) 95–114, 105.

have proved stronger in protecting human rights than the ECHR, such supplementary protection should not be lightly cast aside.[601]

(ii) Relativising Absolute Protections of Conventional Rights by National Constitutions

The utility of the *pro homine* principle was indeed limited in the Strasbourg Court. A prime example is the 1992 *Open Door and Dublin Well Woman v Ireland* case concerning the conflict between freedom of expression and the right to life. In confronting this conflict of rights, the ECtHR simply cut off the argument on Article 60 (the former version of Article 53) of the ECHR invoked by the Respondent Government.[602] Instead, the Court applied the margin of appreciation doctrine and concluded that the restraint imposed on the applicants against receiving or imparting information was disproportionate to the aims pursued.[603] As this case suggests, the ECtHR does not regard Article 53 of the ECHR as an appropriate tool for dealing with conflicting rights as this provision would be 'at odds with the concept of autonomous standards' and diminish 'the reach as well as the authority of the ECtHR case law'.[604] It might be therefore better to say that, within the European system, the margin of appreciation doctrine, not the *pro homine* principle, transforms ECHR concepts 'from an applicant's sword into a defendant's shield'.[605]

Does the *pro homine* principle also relativise the absolute mandates based on the supremacy of international law in favour of national constitutions? An answer can be drawn from the *Melloni* case which represented such a collision between constitutional protection of fundamental rights and EU law systems. On the one hand, the Spanish *Tribunal Constitucional* has

---

601 Brice Dickson, *Human Rights and the United Kingdom Supreme Court* (Oxford University Press 2013) 43.

602 *Open Door and Dublin Well Woman v Ireland*, ECtHR, App Nos 14234/88 and 14235/88, Judgment on Merits and Just Satisfaction of 29 October 1992, paras 78–79.

603 Ibid paras 67–77.

604 Catherine van de Heyning, 'No Place like Home: Discretionary Space for the Domestic Protection of Human Rights' in Patricia Popelier, Catherine Van de Heyning and Piet Van Nuffel (eds), *Human Rights Protection in the European Legal Order: The Interaction between the European and National Courts* (Intersentia 2011) 65–96, 78.

605 Howard Charles Yourow, *The Margin of Appreciation Doctrine in the Dynamics of European Human Rights Jurisprudence* (Brill 1996) 193.

established that the right to participate in an oral trial and to one's own defence constitutes the 'absolute content' of the right to a fair trial.[606] On the other hand, Article 4(a)(1) of the amended European Arrest Warrant Framework Decision 2009/299 specified the conditions under which conviction in a trial *in absentia* cannot constitute a reason for non-surrender of the convicted person. Against the background of this conflict, the *Tribunal Constitucional* decided to refer questions, including the following issue of Article 53 of the CFREU, to the CJEU for a preliminary ruling under Article 267 of the Treaty on the Functioning of the European Union: 'does Article 53 of the Charter [...] allow a Member State to make surrender of a person convicted *in absentia* conditional upon the conviction being open to review in the requesting State, thus affording those rights a greater level of protection than that deriving from European Union Law, in order to avoid an interpretation which restricts or adversely affects a fundamental right recognized by the constitution of the first-mentioned Member State?'

Although the Madrid Court knocked on the Luxembourg Court's door suggesting a possible interpretation of Article 53 of the CFREU, the CJEU simply dismissed it, contending that it 'would undermine *the principle of the primacy of EU law* inasmuch as it would allow a Member State to disapply EU legal rules which are fully in compliance with the Charter where they infringe the fundamental rights guaranteed by that State's Constitution'.[607] Subsequently, the CJEU presented a new formula for regulating the relationship between EU law and national standards under Article 53 of the CFREU as follows:

> It is true that Article 53 of the Charter confirms that, where an EU legal act calls for national implementing measures, national authorities and courts remain free to apply national standards of protection of fundamental rights, provided that the level of protection provided for by the Charter, as interpreted by the Court, and *the primacy, unity and effectiveness of EU law are not thereby compromised*.[608]

In conclusion, the CJEU responded that 'Article 53 of the Charter must be interpreted as not allowing a Member State to make the surrender of a person convicted *in absentia* conditional upon the conviction being

606 Tribunal Constitucional español, Sentencia 91/2000 de 4 de mayo de 2000 para 13.

607 Case C-399/11, *Stefano Melloni v Ministerio Fiscal*, Judgment of 26 February 2013, para 56 (emphasis added).

608 Ibid para 60 (emphasis added).

open to review in the issuing Member State, in order to avoid an adverse effect on the right to a fair trial and the rights of the defence guaranteed by its constitution'.[609] In essence, the *Melloni* ruling clearly asserts that EU law can work not only as a *floor* (minimum standard) but also as a *ceiling* (maximum standard) to limit more protective provisions of national constitutions.[610] Put differently, the CJEU 'forcefully asserted that Article 53 of the EU Charter cannot threaten the supremacy of EU law in any event'.[611]

As a response to the preliminary judgement, the *Tribunal Constitucional* conceded to complete the preliminary ruling of the CJEU by lowering the national level of protection while reminding the Spanish *controlimiti* doctrine elaborated in the *Declaración 1/2004*.[612] In the Declaration, the Madrid Court opened the possibility of 'ultimately rul[ing] in favor of the sovereignty of the Spanish people and the supremacy of the Constitution, through the relevant constitutional procedure'.[613] The Spanish constitutional judges' attitude seems to suggest that the Constitutional Court retains the last word in the event of a clash between the Spanish Constitution and EU law.[614] Aida Torres Pérez offered severe criticism by describing the *Melloni* case as one that moved *from dialogue to monologue* because both the Luxembourg and the Madrid Court eventually 'retreated to the safe havens of EU primacy and constitutional supremacy in a struggle for ultimate authority'.[615] She normatively argues that, to facilitate robust dialogue between the CJEU and national courts, 'even if primacy, unity, and effectiveness [of EU law] were compromised, constitutional rights should not be automatically set aside, but rather the CJEU should examine whether a restriction on those principles might be justified in order

609 Ibid para 64.

610 Fabbrini (n 211) 35–44.

611 Jan Komárek, 'National Constitutional Courts in the European Constitutional Democracy' (2014) 12 *International Journal of Constitutional Law* 525–544, 528 (emphasis added).

612 Tribunal Constitucional español, Sentencia 26/2014 de 13 febrero 2014, Fundamentos jurídicos para 3. See also, BVerfG, 2 BvR 2735/14, Entscheidung vom 15. Dezember 2015, para 78.

613 Tribunal Constitucional español, Decración 1/2004 para 3. See also ibid, Voto particular concurrente que formula la Magistrada doña Encarnación Roca Trías, para 4.

614 Aida Torres Pérez, 'Melloni in Three Acts: from Dialogue to Monologue' (2014) 10 *European Constitutional Law Review* (2014) 308–331, 320.

615 Ibid 329–331.

to accommodate *more protective* constitutional rights'.[616] The pluralist position seems to vindicate the open-minded, substance-oriented interaction between European and domestic legal sources, which are truly favourable to human beings, rather than the absolute primacy of EU law or national constitutions.

To realise such a pluralist idea, the absolutist jurisprudence of the CJEU has been to some extent attenuated in subsequent cases. In *Åkerberg Fransson*, the question arose as to 'whether the charges brought against Mr. Åkerberg Fransson must be dismissed on the ground that he has already been punished for the same acts in other proceedings, as the prohibition on being punished twice laid down by [...] Article 50 of the Charter would be infringed'.[617] It was the legal circumstance where the Swedish *Haparada tingsrätt* asked the CJEU whether the *ne bis in idem* principle laid down in Article 50 of the Charter should be interpreted as precluding criminal proceedings for tax evasion from being brought against a defendant where a tax penalty has already been imposed upon him for the same act of providing false information.[618] Although the main issue of the *Åkerberg Fransson* case was the scope of application of the CFREU as prescribed by Article 51, the CJEU expressly cited the *Melloni* decision in paragraph 29 and explained the relationship between EU law and national standards as follows: '[W]here a court of a Member State is called upon to review whether fundamental rights are complied with by a national provision or measure which, *in a situation where action of the Member States is not entirely determined by European Union law*, implements the latter for the purposes of Article 51(1) of the Charter, national authorities and courts remain free to apply national standards of protection of fundamental rights, provided that the level of protection provided for by the Charter, as interpreted by the Court, and the primacy, unity and effectiveness of European Union law are not thereby compromised'.[619] Following this statement, the Court concluded that 'the *ne bis in idem* principle laid down in Article 50 of the Charter does not preclude a Member State from imposing successively, for the same acts of non-compliance with declaration obligations in the field of VAT [value added tax], a tax penalty and a criminal penalty in so far as the first penalty is not criminal in nature, a matter which is for the

616 Ibid 328 (emphasis added).

617 Case C-617/10, *Åklagaren v Hans Åkerberg Fransson*, Judgment of 26 February 2013, para 14.

618 Ibid para 32.

619 Ibid para 29 (emphasis added).

national court to determine'.[620] *Åkerberg Fransson* implies that where EU law does not completely determine Member States' actions, national authorities may entertain a higher level of protection of fundamental rights than those required by the CFREU.[621]

Later, the CJEU issued *Opinion 2/13* and held that the agreement on the accession of the EU to the ECHR is not compatible with EU law. In ascertaining whether the agreement is liable adversely to affect the specific characteristics of EU law, the Court examined the relationship between Articles 53 of the CFREU and ECHR. In this context, the CJEU noted their relations, citing the *Melloni* judgement, as follows: 'In so far as Article 53 of the ECHR essentially reserves the power of the Contracting Parties to lay down higher standards of protection of fundamental rights than those guaranteed by the ECHR, that provision should be coordinated with Article 53 of the Charter, as interpreted by the Court of Justice, so that *the power granted to Member States by Article 53 of the ECHR is limited* [...] *to that which is necessary to ensure that the level of protection provided for by the Charter and the primacy, unity and effectiveness of EU law are not compromised*'.[622] Despite the potential danger of undermining the primacy of EU law, according to the Court, there is no provision in the draft agreement envisaged to ensure such coordination.[623] Therefore, the CJEU concluded that the EU accession to the ECHR is liable adversely to affect the specific characteristics of EU law and its autonomy.[624] The Opinion seems to express the Court's 'worry that the Member States might now use Article 53 of the Convention to resurrect fundamental rights standards in defiance of *Melloni*'.[625]

Finally, the *Taricco* case narrated by the judges in both Luxembourg and Rome tells us the relativist potential of the *pro homine* principle in the European context. The story started when the *Tribunale di Cuneo* launched a preliminary reference to the CJEU with regard to the compatibility

---

620 Ibid para 37.

621 Bas van Bockel and Peter Wattel, 'New Wine into Old Wineskins: The Scope of the Charter of Fundamental Rights of the EU after *Åkerberg Fransson*' (2013) 38 *European Law Review* 866–883, 878–879.

622 CJEU, Opinion 2/13 of 18 December 2014, para 189 (emphasis added).

623 Ibid para 190.

624 Ibid para 200.

625 Daniel Halberstam, 'It's the Autonomy, Stupid!' A Modest Defense of Opinion 2/13 on EU Accession to the ECHR and a Way Forward' (2015) Public Law and Legal Theory Research Paper Series (University of Michigan), 19 <http://papers.ssrn.com/sol3/papers.cfm?abstract_id=2567591> accessed 30 March 2015.

of Italian provisions regulating limitation periods applicable to tax and financial offences with Article 325 of the TFEU. In the so-called *Taricco I* ruling in 2015, the Court of Justice vindicated the primacy of EU law by requiring domestic courts to disapply national provisions at issue that do not satisfy the requirement of EU law that measures to counter VAT evasion be effective and dissuasive.[626] Because the *Taricco I* provoked turmoil, the Court of Cassation sent references to the Italian Constitutional Court questioning the compatibility of the case law between the Italian Constitutional Court and the CJEU. In a response from Rome, *la Corte costituzionale* indicated the possibility of invoking its own doctrine of *controlimiti* that reflected the notion of respect for national constitutional identity and was constructed on the basis of Article 4(2) of the TEU.[627] Moreover, the constitutional judges paved the way for dialogue with the community judges by asking them to reconsider the interpretation of Article 325 of the TFEU on the basis of its compatibility with Article 49 of the CFREU and the principle of legality.[628] In the Opinion of Yves Bot, advocate general of the CJEU, the application of the Italian constitutional standard of protection 'compromises the primacy of EU law in that it allows an obstacle to be placed in the way of an obligation identified by the Court which is not only consistent with the [CFREU] but also in keeping with the [ECtHR] case law'.[629] In the *Taricco II* judgement, however, the CJEU remarkably cited the *Åkerberg Fransson* judgement's paragraph 29, which in turn invoked the rule affirmed in *Melloni,* although it did not refer to Article 53 of the Charter.[630] It follows from this reasoning that the Community Court made implicit and indirect reference to Article 53 of the CFREU which allows national actors to apply national fundamental rights standards.[631] The *Taricco* case, as Giuseppe Martinico and Giorgio Repetto viewed it, was 'a cumulative approach by which the various catalogues of rights arrive on the scene simultaneously and a different logic

626 Case C-105/14, *Taricco and Others* CJEU, Judgment of 8 September 2015, para 49.

627 Corte costituzionale italiana, Sentenza № 24/2017 del 23 novembre 2016 Considerato in diritto paras 6–8.

628 Ibid para 9.

629 Opinion of Advocate General Bot in Case C-42/17 M A S, M B, para 166.

630 Case C-42/17 M A S, M B, CJEU, Judgment of 5 December 2017, para 47.

631 Matteo Bonelli, 'The Taricco Saga and the Consolidation of Judicial Dialogue in the European Union CJEU' (2018) 25 *Maastricht Journal of European and Comparative Law* 357–373, 364–365.

seems to be emerging vis-à-vis the functioning of the Charter'.[632] The CJEU's attitude in *Taricco II* has an affinity with the diversified application of regional conventions and national constitutions. In line with IACtHR jurisprudence, this attitude embraces a significant implication for the role of the *pro homine* principle in striking an appropriate balance between constitutional and conventional rights.

632 Giuseppe Martinico and Giorgio Repetto, 'Fundamental Rights and Constitutional Duels in Europe: An Italian Perspective on Case 269/2017 of the Italian Constitutional Court and Its Aftermath' (2019) 15 *European Constitutional Law Review* 731–751, 751.

Chapter 2

Domestic Distribution of Conventionality Control Powers

The IACtHR has dynamically developed the doctrine of *control de convencionalidad* to deal with structural human rights violations resulting from domestic norms that are incompatible with international standards. In *Almonacid-Arellano v Chile*, the San José Court for the first time required the judiciary to exercise conventionality control of the self-amnesty law under the Pinochet regime.[633] In the later judgement of *Cabrera Garcia and Montiel Flores v. Mexico* concerning abuse of military jurisdiction, the Court further elaborated the doctrine, particularly as regards the distribution of powers between domestic courts:

> [W]hen a State has ratified an international treaty such as the American Convention, all its bodies, including its judges, are also bound by such Convention, which forces them to see that all the effects of the provisions embodied in the Convention are not adversely affected by the enforcement of laws which are contrary to its purpose and end. *The Judiciary [Los jueces y órganos vinculados a la administración de justicia], in all its levels*, must exercise ex officio a sort of 'conventionality control' between the domestic legal provisions and the American Convention, *evidently within the framework of their respective competence and the corresponding procedural rules*. To perform this task, the Judiciary has to take into account not only the treaty, but also the interpretation thereof made by the Inter-American Court, which is the ultimate interpreter of the American Convention.[634]

This paragraph embraces both *restrictive* and *permissive* aspects concerning the distribution of competences for conventionality control among domestic courts. Concerning the *restrictive* aspect, the first italicised emphasis clearly indicates that conventionality control must be performed by "'all judges", regardless of their formal membership in the Judiciary Branch,

633 *Almonacid-Arellano and Others*, Judgment (n 21) paras 123–125.
634 *Cabrera Garcia and Montiel Flores* (n 35) para 225 (emphasis added).

and regardless of their rank, grade, level or area of expertise'.[635] Compared to the abstract formula 'the Judiciary' in *Almonacid-Arellano*, the *Cabrera Garcia and Montiel Flores* ruling concretised the scope of subjects responsible for conventionality control so as to include ordinary courts as well as the highest courts. In other words, the paragraph envisages *decentralised* or *diffused* conventionality control of domestic law by all judges.

Regarding the *permissive* aspect, the second italicised emphasis signifies that States Parties are granted certain discretion to realise conventionality control at the national level. According to the principle of subsidiarity, which is structurally embedded in international human rights law, the *primary* responsibilities are incumbent on States Parties, and treaty mechanisms are essentially *subsidiary* to national systems.[636] As the IACtHR confirmed in *Liakat Ali Alibux v. Surinam*, human rights conventions do 'not impose a specific model for the regulation of issues of constitutionality and control for conventionality'.[637] This position leaves national freedom of choice to exclusively entrust conventionality control to the *constitutional court* in line with its concentrated powers for constitutionality control. In this sense, the paragraph also opens the possibility of *centralised* conventionality control of domestic law by constitutional judges.

This chapter surveys these two directions of the distribution of powers among domestic courts in the implementation of human rights conventions. It starts with a general observation on the distribution of powers to ordinary courts (Section 1-A) and constitutional courts (Section 1-B) in the control of domestic law in light of national constitutions and community laws. The following section then examines the distribution of powers between domestic judges in a dual direction: decentralised conventionality control by ordinary courts (Section 2-A), and centralised conventionality control by constitutional courts (Section 2-B).

---

635 Concurring Opinion of Judge *ad hoc* MacGregor Poisot, *Cabrera Garcia and Montiel Flores* (n 35) para 19.

636 Paolo G Carozza, 'Subsidiarity as a Structural Principle of International Human Rights Law' (2003) 97 *American Journal of International Law* 38–79, 56–67.

637 *Liakat Ali Alibux* (n 307) para 124.

1. *Relationship between Constitutional and Ordinary Courts*

A. Power Distribution for Ordinary Courts

(i) Consistent Interpretation of Legislation with National Constitutions

Internal and external pressures may prompt ordinary judges to engage in controlling statutes in light of fundamental rights even within the concentrated system of constitutional review.[638] In general, decentralised judicial review systems mandate ordinary judges to interpret ordinary law in conformity with a constitution as well as the annulment of specific norms of ordinary law. This does not mean that ordinary judges in the decentralised model are free from the task of constitution-conformity interpretation. Rather, the interpretative technique is ubiquitous in the jurisprudence of constitutional courts, known as *réserves d'interprétation* in French and as *verfasssungskonforme Auslegung* in German.[639] In Spain, for example, Article 5(3) of the *Ley orgánica del Poder Judicial* expressly provides that '[t]he question of unconstitutionality shall be raised when it is not possible to adapt the rule to the constitutional regulation through interpretation'.[640] Another example is an Italian case in which ordinary judges are able to raise constitutionality questions to the *Corte costituzionale* only if an *interpretazione conforme* of legislation with the Constitution is impossible.[641] With these methods, ordinary courts perform a certain type of constitutionality control by interpreting legislation in conformity with national constitutions before they initiate the preliminary reference to the constitutional court.

If an interpretation cannot resolve the conformity of legislation with national constitutions, the ordinary courts will be forced to set aside the law in substantive terms and to betray the centralised system of constitu-

638 In general, Ferreres Comella (n 442) Part III.

639 For a comparative analysis of European constitutional courts, de Visser (n 52) 291–305.

640 Procederá el planteamiento de la cuestión de inconstitucionalidad cuando por vía interpretativa no sea posible la acomodación de la norma al ordenamiento constitucional.

641 Tania Groppi, 'Constitutional Reasoning in the Italian Constitutional Court' (2014) *Rivista dell'Associazione Italiana dei Costituzionalisti* 1–45, 30.

tional review in favour of a *de facto* diffused system.[642] Having conducted a broad comparative analysis of European constitutional courts, Marrtje de Visser neatly summarises the decentralisation trend of judicial review in Europe: On the one hand, constitutional courts gain some additional measure of control over their caseload by requiring that regular judges seek to interpret legislation in a way that makes it constitutionally valid before they are able to initiate the preliminary reference procedure. On the other hand, the constitutional role and responsibilities of the ordinary judiciary are enlarged as a result of this demand, especially when ordinary courts are overly eager to assess the scope for conciliatory interpretation. In the end, we may thus witness a shift in the division of labour between the constitutional and the ordinary judiciary in favour of the latter, and the introduction of *decentralising* tendencies in the centralised system for constitutional adjudication as it was originally established in many European countries.[643] By means of conformity interpretation of legislation with constitution, the centralised model of judicial review 'is thus based on an unstable distinction between the "power to interpret" (for the ordinary judge) and the "power to set aside" (for the constitutional court)', in contrast to decentralised systems where the distinction does not entail significant consequences.[644]

(ii) Disapplication of Legislation Inconsistent with Community Law

In addition to these internal factors, regional integrations have a significant influence on the distribution of judicial powers among national courts. In the European context, the principle of the primacy of EU law has been recognised as one of the constitutional principles of the EU legal order.[645] The basis of this primacy lies in the very nature of the EU legal order, as a separate and autonomous legal order created by transferring

---

642 Elisabetta Lamarque, 'Interpreting Statutes in Conformity with the Constitution: The Role of the Italian Constitutional Court and Ordinary Judges' (2010) 1 *Italian Journal of Public Law* 87–120, 115-116.

643 De Visser (n 52) 384 (emphasis added).

644 Ferreres Comella (n 442) 474.

645 Armin von Bogdandy, 'Founding Principles' in Armin von Bogdandy and Jürgen Bast (eds), *Principles of European Constitutional Law* (Hart Publishing 2010) 93–111.

competences from the Member States to the EU.[646] The 1964 *Costa v. ENEL* decision established the primacy of EU law by holding that 'the law stemming from the Treaty, an independent source of law, could not [...] be overridden by domestic legal provisions [...] without the legal basis of the Community itself being called into question'.[647] In the 1970 *Internationale Handelsgesellschaft* ruling, the ECJ went a step further with respect to the absolute primacy over 'fundamental rights as formulated by the constitution of that state or the principles of a national constitutional structure'.[648]

The Luxembourg Court then formulated the famous *Simmenthal* doctrine by utilising the primacy of EU law to juxtapose the positions of constitutional and ordinary judges in enforcing Community law:[649]

> *[E]very national court* must, in a case within its jurisdiction, apply Community law in its entirety and protect rights which the latter confers on individuals and must accordingly set aside any provision of national law which may conflict with it, whether prior or subsequent to the Community rule. Accordingly any provision of a national legal system and any legislative, administrative or judicial practice which might impair the effectiveness of Community law by withholding from the national court having jurisdiction to apply such law the power to do everything necessary at the moment of its application to set aside national legislative provisions which might prevent Community rules from having full force and effect are incompatible with those requirements which are the very essence of Community law.[650]

In *Simmenthal*, the ECJ also established the *immediacy* requirement, according to which ordinary judges are obliged 'to do everything necessary at the moment of its application to set aside national legislative provisions which might prevent community rules from having full force and

646 Monica Claes, *The National Courts' Mandate in the European Constitution* (Hart Publishing 2006) 666.

647 Case 6/64 *Costa v ENEL* [1964] ECR 585, 594.

648 Case 11/70 *Internationale Handelsgesellschaft v Einfuhr- und Vorratsstelle für Getreide und Futtermittel* [1970] ECR 1125, para 3.

649 The *Simmenthal* doctrine is also accepted in Community Law of Latin American region. See Karen J Alter, Laurence R Helfer and Osvaldo Saldías, 'Transplanting the European Court of Justice: The Experience of the Andean Tribunal of Justice' (2012) 60 American Journal of Comparative Law 629–664, 657–659.

650 Case 106/77 Amministrazione delle Finanze dello Stato v Simmenthal SpA [1978] ECR 629, paras 21–22 (emphasis added).

effect'.[651] The European version of *Marbury v. Madison* is evaluated as an epoch-making step towards introducing the decentralised system of judicial review.[652]

In accordance with the *Simmenthal* judgement, all domestic judges are obliged to behave as not only as the guardians of national fundamental rights but also the *ordinary judges of Community law*.[653] In subsequent cases, the ECJ has continued such a decentralising approach that bypasses national constitutional courts in the enforcement of EU law.[654] The Court of Justice can interact with national courts in a variety of ways from full centralision to itself (*Cassis de Dijon*), to showing tendency and guidelines (*Dynamic Medien* and *Familiapress*), to granting full decentralisation (*Libert*).[655] The centralised constitutional systems are subject to judicial and executive organs to legislation unless the constitutional court declares that legislation invalid; therefore, the net effect of the *Simmenthal* doctrine is its empowerment of any and all national courts to review any kind of public acts, including acts of parliament.[656] Jan Komárek characterises this as the *displacement* doctrine, according to which 'national constitutional courts are removed from their place in constitutional law and politics and ordinary courts, acting in cooperation with the ECJ, replace them'.[657]

---

651 Ibid.

652 Peter W Schroth, 'Marbury and Simmenthal: Reflections on the Adoption of Decentralized Judicial Review by the Court of Justice of the European Community' (1979) 12 *Loyola of Los Angeles Law Review* 869–902.

653 Monica Claes, *The National Courts' Mandate in the European Constitution* (Hart Publishing 2006) 102.

654 Zdeněk Kühn, 'Wachauf and ERT: On the Road from the Centralized to the Decentralized System of Judicial Review' in Miguel Poiares Maduro and Loïc Azoulai (eds), *The Past and Future of EU Law. The Classics of EU Law Revisited on the 50th Anniversary of the Rome Treaty* (Hart 2010) 151–162.

655 Jan Zglinski, *Europe's Passive Virtues: Deference to National Authorities in EU Free Movement Law* (Oxford University Press 2020) 33-36.

656 Leonard F M Besselink, 'The Proliferation of Constitutional Law and Constitutional Adjudication or How American Judicial Review Came to Europe After All' (2013) 9 Utrecht Law Review 19–35, 25.

657 Komárek (n 612) 526–529.

B. Power Distribution to Constitutional Courts

(i) Individual Complaint Procedures

Despite the purely conceptual distinction between centralised and decentralised models, the roles of constitutional courts have been reinforced in practice. Constitutional framers must decide how far to concentrate these judicial review powers in specially entrusted tribunals, and whether the system's court of last resort on constitutional matters is to be a specialist/non-ordinary or a generalist/ordinary tribunal.[658] To take the example of the German *Bundesverfassungsgericht*, which has been a leading model in the world, constitutional appeals can reach in three main ways: the concrete constitutional review triggered by the referral during a judicial proceeding, the abstract constitutional review (*Normenkontrolle*) directly petitioned by officials, and the individual complaint (*Verfassungsbeschwerde*) invoked by citizens.[659]

As the guardians of constitutional orders, the individual complaint mechanism operated by specialised organs with constitutional jurisdiction works not only for remedying subjective rights but also objective values. The German Federal Constitutional Court has indeed used the *Verfassungsbeschwerde* procedures in a characteristic combination: the *subjectification* of objective constitutional norms by complaining the violation of individual rights, on the one hand, and the *objectification* of substantive constitutional law, in which the constitutional complaint goes beyond specific remedies and extends to the protection of the constitutional order in general, on the other.[660] The Spanish *Amparo* under Article 53(2) of the Constitution, which has greatly influenced Latin American constitutional systems, also permits the *Tribunal Constitucional* to exercise the subjective

658 Frank I Michelman, 'The Interplay of Constitutional and Ordinary Jurisdiction' in Tom Ginsburg and Rosalind Dixon (eds), *Comparative Constitutional Law: Research Handbooks in Comparative Law* (Edward Edgar 2011) 278–297, 279.

659 Justin Collings, 'Introduction' in Matthias Jestaedt, Oliver Lepsius, Christoph Schönberger, Christoph Möllers (eds), *The German Federal Constitutional Court: The Court Without Limits* (Oxford University Press 2020) xv–xvi.

660 Anuscheh Farahat, 'The German Federal Constitutional Court' in Armin von Bogdandy, Peter Huber and Christoph Grabenwarter (eds), *The Max Planck Handbooks in European Public Law: Volume III: Constitutional Adjudication: Institutions* (Oxford University Press 2020) 320–324.

function to protect individuals' fundamental rights as well as 'la defensa objetiva de la Constitución'.[661]

The parallel techniques of subjectifying and objectifying constitutional jurisdiction entails the reallocation of powers between constitutional and ordinary judges. Lech Garlicki explains that '[b]oth procedures – incidental review and the constitutional complaint – modified the idea of the separation of judicial functions in this way: they invite the constitutional courts to participate in the adjudication of individual cases by ordinary jurisdictions, either by resolving preliminary questions of the constitutionality of statutes or by reviewing the constitutionality of final judicial decisions'.[662] Accordingly, although the primary responsibility to protect and respect individuals' fundamental rights rests with ordinary judges, constitutional courts act as subsidiary guardians of such rights by exercising their complaint jurisdiction. Because the jurisdiction dichotomy becomes less sustainable as a feature for classification when several countries adopt systems that mix aspects of a centralised and a decentralised system in Europe and Latin America, the context-specific classifications accurately capture the power distribution in the control of constitutionality, as well as of conventionality, in both regions.[663]

(ii) Rules Prioritising Constitutional Procedures over Community Law Procedures

As a reaction to the external decentralising factor, some States have introduced procedural rules that mitigate the *guerre des juges* in constitutional and ordinary jurisdictions. In Belgium, while the *Cour de Cassation* adopted the *cream cheese* doctrine (*smeerkaasdoctrine*) that the judge must refuse the application of all legal provisions that violate directly applicable international law, the *Cour constitutionnelle* has implicitly maintained the supremacy of the Constitution over treaties.[664] Against this background, there has been a 'parallel system of control with ordinary jurisdictions

---

661 Tribunal Constitucional español, Sentencia STC 1/1981, para 2.

662 Lech Garlicki, 'Constitutional Courts versus Supreme Courts' (2007) 5 *International Journal of Constitutional Law* 44–68, 46–47.

663 Samantha Lalisan, 'Classifying Systems of Constitutional Review: A Context-Specific Analysis' (2020) 5 *Indiana Journal of Constitutional Design* 1–24.

664 Matthias E. Storme, 'The Struggle Concerning Interpretative Authority in the Context of Human Rights: The Belgian Experience' in Rainer Arnold (ed), *The Universalism of Human Rights* (Springer 2013) 223–236, 228–231.

(directly) reviewing the conformity with treaty provisions and the Constitutional Court reviewing the conformity with constitutional provisions'.[665] The Belgian priority rule, Article 26(4) of the special majority act on the Constitutional Court, on 12 July 2009, was thus invented, which 'clearly aims at pragmatically reconciling the centralized constitutional review installed by Article 142 of the Constitution, and the diffuse treaty review installed by the "cream cheese" judgment, because it applies in case of coincidence of constitutional and international human rights'.[666] The text of this new provision reads as follows: 'If before a jurisdiction it is alleged that a [legal provision] violates a fundamental right which is guaranteed in a totally or partially analogous way in a provision of Title II of the Constitution and in a provision of European or international law, the jurisdiction first asks for a preliminary ruling to the Constitutional Court concerning the conformity with the provision of Title II of the Constitution'.

A similar situation can be found in the French legal system, in which Article 55 of the Constitution explicitly recognises the supra-legal rank of treaties. Since the 1975 *IVG* judgement, the Constitutional Council has ruled that it has no jurisdiction to review the conformity of legal provisions in the light of treaties.[667] Subsequently, the *Cour de cassation* and *Conseil d'Etat* have performed the important task of judicial review *ex post* based on treaties, which has substantively complemented the constitutionality control *ex ante* assumed by the *Conseil constitutionnel*.[668] Because these ordinary courts can rely on the ECHR rather than constitutional protection, the 2008 constitutional reform mandated the *ex post* norm-control power to the Constitutional Council and introduced the *QPC*, to ensure priority of the constitutional issue over the treaties issue. Through the *QPC* procedures, 'some violations of ECHR rights are now no longer presented as such, but are rather framed as constitutional cases and hence can be dealt with via constitutional review'.[669]

In France, ironically, the introduction of the *QPC* mechanism itself triggered the *guerre des juges*. Indeed, the *Cour de cassation* responsible for

---

665 Erika de Wet, 'The Reception Process in the Netherlands and Belgium' in Keller and Stone Sweet (n 28) 229–310, 251.

666 Marc Bossuyt and Willem Verrijdt, 'The Full Effect of EU Law and of Constitutional Review in Belgium and France after the *Melki* Judgment' (2011) 7 *European Constitutional Law Review* 355–391, 368.

667 Conseil constitutionnel de la République Française, Décision n° 74–54 DC du 15 janvier 1975.

668 Bossuyt and Verrijdt (n 667) 366–375.

669 Céline Lageot, 'France' in Gerards and Fleuren (n 599) 145–184, 163–165.

conventionality control harshly opposed the *QPC* procedures, and made a preliminary reference to the ECJ regarding the compatibility of the priority rule with Community law. In the 2010 *Melki and Abdeli* ruling, the Luxembourg Court, implicitly relying on the reasoning of the *Conseil constitutionnel*, achieved a compromise that under certain conditions Article 267 TFEU regarding a preliminary ruling does not preclude national legislation which establishes an interlocutory procedure for the review of the constitutionality of national laws.[670] In compromising in favour of constitutional courts, the CJEU also seemed to attenuate the *Simmenthal* immediacy requirement by admitting the temporal discretion in the obligation of national judges to ask for a preliminary ruling.[671] In this sense, this judgement can be considered part of the trend where 'the overall thrust of the Court's approach to questions about decentralised enforcement is merely to establish minimum standards of effective judicial protection, but otherwise leave much to the discretion of each Member State to design their own national remedies and procedural rules'.[672]

Such an optimistic view, however, should not be overestimated, because the CJEU did not change its own stance that the centralised review of legislation could be tolerated to the extent that it does not interfere with the essence of the principle of EU law primacy.[673] The core reasoning in *Melki and Abdeli*, largely based on the *Simmenthal* doctrine, was subsequently confirmed in *A v B and Others* that concerned the centralised judicial review system in Austria.[674] Through these judgements, the Luxembourg Court 'undermined some of the core premises of the reform, particularly the priority of the *Conseil constitutionnel*'s review of the review exercised by ordinary courts'.[675]

---

670 Cases C-188/10 and C-189/10, *Aziz Melki and Sélim Abdeli*, CJEU, Judgment of 22 June 2010.

671 Ibid para 44.

672 Michael Dougan, 'The Vicissitudes of Life at the Coalface: Remedies and Procedures for Enforcing Union Law before the National Courts' in Paul Craig and Gráinne de Búrca (eds), *The Evolution of EU Law*, 2nd ed (Oxford University Press 2015) 407–438, 419.

673 Davide Paris, 'Constitutional Courts as Guardians of EU Fundamental Rights? Centralized judicial Review of Legislation and the Charter of Fundamental Rights of the EU: European Court of Justice (Fifth Chamber), Judgment of 11 September 2014, Case C-112/13, *A v B and Others*' (2015) 11 *European Constitutional Law Review* 389–407, 404.

674 Case C-112/113, *A v B and Others*, CJEU, Judgment of 11 September 2014.

675 Komárek (n 612) 526–527.

The role of constitutional courts within the multilevel framework of fundamental rights protection is embodied in the Austrian *Verfassungsgerichtshof*'s judgement issued on 14 March 2012. There was deep concern in this ruling: If the Constitutional Court were not competent to adjudicate on the rights contained in the CFREU, which largely overlap with the constitutionally guaranteed ECHR rights, it would counter the notion of a centralised constitutional jurisdiction provided for in the Austrian Federal Constitution.[676] By virtue of the principle of equivalence, it was thus clearly affirmed that the rights guaranteed by the CFREU 'constitute a standard of review in general judicial review proceedings' before the Constitutional Court.[677] As Davide Paris noted, this decision 'clearly amounts to an attempt by the Constitutional Court to keep its central position in fundamental rights protection, despite the current pressure toward decentralisation'.[678] In the attempt to recentralise its constitutional jurisdiction, the *Verfassungsgerichtshof* carefully reserved its authority to 'decide on a case-by-case basis which of the rights of the Charter of Fundamental Rights constitute a standard of review for proceedings before the Constitutional Court'.[679] With this cautious attitude, the Constitutional Court plays a role 'not as guarantors of certain rights and freedoms, but as important parts of communicative arrangements which generate decisions that remain open to further revision, and are subject to communicatively generated legitimacy'.[680] In the 2014 *A v B and Others* judgement, the ECJ employed a 'copy and paste' approach to the *Melki and Abdeli* reasoning with regard to the Austrian constitutional review system.[681]

The Austrian precedent was reminded when the Italian Constitutional Court in Judgement No. 269/17 recentralised its power in cases of *doppia pregiudizialità* (double prejudice), namely, disputes that may give rise to questions of constitutionality and, simultaneously, questions of compliance with EU law. In line with the Austrian *Verfassungsgerichtshof*, the Italian *Corte costituzionale* paralleled international and European parameters of fundamental rights for judicial review.[682] In this context, the CJEU

676 Verfassungsgerichtshof Österreich, U 466/11–18 und U 1836/11–13, Erkenntnis vom 14 März 2012, para 34.

677 Ibid para 35.

678 Paris (n 674) 399.

679 U 466/11–18 and U 1836/11–13 (n 677) para 36.

680 Komárek (n 612) 542.

681 Paris (n 674) 402.

682 Corte costituzionale italiana, Sentenza № 269 del 7 novembre 2017 Considerato in diritto para 5.2.

jurisprudence in *Melki and Abdeli* and *A v. B and Others* was cited to affirm that EU law does not preclude the overriding character of the constitutional determination that falls under the competence of the national constitutional courts under certain conditions.[683] This mixture of cooperative intent and the Luxembourg judges and strategic behaviour to recentralise the Roman judges' powers implies 'a way of dealing with constitutional conflict that is able to activate a dialogue without falling into the trap of hierarchical relationships'.[684] As a matter of fact, in a case concerning the refusal to grant a childbirth or maternity allowance to third-country nationals holding a single work permit or a permit for family reasons, *la Corte Suprema di Cassazione* opted to trigger a constitutionality review by *la Corte costituzionale*, and then the latter issued a preliminary reference to the CJEU with Judgement No. 182/2020.[685]

2. *Domestic Centralisation and Decentralisation of Conventionality Control Powers*

A. Decentralising Conventionality Control Powers to Ordinary Courts

(i) Disapplying Legislation Incompatible with Regional Conventions

The previous section revealed the necessity to reconsider the conceptual boundary between constitutional and ordinary jurisdictions, which has been significantly disrupted by internal and external stimuli. In addition to regional community law, human rights conventions become another external factor for decentralising constitutional adjudication.[686] Typically, the *conventionality control* doctrine, in line with the ECJ's *Simmenthal*

683 Ibid.

684 Martinico and Repetto (n 633) 736.

685 Nicole Lazzerini, 'Dual Preliminarity Within the Scope of the EU Charter of Fundamental Rights in the Light of Order 182/2020 of the Italian Constitutional Court', European Papers 25 November 2020, 1–14. See also the list of decisions coherent with and diverging from the Italian Constitutional Court Judgment No 269/2017, available at https://www.cir.santannapisa.it/observatory-practices-inter-legality-italian-high-courts.

686 Mitchel de S-O-l'E Lasser, *Judicial Transformations: The Rights Revolution in the Courts of Europe* (Oxford University Press 2009) 240.

doctrine,[687] converts all domestic judges into the primary and authentic guardians of human rights conventions.[688] The decentralised model of conventionality control would admittedly be beneficial for human rights protection by increasing the opportunities for upholding fundamental rights.

Some State Parties to the ECHR accept the decentralised system of conventionality control, as if the *Simmenthal* doctrine is reloaded in the Strasbourg law.[689] In the States Parties that have adopted the decentralised system of judicial review, such as Sweden, 'all courts and administrative agencies are obliged to refuse to apply a norm that conflicts with the ECHR'.[690] In the cases of Belgium and France where there exist the labour divisions of constitutionality control and conventionality control, the *contrôle de constitutionnalité* is entrusted to the *Cour constitutionnelle*/the *Conseil constitutionnel*, whereas the *contrôle de conventionnalité* is achieved by ordinary and administrative judges. In Spain, the *Tribunal Constitucional* has not expressly recognised its own competences to review the compatibility of legislation with international treaties. It is therefore possible, albeit only theoretically, that 'ordinary judges can refuse to apply a statute on the grounds that it infringes upon a convention right, without having to petition the constitutional court'.[691]

Disapplying domestic law was problematised in the *Almonacid-Arellano* case in which the IACtHR expressly stated the *control de convencionalidad* doctrine for the first time. In monitoring compliance with the judgement in 2010, the Court reviewed whether Chile had carried out the reparation measure to 'ensure that Decree Law No. 2.191 does not continue to hinder the investigation, prosecution and, as appropriate, punishment of those

---

687 Jânia M Lopes Saldanha and Lucas Pacheco Vieira, 'Controle jurisdictional de convencionalidade e reenvio prejudicial interamericano: Um diálogo de ferramentas processuais em favor da efetivação do direito internacional dos direitos humanos' (2013) 19 *Anuario de derecho constitucional latinoamericano* 435–466, 438–440.

688 Concurring Opinion of Judge *ad hoc* MacGregor Poisot, *Cabrera Garcia and Montiel Flores* (n 35) para 24.

689 Giuseppe Martinico, 'Is the European Convention Going to Be "Supreme"? A Comparative-Constitutional Overview of ECHR and EU Law before National Courts' (2012) 23 *European Journal of International Law* 401–424, 412–418; Alec Stone Sweet, 'A Cosmopolitan Legal Order: Constitutional Pluralism and Rights Adjudication in Europe' (2011) 1 *Global Constitutionalism* 53–90, 63–72.

690 Ola Wiklund, 'The Reception Process in Sweden and Norway' in Keller and Stone Sweet (n 28) 165–228, 176–177.

691 Ferreres Comella (n 442) 142.

responsible for similar violations perpetrated in Chile'. For this purpose, the Court started with stating as follows:

> The Court notes that the State took a first step towards fulfilling its duty to ensure that the Decree Law does not continue to represent an obstacle to guaranteeing the right to judicial guarantees and judicial protection in Chile. The Court notes that the effective implementation of this reparation measure is an essential part of complying with the Judgment, as it aims to ensure that violations, such as those in the present case, do not recur by adopting domestic legal measures (legislative, administrative or otherwise) to correct the root causes of violations. While there may be different domestic law measures through which the State could ensure such an outcome, the Court notes that the State considers the most appropriate way to do so is through a legislative amendment.[692]

As this view indicates, legislative reform was considered the most appropriate measure for fundamentally resolving the systemic violation of human rights which existed behind the present individual case. This means that the obligation of *legislative reform* as a part of the obligation of reparation is the principal legal basis by which to coordinate conflicts between the ACHR and domestic law. In this sense, it was welcomed that Chile reported on the initiation of the processing of the bill to interpret the grounds for the exclusion of criminal responsibility in 2008. The IACtHR, however, carefully monitored that, more than two years later, this bill was still pending before the Senate, and urged the state to take any steps that might be necessary to promptly and effectively comply with this reparation measure.[693]

This negative attitude of Chile represented just the tip of the iceberg. In addition to the cases where the States Parties lack intent to comply with the IACtHR's decisions, most of them do not organise competent systems to implement the judgements within their own domestic legal orders.[694] Because these elements are closely related to each other, the judgements ordering non-repetition measures, including legislative reforms, have a

692 *Almonacid-Arellano and Others*, Monitoring Compliance with Judgment (n 334) para 20.

693 Ibid paras 21–22.

694 Jo M Pasqualucci, *The Practice and Procedure of the Inter-American Court of Human Rights* (2nd ed, Cambridge University Press 2013) 330.

very low compliance rate.[695] Against such a reality, even though it may contribute to the fundamental resolution of the systemic violation of human rights, the obligation of legislation might not be a realistic reparation measure to coordinate conflicts between the Convention and domestic law.

An important clue to overcoming this unreality is the *control de convencionalidad* doctrine emphasising judicial functions. In *Almonacid-Arellano*, the IACtHR determined the violation not only of Article 2 of the ACHR, directed at the 'legislature', but also of Article 1(1), aimed at facilitating the judiciary's role. The Court accordingly ordered that the state may not invoke any domestic law to exonerate itself from the Court's order to have a criminal court investigate and punish those responsible for the victim, especially the Decree Law in question.[696] These reparation measures addressed to the judiciary were close to (judicial) *restitutio in integrum*, in comparison with the legislature-oriented reparation measure as a part of guarantees of non-repetition.[697]

It is especially notable in the reasoning that both the reform and disapplication of the Decree Law are categorised into the legal bases for coordinating conflicts between the ACHR and domestic law. In other words, this logic recognises the possibility that the obligation of *disapplication* of legislation works as an alternative to the obligation of legislative *reform*. Oswaldo Ruiz-Chiriboga accurately separated these two kinds of measures for conventionality control: 'There are two reparations that must logically follow the establishment of a breach of Article 2 of the ACHR and the consequent violation of a right or freedom recognised by the Convention: 1) the State must modify, derogate, or otherwise annul or amend the municipal law that breached the Convention, and 2) in the meantime it should not apply that law to the case that was brought before the Court and all other similar cases'.[698] According to this view, the obligation of disapplica-

695 For statistics on the degrees of compliance of the IACtHR's judgments, see Fernando Basch, Leonardo Filippini, Ana Laya, Mariano Nino, Felicitas Rossi and Bárbara Schreiber, 'The Effectiveness of the Inter-American System of Human Rights Protection: A Quantitative Approach to Its Functioning and Compliance with Its Judgments' (2010) 7 *International Journal of Human Rights* 9–35.

696 *Almonacid-Arellano and Others*, Judgment (n 21) paras 151–154.

697 Ibid para 144.

698 Oswaldo Ruiz-Chiriboga, 'The Conventionality Control: Examples of (Un)Successful Experiences in Latin America' (2010) 3 *Inter-American and European Human Rights Journal* 200–219, 205. (the first two emphases are added; last emphasis is in the original text).

tion performed by the judiciary contributes not only to the present case but also to 'all other similar cases' 'in the meantime' legislative change is in process. In the *Almonacid-Arellano* case, the IACtHR indeed confirmed that the 'Decree Law has not been applied by the Chilean courts in several cases since 1998'.[699] Moreover, in the 2010 monitoring compliance resolution, the Court positively assessed the performance of the reparation measures directed in large part at the judiciary.[700] As these developments indicate, the disapplication of the Decree Law by the judiciary has effects similar to guarantees of non-repetition until legislative reform can be achieved.

A complicated question then arises whether the obligation of setting aside unconventional legislation is imposed not only on the special institute equipped with the centralised competences of judicial review but also on ordinary judges lacking such powers. The *Simmenthal*-type of decentralisation realised in the *Radilla Pacheco v. Mexico* case concerning the abuse of military jurisdiction triggered the introduction of the diffused judicial norm-control system. While Article 13 of the Mexican Constitution provides that military jurisdiction subsists for crimes and offences against 'military discipline', Article 57 of the Code of Military Justice broadly defines the term's meaning and refers to the extension of military jurisdiction.[701] Therefore, the IACtHR concluded in the 2009 *Radilla Pacheco* judgement that Mexico failed to comply with Article 2 (Domestic Legal Effects) of the ACHR, in connection with Article 8 (Right to Fair Trial) and Article 25 (Right to Judicial Protection) thereof, upon extending the competence of military jurisdiction to crimes that did not have a strict connection with 'military discipline' or with judicial rights characteristic of the military realm.[702] The San José Court thus ordered the Respondent State to adopt the appropriate legislative reforms of Article 57 of the Code of Military Justice, on the basis of the conventionality control doctrine.[703]

In response, the *Suprema Corte de Justicia la Nación* handed down the 2011 *Radilla Pacheco* judgement, in which it clearly adopted diffused conventionality control by *todos los jueces* of Mexico.[704] To support this position, reference was made to Article 1, the constitutional *pro homine* provision that was newly introduced through the 2011 Human Rights

699 *Almonacid-Arellano and Others*, Judgment (n 21) para 121.

700 *Almonacid-Arellano and Others*, Order (n 334) paras 9–16.

701 *Radilla Pacheco v Mexico* Series C No 209, IACtHR, Judgment on Preliminary Objections, Merits, Reparations and Costs of 23 November 2009, para 283.

702 Ibid paras 288–289.

703 Ibid para 342.

704 *Radilla-Pacheco v Estados Unidos Mexicanos* (n 469) paras 23–36.

Amendments.[705] The Supreme Court particularly put emphasis on Article 1(3), which requires *all national authorities* to realise human rights protection.[706] Consequently, even if ordinary judges are not allowed to invalidate legislation incompatible with constitutional and human rights treaties, they are obliged to *disapply* these norms.[707] This landmark decision is noteworthy because the Mexican judiciary dynamically changed its method of judicial review from the traditional (semi-) centralised version to the diffused version.[708]

Although the Strasbourg Court has not adopted the conventionality control doctrine in an explicit manner, it has alluded to the notion that all state organs are obliged by the ECHR. For example, the 1998 judgement in *The United Communist Party of Turkey and Others v. Turkey* elucidated that '[i]t makes no distinction as to the type of rule or measure concerned and does not exclude any part of the member States' "jurisdiction" from scrutiny under the Convention'.[709] Furthermore, the 1991 *Vermeire v. Belgium* ruling implied the decentralised model of conventionality control in mentioning that '[i]t cannot be seen what could have prevented the Brussels Court of Appeal and the Court of Cassation from complying with the findings of the *Marckx* judgement, as the Court of First Instance had done'.[710]

Another observable practice of decentralised conventionality control comes from the Supreme Court of Justice of Chile in relation to the *Norín Catrimán and Others* case concerning criminal convictions against indigenous leaders. In the 2014 judgement, the IACtHR held that there were multiple violations of ACHR provisions and ordered as legal restitution that '[t]he State must adopt all the administrative, judicial, or any other type of measures required to annul all aspects of the criminal judgments convicting'.[711] In the 2018 order on compliance with the judgement, the

705 Ibid.

706 Ibid.

707 Ibid.

708 Eduardo Ferrer Mac-Gregor and Rubén Sánchez Gil, 'Mexico: Struggling for an Open View in Constittuional Adjudcation' in Tania Groppi and Marie-Claire Ponthoreau (eds), *The Use of Foreign Precedents by Constituional Judges* (Hart Publishing 2013) 301–320, 304–305.

709 *The United Communist Party of Turkey and Others v Turkey*, ECtHR, App No 19392/92, Judgment on Merits and Just Satisfaction of 30 January 1998, para 29.

710 *Vermeire v Belgium*, ECtHR, App No 12849/87, Judgment on Merits of 9 November 1991, paras 25–27.

711 *Norín Catrimán and Others v Chile* (n 189) Declaration para 15.

Inter-American Court admitted partial compliance through various measures but remained open to further supervision of national authorities.[712] In this context, *la Corte Suprema de Justicia de Chile* handed down an epoch-making decision in 2019. In line with the Inter-American order of reparation, the Supreme Court considered that the only possible remedy for provision in the case under review was to declare that the convictions had lost all effect.[713] For that purpose, the Chilean highest court supported the decentralised doctrine of conventionality control at the domestic level as follows:

> Thus, through conventionality control, *the national judges form a part of the inter-American system* in the protection of the standards of compliance and guarantee of such rights, depending on the consequences of this analysis of the functions that each judiciary operator has, being the obligation of all, the authorities and members of the State, systematically and integrally interpret the provisions that inform the legal system, in such a way that their determinations are as consistent and compatible with the international obligations acquired sovereignly by it.[714]

This decision would be praised in that by behaving in the same way as the San José judges, the Santiago judges 'not only enhanced its own authority, but also that of the Inter-American Court's'.[715]

(ii) Interpreting Legislation in Consistency with Regional Conventions

The European centralised judicial review systems are similarly experiencing the 'proliferation' tendency of constitutional adjudication through the practices of consistent interpretation.[716] Within the parallel norm-control

---

712 *Norín Catrimán and Others (Leaders, Members and Activist of the Indigenous Mapuche People) v Chile*, IACtHR, Monitoring Compliance with Judgment, Order of 28 November 2018.

713 Corte Suprema de Justicia de Chile, Sentencia AD 1386–2014 de 16 de mayo de 2019, para 9.

714 Ibid.

715 Jorge Contesse, 'The Supreme Court of Chile as an inter-American Tribunal' I·CONnect (Blog of the International Journal of Constitutional Law, 31 May 2019, available at: http://www.iconnectblog.com/2019/05/the-supreme-court-of-chile-as-an-inter-american-tribunal.

716 Besselink (n 657) 25.

mechanisms in Belgium and France, the special institutions Constitutional Court/Council as well as ordinary and administrative judges take the Strasbourg jurisprudence into account to avoid diverging from constitutional standards.[717] In Germany, the *Bundesverfassungsgericht* dictated in the 2004 *Görgülü* decision that *deutsche Gerichte* must give precedence to interpretation in accordance with the ECHR.[718] In the 2007 *Twin Sentences* Nos. 348 and 349, the Italian *Corte costituzionale* similarly clarified that it is a matter for *giudice comune* to interpret national law in accordance with the ECHR provisions as *norme interposte*.[719] As Oreste Pollicino observed, these statements recharacterised 'the ordinary judge as a decentralised ECHR judge who, for the first time in such a clear way, has been assigned a clear constitutional duty to interpret the domestic law in conformity with the international law of human rights'.[720]

The most sensational tension occurred among Italian constitutional and ordinary judges. In this context, we need to assess the 2007 *Twin Sentences* Nos. 348 and 349 that were the first opportunities for the *Corte costituzionale* to clearly delineate the boundary between constitutional and ordinary judges in conventionality control. Behind the judgements, some Italian common judges tried to bypass the centralised regime of constitutional review by disapplying domestic norms incompatible with ECHR criteria. To mitigate such practices derogating from the centralised system of constitutional adjudication, the Constitutional Court pointed out in the *Sentenze 'gemelle'* that the margin of uncertainty in identifying ECHR provisions 'has led several judgments of the ordinary courts directly to set aside legislative provisions which contrast with the ECHR', and consequently, induced the *Consulta* itself to redistribute labours with common judges as regards conventionality control of domestic law.[721]

This tendency continued even after the 2007 twin judgements. The *Tribunale di Bolzano* made a preliminary reference to the ECJ as regards the question of whether, '[w]hen there is a conflict between a provision of

717 De Wet (n 666) 250; David Szymezak, 'Question prioritaire de constitutionnalité et Convention européenne des droits de l'homme : L'européanisation « heurtée » du Conseil constitutionnel français' (2012) 7 *Jus Politicum* 1–23.

718 *Görgülü* (n 445) para 62.

719 Sentenze № 348 (para 4.7) e 349 (para 6.2) (n 447).

720 Oreste Pollicino, 'The Italian Constitutional Court at the Crossroads between Constitutional Parochialism and Co-operative Constitutionalism. Judgments Nos. 348 and 349 of 22 and 24 October 2007' (2008) 4 *European Constitutional Law Review* 363–382, 377.

721 Sentenza № 348 (n 447) para 4.3.

domestic law and the ECHR, does the reference to the ECHR in Article of the 6 TEU oblige the national court to apply Articles 14 of the ECHR and Article 1 [of Protocol No 12] directly, disapplying the incompatible source of domestic law, without having first to raise the issue of constitutionality before the national constitutional court'? In the 2012 *Kamberaj* ruling, however, the CJEU simply dictated that 'Article 6(3) TEU does not govern the relationship between the ECHR and the legal systems of the Member States and nor does it lay down the consequences to be drawn by a national court in case of conflict between the rights guaranteed by that convention and a provision of national law'.[722]

The obligation of consistent interpretation is explicitly accepted in various national legal systems (see the previous chapter). One of the most open-minded provisions is Article 10(2) of the Spanish Constitution that restructures the constitutional provisions of fundamental rights according to the content of the ECHR.[723] Moreover, Section 3(1) of the 1998 Human Rights Act of the United Kingdom serves as the 'prime remedial measure' through which national judges realise the compatibility of legislative acts with the Convention.[724] In Latin America, the Bolivian *Tribunal Constitucional* confirms its own labours of conventionality control and constitutionality control in terms of Article 256(2) of the 2009 Constitution.[725] Likewise, Article 93 of the 1991 Constitution of Colombia provides the *Corte Constitucional* with the legal basis for dynamically including the ACHR standards within the block of constitutionality.[726] The Peruvian *Tribunal Constitucional* also acknowledges that human rights conventions constitute the block of constitutionality in accordance with Fourth of the

722 Case C 571/10, *Servet Kamberaj v Istituto per l'Edilizia sociale della Provincia autonoma di Bolzano (IPES) and Others*, CJEU, Judgment of 24 April 2012, para 62. See, Giuseppe Bianco and Giuseppe Martinico, 'Dialogue or Disobedience? On the Domestic Effects of the ECHR in Light of the *Kamberaj* Decision' (2014) 20 *European Public Law* 435–450.

723 Patricia Cuenca Gómez, 'La incidncia del derecho interncional de los derechos humanos en el derecho interno: la interpretación del Artículo 10.2 de la Constitución española' (2012) 12 *Revista de Estudios Jurídicos* 1–24, 4.

724 *Ghaidan v Mendoza* [2004] 3 WLR 113, paras 38–49 *per* Lord Steyn. See also, Aileen Kavanagh, *Constitutional Review under the UK Human Rights Act* (Cambridge University Press 2009) Chap 2.

725 Sentencia 1907/2011-R (n 465) Fundamentos III.4. (De los crímenes de lesa humanidad y la CIDH; y, otras Cortes Control de convencionalidad).

726 Corte Constitucional de Colombia, Exp T-357702, Sentencia T-1319–01 de 7 de diciembrede 2001, Consideraciones y Fundamentos para 6 (Solución). See also, Sierra Porto (n 466) 440–446.

Final and Transitory Provisions of the Constitution.[727] In the same vein, the Mexican SCJN integrated constitutional and international parameters for judicial review on the basis of the previously mentioned *pro homine* provision Article 1, particularly paragraph 2, of the Mexican Constitution.[728]

There exists a fundamental difference among the obligations of legislative reform, disapplication and consistent interpretation. On the one hand, the first two obligations of legislative reform and disapplication assume that the domestic law in question is determined as incompatible with international law. Therefore, these obligations are performed as the legal consequences of the breach, that is, the obligation of reparation.[729] On the other hand, the obligation of consistent interpretation relates to the domestic law whose compatibility with the Convention is not definite. The interpretative technique 'take[s] place in cases where the domestic court applies exclusively domestic law but finds that it must interpret it in such a way so as not to conflict with international obligations incumbent upon the State'.[730]

Notwithstanding the essential distinction, the obligation of reparation and consistent interpretation should not be observed independently from each other. Indeed, the performance of consistent interpretation does not depend on whether ordinary judges have the authority to set aside unconstitutional norms within the concentrated system of constitutional adjudication. Judge MacGregor carefully made notice on this point:

> [T]he intensity of the 'diffused conventionality control' will diminish in those systems where the 'diffused constitutionality control' is not allowed, and therefore, not all judges have the power to stop enforcing a law to a specific case. In these cases it is obvious that the judges who lack such jurisdiction, shall exercise the 'diffused conventionality control' with less intensity, *without this implying that they cannot do so* 'within their respective jurisdictions'. This implies that they cannot fail to apply the norm (even though they may not have that power),

727 Tribunal Constitucional de Perú, Exp 0047–2004-AI/TC, Sentencia de 24 de abril de 2006, Fundamentos para 22. See also, Natalia Torres Zúñiga, *El control de convencionalidad: Deber complementario del juez constitucional peruano y el juez interamericano (similitudes, deferencias y convergencias)* (Editorial Académica Española 2013) Chap II.

728 *Radilla-Pacheco v Estados Unidos Mexicanos* (n 469) para 31.

729 Nollkaemper (n 33) Chap 8.

730 Tzanakapoulos (n 420) 155-158.

> and shall, in any case, make a 'conventional interpretation' of it, that is, make a 'consistent interpretation', not only of the national Constitution, but also of the American Convention and the jurisprudence of the Convention. This interpretation requires a creative action in order to achieve compatibility of the national standard in accordance with the conventional parameter and thus achieve the realization of the right or freedom in question, with the broadest and most encompassing reach in terms of the *pro homine* principle.[731]

The *Radilla Pacheco* case well illustrates the essential continuity between these two obligations in the process of conventionality control. Based on the merits decision declaring the violation of Article 2 of the ACHR, the IACtHR ordered Mexico to adopt, within a reasonable period of time, the appropriate legislative reforms in order to make Article 57 of the Code of Military Justice compatible with the international standards of the field and of the Convention.[732] Responding to the judgement, Mexico took steps to reform Article 57 of the Code of Military Justice in 2010. Nevertheless, in monitoring compliance with the judgement both in 2011 and 2013, the Court concluded that the reform initiative was 'insufficient because it does not fully comply with the standards specified in the Judgment'.[733] While the Court ordered Mexico to carry out the appropriate legislative reforms of this article, it is worth noting that the Court rejected the argument made by the representatives of the victim that the state had to make a reform to Article 13 of the Mexican Constitution that regulates military jurisdiction as follows, restating the concept of 'the control of conventionality'.[734]

> [I]t is necessary that the constitutional and legislative interpretations regarding the material and personal competence criteria of military jurisdiction in Mexico be adjusted to the principles established in the jurisprudence of this Tribunal, which have been reiterated in the present case As per this understanding, this Tribunal considers that it is not necessary to order the modification of the regulatory content

731 Concurring Opinion of Judge *ad hoc* MacGregor Poisot, *Cabrera Garcia and Montiel Flores* (n 35) para 37 (emphasis added).

732 *Radilla Pacheco*, Judgment (n 702) para. 342.

733 *Radilla Pacheco v Mexico*, IACtHR, Monitoring Compliance with Judgment, Order of 19 May 2011, paras 17–23; *Radilla Pacheco v Mexico*, IACtHR, Monitoring Compliance with Judgment, Order of 14 May 2013, paras 18–29.

734 *Radilla Pacheco*, Judgment (n 702) paras 337–339.

included in Article 13 of the Political Constitution of the United Mexican States.[735]

This position manifests the requirement of consistent interpretation of domestic law with international law. It is remarkable in the judgement's logic that both the legislative reform of Article 57 of the Code of Military Justice and the consistent interpretation of Article 13 of the Mexican Constitution with the Convention are juxtaposed as the means to coordinate conflicts between the Convention and domestic law.

As a matter of fact, the Mexican Supreme Court faithfully followed the IACtHR judgement that required Article 13 of the Mexican Constitution to be interpreted consistently in line with the ACHR.[736] Relying on the new *pro homine* provision, Article 1(3) of the Constitution, the Supreme Court also noted that all judges in the country had to interpret human rights legislation in accordance with relevant international treaties that Mexico was a party to, ensuring at all times the highest standard of protection in the face of situations that violate the human rights of civilians.[737] The *Corte Suprema* furthermore stated that this interpretation should be observed in all future cases heard by this Court, and decided that all human rights abuse accusations against soldiers had to be sent to the ordinary justice system.[738] It follows that consistent interpretation of Article 13 of the Mexican Constitution in line with the ACHR serves as 'a stopgap measure' until the legislative reform of Article 57 of the Code of Military Justice will be achieved, and thus, has general effects similar to guarantees of non-repetition.[739] In fact, in monitoring compliance in 2013 with the *Radilla Pacheco* judgement, the IACtHR evaluated the ruling of the Supreme Court as a positive contribution and confirmed that from 6 August to 13 September 2012, the Supreme Court took over the hearing of cases related to the restriction of military jurisdiction, deciding in all of them to refer the case to the ordinary justice system.[740]

735 Ibid paras 340–341.

736 *Radilla-Pacheco v Estados Unidos Mexicanos* (n 469) paras 38–43.

737 Ibid para 44.

738 Ibid para 45.

739 Kristin Bricker, 'Military Justice and Impunity in Mexico's Drug War' (2011) 3 *CIGI Security Sector Reform Issue Paper* 2–13, 8.

740 *Radilla Pacheco*, Order 2013 (n 734) para 27.

B. Centralising Conventionality Control Powers to Constitutional Courts

(i) Democracy: Balancing Individual Autonomy and Public Autonomy

Notwithstanding the merits of decentralised conventionality control by ordinary judges, the diffusion of judicial norm-controlling powers to unelected ordinary judges might have negative consequences in terms of democracy and legal certainty. The first risk of diffused conventionality control is that ordinary judges who are unaccountable to nationals may prejudice democratic values by disregarding parliamentary legislation. The *counter-majoritarian difficulty* conundrum is aggravated by ordinary judges who are generally selected through a bureaucratic process, rather than constitutional judges who are typically chosen through a more politicised procedure.[741] Inherently, constitutional review is a mechanism for protecting fundamental rights by reinforcing the rule of law, counteracting the conduct of political organs that possess democratic legitimacy. Therefore, as long as democracy simply means a majoritarian or aggregative form, and constitutionalism solely focuses on individual freedoms, they will come into collision with each other.

Jürgen Habermas conceptualises the *demokratischer Rechtsstaat* to reconcile the potential conflict between constitutionalism and democracy. In his *System of Rights* theory, Habermas elegantly reconciles popular sovereignty deriving from republicanism, and human rights emanating from liberalism.[742] It follows that *public autonomy* arising from popular sovereignty and *private autonomy* based on human rights share *Gleichursprünglichkeit* [co-originality].[743] Concretely speaking, '[c]itizens can make appropriate use of their *public autonomy*, as guaranteed by political rights, only if they are sufficiently independent in virtue of an equally protected *private autonomy* in their life conduct', and in the opposite direction, 'members of society actually enjoy their equal *private autonomy* to an equal extent [...] only if as citizens they make an appropriate use of their *political autonomy*'.[744]

---

741 Víctor Ferreres Comella, 'The Rise of Specialized Constitutional Courts' in Ginsburg and Dixon (n 659) 265–277, 270.

742 Jürgen Habermas, *Faktizität und Geltung: Beiträge zur Diskurstheorie des Rechts und des demokratischen Rechtsstaats* (Suhrkamp 1992) 151–165.

743 Ibid.

744 Jürgen Habermas, 'Constitutional Democracy: A Paradoxical Union of Contradictory Principles?' (2001) 29 *Political Theory* 766–781, 767.

Given the intertwined relations between human rights and popular sovereignty, Habermas emphasises the 'discursive process of opinion- and will formation'.[745] In synchronism with his idea, *deliberative democracy* attracts mass support to overcome the limitations of the majoritarian view. Amy Gutmann and Dennis Thompson define the concept as '[a] form of government in which free and equal citizens (and their representatives), justify decisions in a process in which they give one another reasons that are mutually acceptable and generally accessible, to reach conclusions that are binding in the present on all citizens but open to challenge in the future'.[746] In relation to other forms of democracy, Günter Frankenberg explains that '[d]eliberative democracy [...] picks up, on the level of normative theory, liberal democracy's claim to legitimacy based on reasons [...] and connects its key focus, not on a predetermined will but on the process of its formation, with participatory democracy's claim to popular participation'.[747]

Within the framework of *demokratischer Rechtsstaat*, constitutional courts have an important role to 'keep watch over the system of rights that makes citizens' private and public autonomy equally possible'.[748] To put this in the context of deliberative democracy, constitutional courts first form a part of a communication process regarding constitutional issues.[749] Typically, the *communicative circle* on constitutional problems involves the original judges and parties to the trial; higher courts including the constitutional court within the same trial; the professional interpretative community; a public forum (the media and non-legal audiences); and the whole public sphere of society.[750] Second, constitutional courts guarantee deliberative discourse with political organs. As a notable model, Christopher Zurn advocates the *horizontal dispersal* of constitutional decisional powers: the establishment of self-review panels in the legislative and executive branches of national governments, and various mechanisms for

---

745 Jürgen Habermas, *Between Facts and Norms: Contributions to a Discourse Theory of Law and Democracy*, translated by William Rehg (The MIT Press 1992) 104.

746 Amy Gutmann and Dennis Thompson, *Why Deliberative Democracy?* (Princeton University Press 2004) 3–7.

747 Günter Frankenberg, 'Democracy' in Rosenfeld and Sajó (n 409) 250–258, 255.

748 Habermas (n 746) 263.

749 Patricia Popelier and Aída Araceli Patiño Álvarez, 'Deliberative Practices of Constitutional Courts in Consolidated and Non-consolidated Democracies' in Popelier and others (n 605) 199–231, 201–202.

750 Mark Van Hoecke, 'Constitutional Courts and Deliberative Democracy' ibid, 183–198, 191–193.

interbranch debate concerning constitutional elaboration.[751] In practice, the German *Bundesverfassungsgericht* employed the constitutional principle of democracy to permit the legislature to revoke legal acts of previous legislatures, and claimed that the principle of *Völkerrechtsfreundlichkeit* (openness to international law) does not include the constitutional obligation of unconditional compliance with international law.[752]

However, these contributions of constitutional courts should be reconsidered in the context of constitutional democracy *beyond the State*.[753] Rainer Nickel points out that 'in a new, globalized environment where the execution of diffuse powers by diffuse actors blurs the line between public authority and private power, the well-ordered theory of the *democratic Rechtsstaat* seems to lose its empirical foundation *and* its persuasiveness altogether'.[754] The blurring of the boundary between private and public autonomy is highly worrisome when international courts radically reinforce the protection of fundamental rights while their decision-making is beyond national control.[755]

With regard to the transnational roles of constitutional courts, the European constitutional democracy doctrine suggested by Komárek provides a fresh analytical perspective. He explains that '[t]he role of national constitutional courts related to the Europeanized *individual autonomy* thus consists in defending the rights of those who do not benefit from integration and whose voice can be structurally undermined by it'.[756] However, according to his theory, the role 'should not be understood as constitutional courts' simple defense of national constitutions or national democracy' but rather as 'putting limits on the currently too wide *individual autonomy*, which is not placed into a communicative arrangement with its political counterpart'.[757]

---

751 Christopher F Zurn, *Deliberative Democracy and the Institutions of Judicial Review* (Cambridge University Press 2007) 301–312.

752 BVerfG, 2 BvL 1/12, Entscheidung vom 15. Dezember 2015, paras 53–54, 67.

753 Steven Wheatley, *The Democratic Legitimacy of International Law* (Bloomsbury Publishing 2010) Chap 8.

754 Rainer Nickel, 'Private and Public Autonomy: Jürgen Habermas' Concept of Co-Originality in Times of Globalisation and the Militant Security State' in Martin Loughlin and Neil Walker (eds), *The Paradox of Constitutionalism* (Oxford University Press 2007) 147–167, 166 (emphasis in original text).

755 Geir Ulfstein, 'The International Judiciary' in Klabbers and Others (n 26) 126–152, 147.

756 Komárek (n 612) 537–543 (emphasis added).

757 Ibid.

The transnational functions of constitutional courts should also be re-evaluated in the implementation of regional human rights conventions. Víctor Ferreres Comella, who at an early stage captured the decentralising phenomenon of constitutional adjudication in Europe, voices concern that the ECtHR endorses 'a very broad conception of the sphere of privacy of public figures'.[758] In parallel to Komárek's *European constitutional democracy* doctrine cited above, Ferres Comella emphasises the necessity of coordinating individual and public autonomy through constitutional courts as follows:

> In so far as the ECHR does not perform a minimal function but is instead at the vanguard of human-rights discourse in an increasing number of cases, the establishment of a system of checks and balances between the national institutions and the ECHR becomes important. The democratic nations that are parties to the European Convention on Human Rights should be able to voice their reasoned disagreement in controversial cases. The national parliaments are important settings where this disagreement can be expressed, and constitutional tribunals provide an ideal forum to continue the domestic conversation about the acceptability of the ECHR's rulings.[759]

This normative argument may be empirically grounded in the *Von Hannover v Germany* case concerning the conflict between Articles 8 (right to respect for private and family life) and 10 (freedom of expression) of the ECHR. Concerning these competing rights, the German *Bundesverfassungsgericht* ruled in favour of the media's freedom regarding public autonomy, while the Strasbourg Court issued *Von Hannover No. 1* in favour of the plaintiff concerning individual autonomy.[760] However, the ECtHR highly evaluated in *Van Hannover No. 2* that 'the German Constitutional Court, for its part, had [...] undertaken a detailed analysis of the [ECtHR's] case law' and concluded that national courts have not failed to comply with their positive obligations under Article 8 of the ECHR having regard their margin of appreciation.[761] This dialectic interaction indicates that national constitutional courts play a significant role in filling the gap between

---

758 Ferreres Comella (n 442) 150.

759 Ibid 151.

760 *Von Hannover v Germany (No. 1)*, ECtHR, App No 59320/00, Judgment on Merits of 24 June 2004.

761 *Von Hannover v Germany (No. 2)*, ECtHR (Grand Chamber), App No 40660/08, Judgment on Merits and Just Satisfaction of 7 February 2012.

bloated individual autonomy and prejudiced public autonomy through supranational human rights adjudication.

The democratic role of constitutional courts becomes significant particularly in cases of transitional justice, as evinced by the election process in Bosnia and Herzegovina. The State Party's Constitution, adopted within the framework of the Dayton Agreement, provides in its Preamble that Bosniacs, Croats and Serbs are described as constituent peoples. In the *Sejdić and Finci* case, the applicants complained of their ineligibility to stand for election to the House of Peoples and the presidency on the grounds of their Roma and Jewish origin.[762] The ECtHR admitted the government's position that the exclusionary constitutional provisions that 'put in place a very fragile ceasefire' and were 'designed to end a brutal conflict marked by genocide and "ethnic cleansing"' aimed at 'the restoration of peace', which is broadly compatible with the general objectives of the Convention's Preamble.[763] However, the Strasbourg judges assessed that the maintenance of the system in any event did not satisfy the requirement of proportionality and held the violation of Article 14 taken in conjunction with Article 3 of Protocol No. 1, and that of Article 1 of Protocol No. 12.[764]

In the aftermath of *Sejdić and Finci*, the Constitutional Court of Bosnia and Herzegovina declared the relevant provisions unconstitutional of the Election Act 2001, ordered the Parliamentary Assembly to amend those provisions within a limited period, and, given the failure thereof, adopted a ruling on the non-enforcement of its decision.[765] Even after similar decisions by the ECtHR in *Zornić* and *Pilav*, the unconstitutional and unconventional situation was not remedied by the political sector.[766] Against the background of the government's failure to implement the decision of

---

762 Marko Milanovic, 'Sejdić &Finci v Bosnia and Herzegovina' (2010) 104 *American Journal of International Law* 636–641.

763 *Sejdić and Finci v Bosnia and Herzegovina*, ECtHR (Grand Chamber), App Nos 27996/06 and 34836/06, Judgment on Merits and Just Satisfaction of 22 December 2009, para 45. See also, Martin Wählisch, *Peacemaking, Power-sharing and International Law: Imperfect Peace* (Bloomsbury 2019) 69–71.

764 Ibid paras 47–50, 56.

765 Constitutional Court of Bosnia and Herzegovina, Decision of No. U 9/09 of 26 November 2010.

766 *Zornić v Bosnia and Herzegovina*, ECtHR, App No 3681/06, Judgment on Merits and Just Satisfaction of 15 July 2014; *Pilav v Bosnia and Herzegovina*, ECtHR, App No 41939/07, Judgment Merits and Just Satisfaction of 9 June 2016.

the Constitutional Court and its ancillary orders, the ECtHR took a stricter position in applying Article 46 of the ECHR in the fourth *Baralija* case:

> Consequently, having regard to these considerations, as well as to the large number of potential applicants and the urgent need to put an end to the impugned situation, the Court considers that the respondent State must, within six months of the date on which the present judgment becomes final, amend the Election Act 2001 in order to enable the holding of local elections in Mostar. Should the State fail to do so, the Court notes that the Constitutional Court, under domestic law and practice, has the power to set up interim arrangements as necessary transitional measures.[767]

This message from Strasbourg judges to the Sarajevo judges suggests the former's expectation that the latter would not merely exert its power to behave as the 'negative legislator', merely striking down the norms which are inconsistent with the Constitution, but rather take the role of the active legislator in adopting the interim arrangements as temporary measures that will resolve the issue until a permanent solution is adopted by the legislators.[768]

The fine-tuning function of constitutional courts would be more problematic in the implementation of the ACHR given the IACtHR's judicial activism. The Court's radical expansion of Convention rights and freedoms has often been the target of criticism, and the gap between individual and public autonomy reaches a greater extent in the Latin American region.[769] Nevertheless, the inter-American human rights system also has an institutional gap in safeguarding public autonomy against overblown individual autonomy. For example, the judges of the San José Court are elected under less politicised procedures because politics has negatively influenced elections in Latin America.[770] This manner of choosing judges contrasts with the European human rights system in which judges are se-

767 *Baralija v Bosnia and Herzegovina*, ECtHR, App No 30100/18, Judgment on Merits and Just Satisfaction of 29 October 2019, para 62.

768 Dženeta Omerdić and Harun Halilović, 'The Case of Baralija v Bosnia and Herzegovina: A new Challenge for the State Authorities of Bosnia and Herzegovina?' (2020) 4 *Društvene i humanističke studije* 217–238, 228–233.

769 Diana P Hernández Castaño, *Legitimidad democrática de la Corte Interamericana de Derechos Humanos en el control de convencionalidad* (Universidad Externado de Colombia 2015) Chap 3.

770 Pasqualucci (n 695) 483–486.

lected by the CoE Parliamentary Assembly, which is composed of political representatives appointed by national parliaments.[771]

Despite these circumstances, it should be carefully assessed whether constitutional courts in Latin American countries have the ability to reconcile the discrepancy between individual and public autonomy. Generally speaking, if the ordinary judges under a past dictatorship are not removed by a new democratic government, the constitutional judges are expected to show sensitivity to the liberal and transformative spirit of the new Constitution.[772] Nevertheless, Latin American courts are in a process of democratisation and their roles are still part of an open-ended discussion.[773] As an embryonic example in the unconsolidated democracies of Latin America, the Colombian *Corte Constitucional* issued an interesting ruling on 10 October 2013. Referring to the precedent case *López Mendoza v. Venezuela*, in which the IACtHR provided systematic interpretation regarding Article 23 ACHR (right to participate in government), the Constitutional Court cast a cautious eye at unconditional obedience to the San José jurisprudence by distinguishing the contexts of the Venezuelan and the Colombian cases. Consequently, the *Corte Constitucional* adopted its own interpretation of the ACHR provision with regard to the *Legislador*'s democratic role.[774]

As a democratic challenge from a national constitutional court to the regional court, the *El Mozote* case beautifully illustrates the relativist theories on international and national authorities in light of constitutional reasoning. This case concerned the alleged massacres that occurred during the period of the so-called counterinsurgency operations deployed against civilians on a massive scale by the Salvadoran army during the civil war in that country. Although the 1992 the Chapultepec Peace Accord that ended hostilities clearly mentions 'the need to clarify and put an end to any indication of impunity', the Legislative Assembly of the Republic of El Salvador enacted the 1993 Law of General Amnesty for the Consolidation of Peace to extend the benefit of unrestricted amnesty under the 1992 National Reconciliation Law. In the merits phase on 25 October 2012, the IACtHR resolutely maintained its jurisprudence on amnesty laws. Despite

771 Ferreres Comella (n 442) 148.

772 Ibid 270.

773 Popelier and Patino Alvarez (n 750) 206–208.

774 Corte Constitucional de Colombia, Exp T-3005221, Sentencia SU712/13 de 17 octubre de 2013, para 7.6 (La competencia atribuida constitucionalmente es compatible con la Convención Americana sobre Derechos Humanos).

the apparently democratic process through which the Law of General Amnesty was adopted, it was regarded as evidently incompatible with the ACHR and lacking legal effect.[775] We should not overlook in this context the concurring opinion of Judge Diego García Sayán, which was adhered to by Judges Leonardo A. Franco, Margarette May Macaulay, Rhadys Abreu Blondet and Alberto Pérez Pérez. Their opinion complemented the majority position in terms of the special conditions of transitional justice as follows:

> In these [transitional situations between armed conflicts and peace], taking into consideration that none of those rights and obligations is of an absolute character, it is legitimate that they be weighed in such a way that the satisfaction of some does not affect the exercise of the others disproportionately. Thus, the degree of justice that can be achieved is not an isolated component from which legitimate frustrations and dissatisfactions can arise, but part of an ambitious process of transition towards mutual tolerance and peace.[776]

In line with this thoughtful opinion, the Constitutional Chamber of the Supreme Court of El Salvador in the judgement of 13 July 2016 tactfully orchestrated its constitutional reasoning in favour of both international and national mandates. As a starting point for dialogue, the constitutional guardian evaluated the inter-American authority in that the latter 'without disregarding the sovereign right that States retain to decree amnesties in situations of post-armed conflict, has ruled on the incompatibility of certain amnesty laws – specifically self-amnesties – with international law and with the international obligations of states'.[777] By offering a friendly reappraisal and at the same time, by recharacterising Inter-American jurisprudence as developed mainly in 'self' amnesty cases, the Constitutional Chamber skilfully arranged its own field to create jurisprudence on 'post-armed conflict' amnesty in terms of constitutional reasoning, which was corroborated with a constitutional comparative analysis of transitional cases including Argentina and Colombia.[778] To differentiate itself from

775 *The Massacres of El Mozote and Surrounding Areas v El Salvador*, IACtHR, Series C No 252, Judgment on Merits, Reparations and Costs of 25 October 2012, para 296.

776 Ibid, Concurring Opinion of Judge Diego García Sayán, para 38.

777 Sala de lo Constitucional de la Corte Suprema de Justicia de El Salvador, Inconstitucionalidad 44–2013/145–2013, Sentencia de 13 de julio de 2016, Considerando IV.6.A.

778 Ibid Considerando V.1.A.

the Inter-American Court that links strict international obligations with 'all' violations of protected rights, the Salvadorean Court identified the actually relevant criteria to be applied only in 'serious' violations of human rights.[779] Within the reformulated framework, the proportionality was even more closely evaluated between 'the need to ensure certain legitimate public interests – such as peace, political stability and national reconciliation – and the state's inalienable obligation to investigate and sanction violations of fundamental rights'.[780]

Although the IACtHR and the Constitutional Chamber proceeded along different paths, they eventually joined together in the conclusion that the *Ley de Amnistía General para la Consolidación de la Paz* was subject to control of constitutionality and conventionality. As the subsequent stage of supervising judgement compliance, the San José judges positively evaluated the San Salvadorean judges' efforts to align the constitutional and conventional jurisprudence regarding the prohibition of amnesty.[781] This Salvadorean approach in *El Mozote* elaborated a thought-provoking constitutional reasoning that respectfully aims to relativise the IACtHR's absolutist doctrines. On this point, Carlos Arturo Villagrán Sandoval and Fabia Fernandes Carvalho Veçoso have made an insightful comment that the most interesting aspect of the Salvadorean decision was that it presented the Chamber as 'a catalyst in the bottom-up construction of democratic values in a dialectic manner'.[782] We may observe the dual aspect of such bottom-up democratisation: First, the Constitutional Chamber constructively criticised the IACtHR's comparative method for ascertaining the international *corpus juris.* As we confirmed above, the Inter-American comparative approach has been a target of criticism for 'undertak[ing] a fairly superficial reading of the law of the other countries involved, particularly in the absence of IACtHR cases dealing with the same set of laws in the other jurisdictions'.[783] The Constitutional Chamber, in order to overcome such a flaw stemming from the top-down approach of the Inter-American

779 Ibid Considerando V.2.A.

780 Ibid Considerando V.2.B.

781 The Massacres of El Mozote and Surrounding Areas v El Salvador, IACtHR, Order on Monitoring Compliance with Judgment of 31 August 2017, para 17.

782 Carlos Arturo Villagrán Sandoval and Fabia Fernandes Carvalho Veçoso, 'A Human Rights' Tale of Competing Narratives' (2016) 8 *Revista Direito e Práxis* 1603–1651.

783 Lucas Lixinski, 'The Consensus Method of Interpretation by the Inter-American Court of Human Rights' (2017) *Canadian Journal of Comparative and Contemporary Law* 65–95, 79.

Court, intended to build a bottom-up democratic consensus among States Parties by comparing constitutional peers' practices in this region. Second, the Constitutional Chamber attenuated the IACtHR's ultimate authority in exercising control of conventionality, claiming its better placed position than that of the Inter-American Court's top-down standpoint for assessing constitutional proportionality to reflect democratic values in the sensitive context of transitional justice. As is implied in the Salvadorean case, such a double bottom-up construction of democratic consensus through reasonable constitutional reasoning contributes to reinforcing, rather than demolishing, the legitimate authority of international law.[784]

Another case that illustrates the synergy between regional and constitutional courts for democratic decision-making is found in the legal dispute over same-sex marriage in Costa Rica. Asked by the government of Costa Rica for its interpretation of the recognition of the rights of same-sex couples under the ACHR, the IACtHR issued its advisory opinion. Invoking the doctrine of conventionality control, the Court declared that Article 54 of the Civil Code of Costa Rica must be interpreted pursuant to the standards that those who wish to have their records and/or their identity documents comprehensively rectified in order to conform to their self-perceived gender identity, may effectively enjoy this human right recognised in Articles 3, 7, 11(2), 13 and 18 of the American Convention.[785] Along with the obligation of consistent interpretation, the advisory opinion manifested more generally that 'States must ensure access to all the legal institutions that exist in their domestic laws to guarantee the protection of all the rights of families composed of same-sex couples, without discrimination in relation to families constituted by heterosexual couples'.[786] Moreover, the Inter-American judges recognised that 'some States must overcome institutional difficulties to adapt their domestic law and extend the right of access to the institution of marriage to same-sex couples, especially when there are rigorous procedures for legislative reform, which may demand a process that is politically complex and requires time'.[787] As a responsive dialogue of judges in San José, the Constitutional Chamber of

784 The Salvadorian case is suggestive for the Colombian context. See, Juana I Acosta-López, 'The Inter-American Human Rights System and the Colombian Peace: Redefining the Fight Against Impunity' (2016) 110 *American Journal of International Law* 178–182, 181–182.

785 *Gender Identity, and Equality and Non-discrimination with Regard to Same-sex Couples* (n 159) para 171.

786 Ibid para 228.

787 Ibid para 226.

the Supreme Court followed the Inter-American Advisory Opinion and set a deadline of 18 months for the entry into force of the unconstitutionality of the relevant provisions of the Family Code, which urged the Legislative Assembly to amend the laws.[788] As a fruitful result produced by the dialogue between national and Inter-American judges involving political actors, same-sex civil marriage came into effect in Costa Rica on 26 May 2020, which made it the first country in Central America to take this step.

(ii) Legal Certainty: Balancing Predictability and Acceptability

The second risk of diffused conventionality control is that *legal certainty* may be damaged when different ordinary judges reach a different conclusion regarding the application and interpretation of human rights conventions. Legal certainty has been a guiding principle of European legal systems, in contrast to the *legal indeterminacy* which governs American lawyers.[789] In parallel with the national sphere, the ECtHR has regarded the principle of legal certainty as 'inherent in the right of the Convention for the Protection of Human Rights'.[790] The IACtHR also invokes legal certainty in combination with procedural balance among the parties in cases of massacres involving a flood of victims and complicated facts.[791] Legal certainty has formal and substantive meanings. Elina Paunio, citing the hermeneutical footsteps of legal theorists such as Aulis Aarnio and Alexander Peczenik, elucidates that *formal legal certainty* implies that 'laws and, in particular, adjudication must be predictable: laws must satisfy requirements of clarity, stability, and intelligibility so that those concerned can with relative accuracy calculate the legal consequences of their actions

788 Sala Constitucional de la Corte Suprema de Justicia de Costa Rica, Exp 15–013971–0007-CO, Res № 2018012782 de 8 de agosto del 2018 See also, Ana María Ruiz González, 'Supreme Court of Justice of Costa Rica (Corte Suprema de Justicia de Costa Rica) Costa Rica [cr]' in Rainer Grote, Frauke Lachenmann, Rüdiger Wolfrum (eds), *Max Planck Encyclopedia of Comparative Constitutional Law* (Oxford University Press2019), updated in 2019, paras 20–22.

789 James R Maxeiner, 'Legal Certainty: A European Alternative to American Legal Indeterminacy?' (2006–2007) 15 *Tulane Journal of International and Comparative Law* 541–607, 545–553.

790 *Marckx v Belgium*, ECtHR, App No 6833/74, Judgment of 13 June 1979, para 58.

791 *The 'Las Dos Erres' Massacre v Guatemala*, IACtHR, Series C No 211, Judgment on Preliminary Objection, Merits, Reparations, and Costs of 24 November 2009, para 63.

as well as the outcome of legal proceedings'.[792] Moreover, *substantive* legal certainty means 'the rational acceptability of legal decision-making'.[793] Habermas' theory on the *indeterminacy of law* suggests a procedural guarantee for reconciling both formal and substantive concepts of legal certainty. Although Habermas focuses on the investigation of the legitimacy of legal norms and not on legal certainty, his view highlights their inherent indeterminacy, and thereby covers both formal and substantive legal certainty.[794] In fact, he acknowledges that 'court rulings must satisfy simultaneously the conditions of *consistent decision-making* and *rational acceptability*'.[795] The theoretical framework of *procedure-dependent certainty of law* reckons from the start with a 'discursively regulated competition among different paradigms'.[796] Replacing the proceduralist approach to legal certainty in the implementation of human rights conventions, it implies a *judicial dialogue* between human rights courts and domestic courts for converging their interpretations.[797]

In addition to the democratic values examined above, legal certainty guaranteed through judicial dialogue is another key factor for distributing labour between constitutional and ordinary judges in conventionality control. In order to reconcile the decentralising tendency of constitutional review in Europe and the guarantee of legal certainty, Ferres Comella normatively suggests the following amendment to the centralised system of constitutional adjudication: [O]rdinary judges may engage in rather strained interpretations of statutes (and may even formally disregard them) only if the ECHR's precedents are sufficiently clear. When, in contrast, the legitimacy of the national law under the existing case law is more controversial, ordinary courts should ask the constitutional court to intervene and express their position.[798] In *Horncastle*, for example, Lord Phillips sent a message raising an objection to the interpretation made by the ECtHR Chamber 'so that there takes place what may prove to be a valuable dia-

792 Elina Paunio, 'Beyond Predictability: Reflections on Legal Certainty and the Discourse Theory of Law in the EU Legal Order' (2009) 10 *German Law Journal* 1469–1493, 1469.

793 Ibid.

794 Nupur Chowdhury, *European Regulation of Medical Device and Pharmaceutical: Regulatee Expectations of Legal Certainty* (Springer 2014) 58.

795 Habermas (n 746) 198 (emphasis in orginal text).

796 Ibid 223–224.

797 Paunio (n 793) 1476.

798 Ferreres Comella (n 442)145–146.

logue between this court and the Strasbourg Court'.[799] In the *Al-Khawaja* ruling, the ECtHR Grand Chamber duly received the message from the Supreme Court of the United Kingdom and reformulated the Strasbourg principles.[800]

A revised model of concentrated constitutional adjudication in terms of legal certainty may be found in the Italian constitutional review system. In the 2015 *Judgement No 49*, the Italian *Corte costituzionale* had another occasion to elaborate the conventionality control framework in light of legal certainty. Regarding the ECtHR's responsibility for the *certezza* and *uniformità* of human rights protection, the Constitutional Court rejected the notion that the ECHR has turned national courts into passive recipients of an interpretative command issued elsewhere in the form of a court ruling, irrespective of the conditions that gave rise to it.[801] It is true that ordinary courts are regulated by the primary constitutional requirement of *stabile assetto* (equilibrium) *interpretativo*, according to which they cannot disregard the *consolidata interpretazione* of fundamental rights made by the Strasbourg Court as the ultimate instance.[802] However, the interpretative equilibrium must be coordinated with a synthesis between the interpretative autonomy of the ordinary courts and their duty to cooperate in ensuring that the meaning of fundamental rights ceases to be a matter of dispute.[803] Therefore, ordinary courts are required to follow only *diritto consolidato* of ECtHR jurisprudence, which corresponds to the 'well-established case law of the Court' under Article 28 ECHR.[804] In the absence of such a *diritto consolidato* under Strasbourg law, ordinary courts may avoid the need to refer a question of the constitutionality of the ECHR provisions by interpreting them in a manner in conformity with the Constitution.[805]

The Italian *Consulta*'s judgement may contribute to coordinating both *formal* and *substantive* legal certainty. On the one hand, it demarcates

---

799 *R v Horncastle and others* [2009] UKSC 14, para 11 (emphasis added). See also, Merris Amos, 'The Dialogue between United Kingdom Courts and the European Court of Human Rights' (2012) 61 Int'l & Comp. LQ 557.

800 *Al-Khawaja and Tahery v the United Kingdom*, ECtHR (Grand Chamber), App Nos 26766/05 and 22228/06, Judgment on Merits and Just Satisfaction of 15 December 2011.

801 Corte costituzionale italiana, Sentenza № 49 del 1 maggio 2015, para 7.

802 Ibid.

803 Ibid.

804 Ibid.

805 Ibid.

the scope of consistent interpretation by ordinary judges in light of the *predictability* of ECHR rights. On the other hand, speaking in its own defence, the Italian *Corte costituzionale* explains that a judgement is based on argumentation within the perspective of *cooperazione* and *dialogo* between the courts rather than the vertical imposition of a particular interpretation which has not yet become established within Strasbourg case law.[806] To borrow the words of Giuseppe Martinico, this should be characterised not as a rebellious attitude embracing a feeling of mistrust towards Strasbourg jurisprudence but as *disobbedienza funzionale* for the ultimate purpose of achieving the effective protection of human rights.[807] Coordination between formal and substantive legal certainty by constitutional courts would be more important in relation to the *evolutive* or *dynamic* interpretation by human rights courts. Confronting such a *creatività* in the jurisprudence of human rights courts, national constitutional courts form a significant part of the communicative process for reconciling its predictability and acceptability simultaneously.[808]

Notwithstanding these advances, *Sentenza no 49/2015* is not without criticism in terms of legal certainty. In the later judgement in *GIEM SRL and Others v. Italy*, in which legal certainty and predictability inherent in the principle of legality under Article 7 ECHR were in question, the Strasbourg judges send a signal to the Roman judges: 'its judgments all have the same legal value. Their binding nature and interpretative authority cannot therefore depend on the formation by which they were rendered'.[809] More specifically, Judge Paulo Pinto de Albuquerque offered the criticism that the criteria the Italian Constitutional Court set forth in order to identify *consolidata interpretazione* reveals their propensity to create a situation of dangerous legal uncertainty, to the extent that it provided no further guidance to ordinary judges since the sentence.[810] The door opened by the Italian *Corte costituzionale* should not be closed by it for future deliberation as regards the *acceptability* of the Strasbourg law.

---

806 Ibid.

807 Giuseppe Martinico, 'Corti constituzionali (o supreme) e "disobbedienza funzionale": Critica, dialogo e conflitti nel rapporto fra diritto interno e diritto delle Convenzioni (CEDU e Convenzione americana sui diritti umani)' *Diritto Penale Contemporaneo*, 28 Aprile 2015.

808 Sentenza №49/2015 (n 802) para 7.

809 *GIEM SRL and others v Italy*, ECtHR (Grand Chamber), App No 1828/06 and others, Judgment on Merits of 28 June 2018, para 252.

810 Ibid Partly Concurring, Patly Dissenting Opinion of Judge Paulo Pinto de Albuquerque, paras 43–56.

In Latin America, the rationale of legal certainty for triggering the centralisation of conventionality control powers within constitutional courts is exemplified by the *Gelman* case concerning enforced disappearance in Uruguay within the scheme of *la Operación Cóndor*. In shifting from a military regime to a constitutional democratic system, the Uruguayan parliament in 1986 promulgated the Expiry Law to grant amnesty to those responsible for such crimes. La Ley de Caducidad was publicly supported through the exercise of direct democracy in 1989 and 2009. Against this background, the IACtHR rendered judgement on the merits on 24 February 2011. The *Gelman* ruling was slightly different from precedents regarding self-amnesty in that the Expiry Law in question allegedly gained democratic legitimacy. For the San José Court, the primary mission was to defend its individual-oriented case law from the risk of majoritarian rule:

> The fact that the Expiry Law of the State has been approved in a democratic regime and yet ratified or supported by the public, on two occasions, namely, through the exercise of direct democracy, does not automatically or by itself grant legitimacy under International Law. [...] The democratic legitimacy of specific facts in a society is limited by the norms of protection of human rights recognized in international treaties, [...] in such a form that the existence of one true democratic regime is determined by both its formal and substantial characteristics, and therefore, particularly in cases of serious violations of non-revocable norms of International Law, the protection of human rights constitutes an impassable [*infranqueable*] limit to the rule of majority.[811]

In this context, *la Corte Interamericana* highly evaluated the Supreme Court of Justice of Uruguay's *Sabalsagaray* judgement in 2009, in which the Expiry Law was disregarded as unconstitutional, as an *adecuado control de convencionalidad*.[812] In the aftermath of *Gelman*, however, *la Corte Suprema de Justicia* clearly showed a sense of rebellion against the Inter-American top-down decision. Indeed, its judgement of 22 February 2013 declared the unconstitutionality of Articles 2 and 3 of Law No 18831, which was enacted for implementing the IACtHR judgement on violating the constitutional principle of non-retroactivity. To justify their own constitutional logic, the Uruguayan highest judges emphasised that 'while it is beyond any discussion that the IACtHR is the final interpreter of the ACHR –

---

811 *Gelman*, Judgment (n 464) paras 238-239.
812 Ibid para 239.

naturally within the sphere of its jurisdiction – it cannot be denied that the final interpreter of the Constitution of the Oriental Republic of Uruguay is the Supreme Court of Justice'.[813]

Shortly after receiving this harsh contestation from Montevideo, the San José Court in turn issued an order on compliance with the judgement in 2013. To counter the Supreme Court's argument distinguishing Inter-American and constitutional authorities, the IACtHR resolutely reiterated that according to international law which the State had accepted in a democratic and sovereign manner, it is unacceptable that once the Inter-American Court has issued a judgement with the authority of *res judicata*, the domestic law or its authorities should seek to leave it without effects.[814] Consequently, the San José judges signalled that the Montevideo judges' decision in 2013 constituted an obstacle to the full compliance of the Inter-American judgement by producing adverse effects against access to justice by victims of grave human rights violations.[815]

In receiving this signal from the IACtHR, the Supreme Court of Justice unanimously dismissed on 30 May 2019 the appeal filed by the defence in the case concerning the 'very seriously aggravated homicide' of victim Gerardo Alter, on the basis that 'the period of the *de facto* regime cannot be counted to calculate the statute of limitations for this criminal action, since the victim was prevented from seeking the relevant investigations during that time'.[816] The Inter-American Commission on Human Rights positively evaluated this decision as 'one step closer to investigation of events in that case', but, at the same time, expressed its concern about 'the persistence in criminal law proceedings of some statutory interpretations that insist on applying a statute of limitations to serious human rights violations committed during the Uruguayan dictatorship'.[817] In the most recent order on compliance with the judgement, which came in 2020, the IACtHR shared the Commission's evaluation and concern, and noted that 'sufficient juridical security does not exist' for complying with

813 Corte Suprema de Justicia de Uruguay, Gelman, Caso 20/2013, Proceso de Inconstitucionalidad. Sentencia de 22 de febrero de 2013, Considerando III.a.

814 *Gelman*, Order (n 375) para. 90.

815 Ibid.

816 IACHR, Press Release: IACHR Notes Uruguay Court Decision Limiting the Application of Statute of Limitations to Crime Committed during the Dictatorship, June 24, 2019, available at https://www.oas.org/en/iachr/media_center/PReleases/2019/158.asp.

817 Ibid.

the judgement.[818] In the meantime, to overcome a fragmented situation where plural 'judicial interpretations persist', the Inter-American judges once again expected the Montevideo judges to play 'the important role that the Supreme Court of Justice of Uruguay – as the national tribunal of the highest hierarchy – has, within the scope of its competences, in the compliance with or implementation of the Inter-American Court Judgment'.[819] The *Gelman* case reveals that centralised conventionality control by constitutional courts is desirable to ensure legal certainty as well as democratic legitimacy at the national level.

---

818 *Gelman v Uruguay*, IACtHR, Monitoring Compliance with Judgment, Order of 19 November 2020, para 31.

819 Ibid paras 32–33.

Conclusion

Although patients are sovereign over their own health and doctors are complementary to medical care in theory, their relationship is not simply dualistic or monistic but rather more complicated in practice. On the one hand, doctors often proactively employ their expertise, which is accumulated at the universal level, to manage the health conditions of patients. On the other hand, when patients feel that the experts misdiagnose or prescribe a suboptimal drug, or when they are confident they are the 'true experts' for their own bodies, they may engage in dialogue with the medical experts to treat their own diseases independently.[820] This figuration of *co-constitutive relationality* may be applied similarly to the practices of conventionality control. This monograph has surveyed the parallel dynamism between 'constitutionalised international adjudication' (Part I) and 'internationalised constitutional adjudication' (Part 2) by focusing on the practice of conventionality control of domestic law in the European and Inter-American systems of human rights. Chapter 1 of each Part revealed that the interpretation and application of conventionality control parameters combine unifying and diversifying approaches depending on the protection level of universal, regional and constitutional norms in light of the *pro homine* principle embedded in 'more favourable' clause. In addition, Chapter 2 of both Parts demonstrated that the allocation of conventionality control powers can also be centralised and decentralised depending upon the nature of the labour among regional, constitutional and ordinary courts. The results of the analysis is summarised in **Chart 2.**

As noted in the last part of the Introduction, this project purports to create one normative model of conventionality control based on those adjudicatory practices at the international and domestic levels. Given the dynamism of top-down constitutionalisation and bottom-up internationalisation of adjudication in Europe and Latin America, the so-called *static validity* theory (dualism or monism) or the *practical coordination* theory cannot be a panacea to address this phenomenon. Therefore, the monograph, finally, elaborates a *dynamic process* theory that may explain, in

820 This possibility is pointed out in a discussion with Professor Andreas Føllesdal, who questioned that 'So the worries may be that the "experts" misdiagnose, or prescribe a suboptimal drug..?'.

both the empirical and normative senses, the doctrine of conventionality control.

	Chapter 1 Conventionality Control Parameters	**Chapter 2 Conventionality Control Powers**
Part I Constitutionalisation of International Adjudication	**Interpretation of conventionality control parameters**	**International distribution of conventionality control powers**
Section 2-A Unification-Centralisation	*Unifying* regional and universal standards	*Centralising* powers to regional courts
Section 2-B Diversification-Decentralisation	*Diversifying* regional and universal standards	*Decentralising* powers to domestic courts
Part II Internationalisation of Constitutional Adjudication	**Application of conventionality control parameters**	**Domestic distribution of conventionality control powers**
Section 2-A Unification-Centralisation	*Unifying* regional and constitutional standards	*Centralising* powers to constitutional courts
Section 2-B Diversification-Decentralisation	*Diversifying* regional and constitutional standards	*Decentralising* powers to ordinary courts

Chart 2. Summary of Chapters

1. Reconstructing Pyramid

A. Pyramid Model: Closedness, Formalism and State-Centrism

The pyramidal concept of the relationship between international and domestic law has been developed through monism theories.[821] Based on Adolf Merkl's idea of a *rechtlicher Stufenbau* (hierarchically structured legal pyramid), Hans Kelsen advocated in his *Reine Rechtslehre* that '[t]he legal order is not of legal norms of equal rank but a pyramid structure of different layers of legal norms'.[822] According to this Kelsenian theory, as depicted in **Figure 1** below, there are two theoretically equal possibilities: monism with the supremacy of international law and monism with the

821 Paul Gragl, *Legal Monism: Law, Philosophy, and Politics* (Oxford University Press 2018).

822 Hans Kelsen, *Reine Rechtslehre*, 2nd ed (Deuticke 1960) 228ff.

supremacy of the constitution.[823] However, as the present monograph has proved in the context of conventionality control, the contemporary state of affairs poses huge challenges to the supremacy of international law and constitutional law, respectively. In the present context of international adjudication, the literature also proved that 'international constitutional judicial review is not concentrated in a single "world court", as Kelsen might have wished, but rather shared by a many international courts and tribunals within the fragmented and pluralized international system'.[824] It is a remarkable trend that contemporary public law scholars have inherited and refined the *moderate monism* theory to seek constitutionalist approaches to international law.[825] For the present purpose, it is furthermore notable that constitutionalism beyond the state 'regards the unity, universality, and supremacy of the global constitutional legal order vis-à-vis domestic legal orders'.[826]

Nonetheless, the monist figure of a pyramid has been challenged by legal pluralists who, by amplifying dualist perspectives, presuppose the interplay of various layers of law and politics according to rules ultimately set by each layer for itself.[827] Should the legal pyramid be deconstructed due to the internationalisation of constitutional law? Armin von Bogdandy, one of the most prominent critics, answers this question by arguing that the pyramid model should be reconstructed in light of legal pluralism to promote 'the insight that there is an interaction among the different legal orders'.[828] Von Bogdandy admits that, given the state of development of international law, there should be the possibility of placing legal limits on the effect of international law within the domestic legal order if it severely conflicts with constitutional principles.[829] However, his answer is 'not to be understood as monism with the constitution at the apex' but as

823 Ibid 321ff.

824 Tomer Broude, 'The Constitutional Function of Contemporary International Tribunals, or Kelsen's Visions Vindicated' (2012) 4 *Göttingen Journal of International Law* 519–549, 521–522.

825 Thomas Kleinlein, 'Alfred Verdross as a Founding Father of International Constitutionalism?' (2012) 4 *Goettingen Journal of International Law* 385–416.

826 Jean L Cohen, *Globalization and Sovereignty: Rethinking Legality, Legitimacy, and Constitutionalism* (Cambridge University Press 2012) 47–48.

827 Krisch (n 406) 69.

828 Armin von Bogdandy, 'Pluralism, Direct Effect, and the Ultimate Say: On the Relationship between International and Domestic Constitutional Law' (2008) 6 *International Journal of Constitutional Law* 397–413, 399–401.

829 Ibid.

a theory of pluralism of legal orders in which the normative independence of international law is not put into question.[830]

From the perspective of legal pluralism, the pyramidal concept can be revised in three aspects. First, the hierarchical pyramid is overly holistic, *close-minded* to the extent that it projects 'a holistic ambition, an ambition to construct a comprehensive, justified political order'.[831] The present volume's whole analyses rather envision an open-minded scheme of conventionality control in line with legal pluralism as Nico Krisch explains its attribute: 'Pluralism's institutional openness thus corresponds with the openness and fluidity of postnational society in a way constitutionalism, tailored to less heterogeneous societies, does not'.[832]

Second, the monist pyramid model adheres to *formalism*, one of the tenets of legal positivism, represented by a formal hierarchy that determines the validity of norms in conflict.[833] As this monograph has demonstrated, however, the decisive element for governing these relations is shifted from a formal hierarchy to *substantive* protection. In this regard, Anne Peters proposed a *nonformalist, substance-oriented* approach, integrating the constitutionalist and pluralist standpoints. Having empirically analysed the interaction between international law and national constitutions, she suggested that '[t]he ranking of the norms at stake should be assessed in a more subtle manner, according to their *substantial* weight and significance'.[834]

Third, the pyramid should be customised for contemporary global law as is illustrated by Rafael Domingo. He expresses the criticism that 'Kelsen's error was to place the state – for him, a personification of the legal order – and not the human person as such at the center of his whole normative system'.[835] The new pyramid model that Domingo instead proposes, 'unlike Kelsen's, would not comprise superimposed normative layers, each dependent on another up through the fundamental norm (*Grundnorm*), but rather a wide base in which each point – that is, each

830 Ibid.

831 Nico Krisch, 'Global Administrative Law and the Constitutional Ambition' in Petra Dobner and Martin Loughlin (eds), *The Twilight of Constitutionalism?* (Oxford University Press 2010) 245–266, 254.

832 Krisch (n 406) 26.

833 D'Aspremont (n 160) 25–26.

834 Peters (n 411) 195–198 (emphasis added).

835 Rafael Dominigo, *The New Global Law* (Cambridge University Press 2010) 147–149.

person – would be projected in the apex'.[836] This humanised pyramid, beyond the context of human rights protection, 'integrates the local and the global across all existing and developing branches of law'.[837]

B. Reconciling Constitutionalism and Legal Pluralism Beyond the State

It has increasingly been accepted that constitutionalist and legal pluralist perspectives should be reconciled, in the name of *constitutional pluralism*. Niel MacCormick, the father of this prevalent strand of thought, made a jurisprudential attempt to overcome 'a narrow one-state or Community-only perspective, a monocular view' within the framework of European integration.[838] By revising H L A Hart's concept of *internal point of view*, MacCormick seeks the cognitive possibility of acknowledging differences of perspective, instead of a volitional commitment to a monocular vision dictated by sovereignty theory.[839] From such pluralised viewpoints, there is 'no compulsion to regard sovereignty, or even hierarchical relationships of superordination and subordination, as necessary to our understanding of legal order in the complex interaction of overlapping legalities'.[840] Having noted the risk of normative conflicts in *radical pluralism*, MacCormick subsequently attenuated his position by espousing *pluralism under international law*.[841]

The idea of constitutional pluralism has widely spread in both theory and practice, and consequently, has multiply diversified within and beyond the context of European integration: socio-teleological constitutionalism (Joseph Weiler), epistemic meta-constitutionalism (Niel Walker), cosmopolitan constitutionalism (Matthias Kumm), contrapunctual law (Miguel Poiares Maduro) and so on.[842] As another framework, Mireille Delmas-Marty coined the concept of *pluralisme ordonné* 'to move beyond

836 Ibid.

837 Ibid.

838 Niel MacCormick, 'Beyond the Sovereign State' (1993) 56 *Modern Law Review* 1–18, 5.

839 Ibid 6.

840 Ibid 10 (emphasis added).

841 Niel MacCormick, *Questioning Sovereignty* (Oxford University Press 1999) 113–121.

842 Matej Avbelj and Jan Komárek, 'Introduction' in Matej Avbelj and Jan Komárek (eds), *Constitutional Pluralism in the European Union and Beyond* (Hart 2012) 1–15, 4–7.

the universal/relative dichotomy and explore the possibility of a law that would order complexity without eliminating it'. In another approach, Ingolf Pernice suggested *multilevel constitutionalism*, or its German term *Verfassungsverbund*, which can articulate 'a theoretical approach to conceptualize the constitutional European system as an interactive process of establishing, dividing, organizing, and limiting powers, involving national constitutions and the supranational constitutional framework, considered two independent components of a legal system governed by constitutional pluralism instead of *hierarchies*'.[843] Instead of the characterisation *multilevel* that might reproduce a hierarchical idea, Bustos Gilbert envisions *constitución red* to illustrate the multiple links corresponding to each constitutional place independent from and interactive with each other.[844] In a similar vein, the *réseau* model is advocated by Ost and Kerchove to explain the emergence of the complex relationship between legal orders against the background of the *bougés* of the pyramidal model.[845] In line with these doctrines, Anne Peters sophisticates her position of global constitutionalist into *constitutionalising fragmentation*, according to which 'constitutional principles and procedures are needed to constructively deal with pluralism (and with fragmentation)'.[846]

For the present purpose of reconfiguring the monist model of conventionality control, the camp of legal pluralism provides us with the *relation-*

843 Ingolf Pernice, 'The Treaty of Lisbon: Multilevel Constitutionalism in Action' (2009) 15 *Columbia Journal of European Law* 349–407 (emphasis added). See also, Ingolf Pernice, 'Theorie und Praxis des Europäischen Verfassungsverbundes' in Calliess (ed), *Verfassungswandel im europäischen Staaten- und Verfassungsverbund* (Mohr Siebeck 2007) 61–92, 78–84.

844 Bustos Gisbert, 'Elementos constitucionales en la red global' (2012) 60 *Estudios de Deusto* 21–43, 26.

845 Ost and van de Kerchove, *De la pyramide au réseau? Pour une théorie dialectique du droit* (Publications des Facultés universitaires Saint-Louis 2002) Chap I. See also, Boris Barraud, *Repensar la pyramide des normes à l'ère des réseaux : Pour une conception pragmatique du droit* (L'Harmattan 2012) 65–74.

846 Anne Peters, 'Fragmentation and Constitutionalization' in Anne Orford and Florian Hoffmann (eds), *The Oxford Handbook of the Theory of International Law* (Oxford University Press 2016) 1011–1032, 1023–1026. See also, Turkuler Isiksel 'Global Legal Pluralism as Fact and Norm' (2013) 2 *Global Constitutionalism* 160–195, 190 (arguing that 'a relatively consolidated form of global constitutionalism, rather than unregulated global legal pluralism, is the best way to ensure a healthy pluralism of human values').

al concept of law.[847] On the parameters of conventionality control, as each Chapter 1 of Parts I and II demonstrates, their interpretation and application can be directed in two contrasting ways, either unification or diversification, among universal standards, regional conventions and national constitutions. This dynamic interaction of different sources of different orders can no longer be explained by the single rule of recognition within respective legal orders. Inheriting the challenge of MacCormick to generalise Hart's theory, Ralf Michaels endorses the concept of *external rules of recognition* to establish the relation with other legal orders.[848] With such tertiary rules of external recognition complementing secondary rules of internal recognition, legal systems are not conceived as independently autopoietic but rather 'mutually constitute each other through mutual recognition' in an 'allopoietic' manner.[849]

On the powers of conventionality control, as each Chapter 2 of Parts I and II prove, their allocation can also be shifted in opposite directions, either centralisation or decentralisation, among regional, constitutional and ordinary courts. This context-based gradation of power allocation between different judicial organs of different legal orders cannot be elucidated by a self-standing, monolithic understanding of authority. Rather, as Nicole Nicole Roughan theorises *relative authority*, we need to conceive the legitimacy of overlapping or interactive authorities as relative.[850] The relativity condition does not cast aside any values attaching to particular authorities by the presence of other authorities wielding more or better resources, but rather 'places the onus *upon the authorities* to interact appropriately so that subjects can rely upon those authorities to realize their own justifications'.[851]

---

847 Maksymilian Del Mar, 'Legal Reasoning in Pluralist Jurisprudence: The Practice of The Relational Imagination' in Nicole Roughan and Andrew Halpin (eds), *In Pursuit of Pluralist Jurisprudence* (Cambridge University Press 2017) 40–63.

848 Ralf Michaels, 'Law and Recognition: Towards a Relational Concept of Law' in Nicole Roughan and Andrew Halpin (eds), *In Pursuit of Pluralist Jurisprudence* (Cambridge University Press 2017) 90–115, 99–101.

849 Ibid 91.

850 Nicole Roughan, *Authorities: Conflict, Cooperation, and Transnational Legal Theory* (Oxford University Press 2016) 136.

851 Ibid 142 (emphasis in the original text).

2. *Constructing a Trapezium*

A. Trapezium Model: Openness, Substantivism and Human-centrism

Inspired by those constitutional pluralist concepts, this monograph presents **Figure 2**, which depicts the *trapezium* model as an alternative to the pyramid model. While the summit of the pyramid fixes either international or constitutional law as the supreme norm, the upper base of the trapezium model consists of both legal sources. The trapezium vision has already been devised by some commentators in relation to Article 75(22) of the Argentine constitution, which places human rights treaties and the national constitution at the same rank.[852] As most famous advocate, Flávia Piovesan, envisions a change from a 'hermetically-closed pyramid focusing on the *State approach*' to 'the permeable trapezium focusing on the *human rights approach*'.[853] Inheriting traits from both constitutionalism and legal pluralism, this paper identifies three features of the novel trapezium in contrast to the traditional pyramid.

The author identifies the following three features of the trapezium model of conventionality control in light of constitutional pluralism. First, equating international standards with constitutional standards *opens up* closed constitutions to international society. The notion of *permeability*, which Piovesan accentuates in her figure, enables a legal order to incorporate the normative principles and content emanating from other legal orders.[854] In this respect, we should carefully reject the overly simplified understanding that constitutionalism is a structurally hierarchical and

852 Víctor Bazán, 'La interacción del derecho internacional de los derechos humanos y el derech interno en Argentina' (2007) 5 *Estudios Constitucionales* 137–183, 142; Calogero Pizzolo, 'Los mechanismos de protección en el sistema interamericano de derechos humanos y el derecho interno de los países miembros: El caso argentino', in R. Méndez Silva (ed.), *Derecho internacional de los derechos humanos. Memoria del VII Congreso Iberoamericano de Derecho Constitucional* (2002) 505–519, 514.

853 Flávia Piovesan, 'Direitos humanos e diálogo entre juridições' (2012) 19 *Revista Brasileira de Direito Constitucional* 67–93, 68–72 (emphasis in original text).

854 For the relationship between these concepts, see Mattias Wendel, *Permeabilität im europäischen Verfassungsrecht: Verfassungsrechtliche Integrationsnormen auf Staats- und Unionsebene im Vergleich* (Mohr Siebeck 2011) 28–30. See also, Mariela Morales Antoniazzi, 'El nuevo paradigma de la apertura de los órdenes constitucionales: una perspectiva sudamericana', in Armin von Bogdandy and José María Serna de la Garza (eds), *Soberanía y Estado abierto en América Latina y Europa* (Biblioteca Jurídica Virtual 2014) 233–282, 243–247.

holistic concept. Just as Giuseppe Martinico rebuffed Krisch's narrow conception, constitutionalists also apprehend openness as the 'established "friendless" within a constitution towards legal sources that are, from a formal point of view, external to those governed by the national system'.[855] The constitutionalist *Offenheit* (openness) is represented by Klaus Vogel's *offene Staatlichkeit* theory[856] and by Peter Häberle's *cooperative Verfassungsstaat* theory.[857] In this way, the constitutional openness based on which plural constitutional orders interact necessarily endorses the *rehabilitación* of the state, converting it into the principal space for human rights protection.[858]

Second, to introduce the anti-formalist approach into the trapezium model, the author envisages that the common values recognised in both international law and national constitutions are placed on its upper level. By crowning these common values independent from the formal hierarchy, 'the domestically rather powerless notion of the *supremacy of international law* would be replaced by a notion of the *supremacy of universal values* that would be able to pierce the divide between the domestic and international sphere'.[859] At the same time, 'a constitution is no longer supreme by the formalities in its approbation – *formal supremacy* –, but rather by the contents which it regulates and proclaims – *supremacy of contents* –'.[860] These parallel positions resonate with Peter's nonformalist, substantive perspective form in which 'certain less significant provisions in state constitutions would have to give way to important international norms. Inversely, [domestic] fundamental rights guarantees should prevail

855 Giuseppe Martinico, 'Constitutionalism, Resistance and Openness: Comparative Law Reflections on Constitutionalism in Global Governance' (2016) 35 *Yearbook of European Law* 318–340, 320.

856 Klaus Vogel, *Die Verfassungsentscheidung des Grundgesetzes für die internationale Zusammenarbeit* (Mohr Siebeck 1964) 42.

857 Peter Häberle, *Der kooperative Verfassungsstaat aus Kultur und als Kultur: Vorstudien zu einer universalen Verfassungslehre* (Duncker & Humblot GmbH 2013) 96–116.

858 Mauricio Iván Del Toro Huerta, 'La aperture constitucional al derecho internacional de los derechos humanos en la era de la Mundialización y sus consecuencias en la práctica judicial' (2005)112 *Boletín Mexicano de Derecho Comparado* 325–363, 331–343.

859 Janne E Nijman and André Nollkaemper, 'Beyond the Divide', in Janne E Nijman and André Nollkaemper (eds), *New Perspectives on the Divide Between National and International Law* (2007) 341–360, 342–348 (emphasis added).

860 Boris Wilson Arias López, 'Entre la Constitución y los tratados de derechos humanos' (2014) 38 *Derecho y Cambio Social* 1–13, 11 (emphasis added).

over less important [international] norms (independent of their locus and type of codification)'.[861]

Third, above all, the substantive values shaped by an open interaction between international and national legal sources are construed for the sake of *persons*, not for states. This notion is expressed in the Roman maxim 'hominum causa omne jus constitutum est' (all law is created for the benefit of human beings).[862] In the human-centric trapezium, the *pro homine* principle constitutes the core element in lieu of the supremacy of international law or constitutional law. To locate human beings at the centre of the legal system, we can consider implications from two relevant illustrations, which attempt to humanise the Kelsenian pyramid just as this paper does. For this attempt, Norberto Garay Boza's illustration, *the structural inversion of the Kelsenian pyramid*, is highly suggestive.[863] In his model, the conformity of domestic norms with international human rights criteria is controlled in light of the principle of *progressiveness*, a concept that is interchangeable with the *pro homine* principle.[864] In contrast with our trapezium schema, the inverse pyramid vision might be problematic from the legal pluralist perspective because it seems to place *a priori* priority of international human rights standards over constitutional ones.[865] Nevertheless, the author supports Boza's argument that if the content of infra-legal regulations are ampler than those of legislation in light of international human rights standards, priority should be given to the former rather than to the latter. This humanity-oriented idea enlightens our trapezium to admit that even hierarchically inferior norms take precedence if they contain the most favourable protection to persons. It follows that the formal supremacy of international law would be powerless to counter more protective legislation and other forms, without prejudice to the formal supremacy of constitution in relation to other national norms.

---

861 Peters (n 411) 197.

862 *Prosecutor v. Tadić*, ICTY, Case No. IT-94–1, Appeals Chamber, Interlocutory Appeal on Jurisdiction, Judgment of 2 October 1995, para. 97.

863 Norberto E Garay Boza, 'Gobernar desde abajo: Del control de convencionalidad a la instrumentalización de la inversión estructural de la pirámide kelseniana' (2012) 5 *Inter-American and European Human Rights Journal* 124–147, 128–137.

864 Ibid. As to the interchangeability between the principle of progressiveness and the *pro homine* principle, see Brewer-Carías (n 449) 59–61.

865 Ibid.

B. Uni/Diversified Parameters and De/Centralised Powers of Conventionality Control

The newly configured trapezium is more suitable than the traditional pyramid to explicate the practice of conventionality control examined in this monograph. In Chapter 1 of both Parts I and II, which blends unifying and diversifying approaches, the *pro homine* principle embedded in 'more favourable' clauses entails three correlated features. First, a 'more favourable' interpretative clause '*opens the door* for the use of other instruments (international or national) as relevant tools and [...] precludes restrictive interpretations' of the rights and freedoms recognised thereby.[866] The *pro homine* principle, as often stipulated in conjunction with 'consistent interpretation' clauses, promotes *open-minded* dialogue between international and national legal actors, and thereby builds important momentum to transform the state into the *estatalidad abierta*.[867] Second, 'more favourable' clauses do 'not decide the precedence on the basis of the hierarchical position of the norm nor of a specific court, but instead on the basis of *substantive* criteria'.[868] The *pro homine* principle likewise demands that decision makers consider various international and national norms and select the most protective *substance* regardless of their hierarchy.[869] Third, 'more favourable' clauses, compared to the traditional value-oriented doctrine of restrictive interpretation in favour of State sovereignty, typify the new trend where 'in case of doubt, the interpretation more favourable to the private party must be preferred'.[870] The *pro homine* principle, as graphically expressed by the Latin maxim itself, also requires the norms in question to be interpreted and applied in the most favourable ways to *persons*.[871]

866 Lixinski (n 171) 597 (emphasis added).

867 Morales Antoniazzi (n 856) 250.

868 Van de Heyning (n 605) 72 (emphasis added).

869 Humberto Henderson, 'Los tratados internacionales de derechos humanos en el orden interno: la importancia del principio *pro homine*' (2004) 39 *Revista IIDH* 71–99, 92.

870 Luigi Crema, 'Disappearance and New Sightings of Restrictive Interpretation(s)' (2010) 21 *European Journal of International Law* 681–700, 690–691. Although Crema did not consider 'more favorable' clauses in this article such as Article 29(b) ACHR (at 688, footnote 53), he evaluated the *pro homine* principle, embedded in this provision, as a new trend.

871 Mónica Pinto, 'El principio *pro homine*: criterios de la hermenéutica y pautas para la regulación de los derechos humano', in Martín Abregú and Christian

Chapter 2 of both Parts I and II also reveals the context-based variability between the *concentration* and *decentralisation* of conventionality control powers among regional, constitutional and ordinary courts. At the international level, the positive aspect of subsidiarity enables regional courts to *open up* the state black box to identify the pertinent remedial measures and national organs that depend on the *substantive* inability and unwillingness of the latter to protect *human* rights. Inversely, the negative aspect of subsidiarity requires regional courts to be *openly* deferential to States Parties to the extent that national authorities *substantively* behave as the primary guardians of *human* rights. At the domestic level, the task of conventionality control is *open* to all ordinary judges who are required to exercise their *substantive* mandates to disapply and consistently interpret legislation in accordance with *human* rights parameters under the Conventions. The inter-authority relationship for conventionality control, however, is *openly* flexible so that constitutional judges may be trusted when necessary to strike a *substantive* balance between *human* rights and legal certainty and democracy.

The normative trapezium model of conventionality control may be conditioned by taking into account the empirical comparative differences between the ACHR and the ECHR context. As regards the parameters of conventionality control, while the *pro homine* principle reflected in Article 29(b) ACHR has been widely accepted in Latin America, the regional and national courts in Europe have not manifestly adopted the principle. Even when referring to the 'more favourable' provision, Article 53 ECHR, they limit its purpose only to preserving national discretion in human rights protection. In cases of conflicting rights, whereas the San José Court employs the *pro homine* principle, the Strasbourg Court instead prefers the margin of appreciation doctrine. The cautious attitude of European judiciaries can lead to a convincing counterargument that the *pro homine* principle does not work at all in the ECHR implementation. With respect to the powers of conventionality control, the Inter-American Court has been relatively interventionist by means of positive subsidiarity by diminishing national discretion to combat the culture of impunity. Under the influence of the IACtHR's doctrine mandating all judges to exercise conventionality control, ordinary judges in Latin American countries tend to behave as Inter-American guardians in the diffused fashion of judicial review. In contrast, the European Court has maximally shown its deference to national

---

Courtis (eds), *La aplicación de los tratados sobre derechos humanos por los tribunales locales* (Centro de Estudios Legales y Sociales 1997) 163–171, 164–165.

authorities in light of negative subsidiarity. Several constitutional courts in Europe have developed to concentrate their own authorities to manage the relations between a conventional and a constitutional bill of rights.

Those disparities, however, should not be taken as a clear-cut contrast between the Latin American and European attitudes but rather corroborate the normative trapezium model by progressively converging with each other from different angles. Inter-American jurisprudence started to recognise a certain degree of national discretion when domestic authorities, particularly constitutional courts, achieved adequate conventionality control for the sake of individuals in a minute balance with legal certainty and democracy. In this sense, the *pro homine* principle embedded in Article 29 ACHR and the margin of appreciation doctrine can move in concert, aiming at the ultimate purpose of the Inter-American human rights system.[872] On the European side, indirectly through the development of Article 53 CFREU as the counterpart of Article 53 ECHR, the idea of *pro homine* can be implied to attenuate the absolute supremacy of either international or constitutional law. By granting a margin of appreciation to States Parties, the European approach rather 'allows the consideration of a role of the state' as an 'expression of the principle of good faith' in interpreting human rights.[873] In essence, the Inter-American and European experiences of conventionality control are two sides of the same coin, and probably, their converging realities will let us get closer to the ideal of *ius constitutionale commune regionale*.

---

872 José Luis Caballero Ochoa, 'La cláusula de interpretación conforme y el principio *pro persona* (artículo 1º., segundo párrafo, de la Constitucion)' in Miguel Carbonell and Pedro Salazar (eds), *La reforma constitucional de derechos humanos: un nuevo paradigma* (Instituto de Investigaciones Jurídicas de la Universidad Nacional Autónoma de México 2012) 103–133, 119–121. See also, Separate Opinion of JudgeMacGregor Poisot, *Gelman*, Order (n 375) para 72.

873 Crema (n 872) 699.

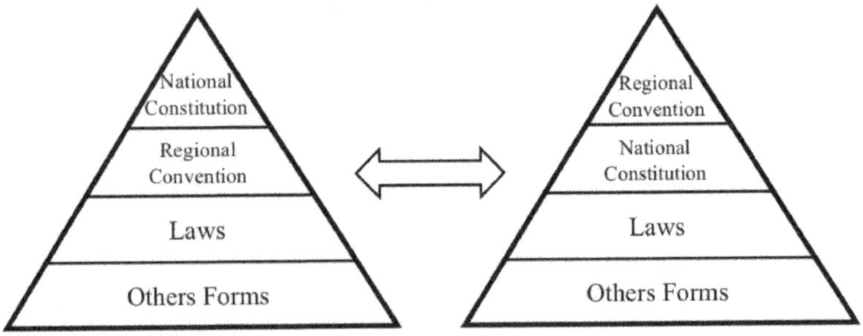

Figure 1. The Monism Pyramids: Supremacy of National Constitution or Regional Convention

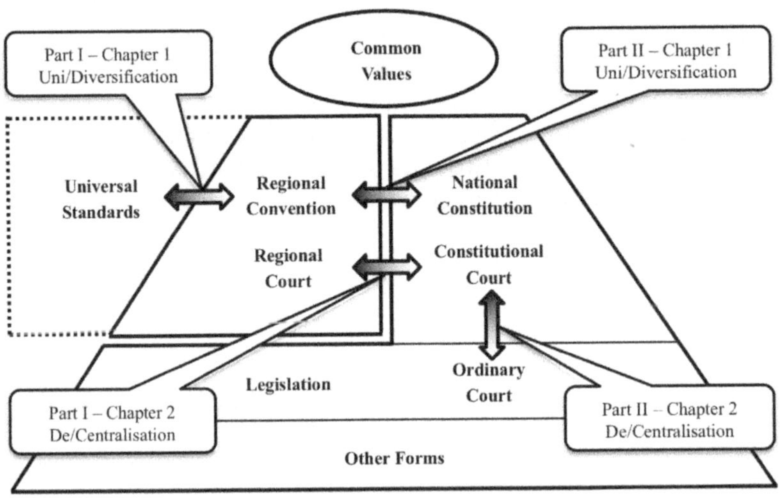

Figure 2. The Constitutional Pluralist Trapezium of Conventionality Control

Bibliography

Permanent Court of International Justice / International Court of Justice

Factory at Chorzów (Germany vs Poland), PCIJ, Series A No 9, Judgment on Jurisdiction of 26 July 1927, 21

Exchange of Greek and Turkish Populations, PCIJ, Series B No 10, Advisory Opinion of 21 February 1925

Jurisdiction of the Courts of Danzig (Advisory Opinion), PCIJ Rep Series B No 15 (1928) 17–18.

Legal Consequences for States of the Continued Presence of South Africa in Namibia (South West Africa) notwithstanding Security Council Resolution 276 (1970), ICJ Reports 1971

LaGrand (Germany vs United States of America), Judgment, ICJ Report 2001

Arrest Warrant of 11 April 2000 (Democratic Republic of the Congo vs Belgium), Judgment, ICJ Report 2002

Avena and Other Mexican Nationals (Mexico vs United States of America), Judgment, ICJ Report 2004

Dispute regarding Navigational and Related Rights (Costa Rica v Nicaragua), Judgment, ICJ Reports 2009

Ahmadou Sadio Diallo (Republic of Guinea v. Democratic Republic of the Congo, Merits, Judgment, ICJ Reports 2010 (Separate opinion of Judge Cançado Trindade; Joint Declaration of Judges Keith and Greenwood)

Whaling in the Antarctic (Australia v Japan: New Zealand intervening), Judgment, ICJ Reports 2014

Jadhav (India v. Pakistan), Judgment, ICJ Reports 2019, 418

Human Rights Committee

General Comment No 33 on Obligations of States parties under the Optional Protocol to the International Covenant on Civil and Political Rights, HRC, UN Doc CCPR/C/GC/33 (2009)

Judge v *Canada*, HRC, Communication No 829/1998, UN Doc CCPR/C/78/D/829/1998, View of 13 August 2003

Correia de Matos v Portugal, HRC, Comm No 1123/2002, UN Doc CCPR/C/86/D/1123/2002, Views of 28 March 2006

Elgueta v. Chile, HRC, Comm No 1536/2006, CCPR/C/96/D/1593/2006, Decision of 28 July 2009 (Individual Opinion of Helen Keller and Fabián Salvioli)

Yaker v France, HRC, Comm No 2747/2016, UN Doc CCPR/C/123/D/2807/2016, View of 17 July 2018 UN Doc. CCPR/C/123/D/2747/2016

Hebbadi v. France, Communication No. 2807/2016, View of 17 July 2018, UN Doc CCPR/C/123/D/2807/2016

Council of Europe

[Judgments, Decisions and Opinions of the European Court of Human Rights]

Ireland v the United Kingdom, ECtHR (Plenary), App no 5310/71, Judgment on Merits of 18 January 1978

Tyrer v the United Kingdom, ECtHR, App No5856/72, Judgment on Merits of 25 April 1978

Marckx v Belgium, ECtHR, App No 6833/74, Judgment of 13 June 1979

Rees v the United Kingdom, ECtHR (Plenary), App. No. 9532/81, Judgment on Mertis of 17 October 1986

Vermeire v Belgium, ECtHR, App No 12849/87, Judgment on Merits of 9 November 1991

Open Door and Dublin Well Woman v Ireland, ECtHR, App Nos 14234/88 and 14235/88, Judgment on Merits and Just Satisfaction of 29 October 1992

Loizidou v Turkey, ECtHR (Grand Chamber), App No 15318/89, Judgment on Preliminary Ojbections of 23 March 1995

Brualla Gómez de la Torre v Spain, ECtHR, App No 155/1996/774/975, Judgment on Merits and Just Satisfaction of 19 December 1997

The United Communist Party of Turkey and Others v Turkey, ECtHR, App No 19392/92, Judgment on Merits and Just Satisfaction of 30 January 1998

Sheffield and Horsham v the United Kingdom, ECtHR (Grand Chamber), App Nos 22985/93 and 23390/94, Judgment on Merits of 30 July 1998

Kudła v Poland, ECtHR, App No 30210/96, Judgment on Merits and Just Satisfaction of 26 October 2000

Karner v Austria, ECtHR, App No 40016/98, Judgment on Merits and Just Satisfaction of 24 July 2003

Christine Goodwin v the United Kingdom, ECtHR (Grand Chamber), App No 28957/95, Judgment on Merits and Just Satisfaction 11 July 2002

Maestri v Italy, ECtHR (Grand Chamber), App No 39748/98, Judgment on Merits and Just Satisfaction of 17 February 2004

Von Hannover v Germany (No 1), ECtHR, App No 59320/00, Judgment on Merits of 24 June 2004

Broniowski v Poland, ECtHR (Grand Chamber), App. No 31443/96, Judgment on Merits of 22 June 2004

Okyay and Others v. Turkey, ECtHR, App No 36220/97, Judgment on Merits and Just Satisfaction of 12 July 2005

Hirst v the United Kingdom (No 2), ECtHR (Grand Chamber), App No 74025/01, Judgment on Merits and Just Satisfaction of 6 October 2005

Xenides-Arestis v Turkey, ECtHR, App No 46347/99, Judgment on Merits of 22 December 2005

Scordino v Italy (No 1), ECtHR (Grand Chamber), App No 36813/97, Judgment on Merits and Just Satisfaction of 29 March 2006

Hutten-Czapska v Poland, ECtHR (Grand Chamber), App No 35014/97, Judgment on Merits and Just Satisfaction of 19 June 2006

Wolkenberg and Others v Poland, ECtHR, App No 50003/99, Decision of 4 December 2007

E B v France, ECtHR, App no 43546/02, Judgment on Merits and Just Satisfaction of 22 January 2008

Demir and Baykara v. *Turkey*, ECtHR (Grand Chamber), App No 34503/97, Judgment on Merits and Just Satisfaction of 12 November 2008

Burdov v Russia (No 2), ECtHR, App No. 33509/504, Judgment on Merits and Just Satisfaction of 15 January 2009

Sujagic v Bosnia Herzegovina, ECtHR, App No 27912/02, Judgment on Merits and Just Satisfaction of 3 November 2009

Sejdić and Finci v Bosnia and Herzegovina, ECtHR (Grand Chamber), App Nos 27996/06 and 34836/06, Judgment on Merits and Just Satisfaction of 22 December 2009

Demopoulos and Others v Turkey, ECtHR (Grand Chamber), App Nos 46113/99 and Others, Decision of 1 March 2010

Rumpf v Germany, ECtHR, App No 46344/06, Judgment on Merits and Just Satisfaction of 2 September 2010

Nagovitsyn and Nalgiyev v Russia, ECtHR, App Nos 27451/09 and 60650/09, Decision of 23 September 2010

Maria Atanasiu and Others v Romania, ECtHR, App Nos 30767/05 33800/06, Judgment on Merits and Just Satisfaction of 12 October 2010

Zadrić v Bosnia and Herzegovina, ECtHR, App No 18804/04, Decision of 16 November 2010

Greens and M T v the United Kingdom, ECtHR, App Nos 60041/08 and 60054/08, Judgment on Merits and Just Satisfaction of 23 November 2010

A, B and C v Ireland, ECtHR (Grand Chamber), App No 25579/05, Judgment on Merits and Just Satisfaction of 16 December 2010

Vassilios Athanasiou and Others v Greece, ECtHR, App No 50973/08, Judgment on Merits and Just Satisfaction of 21 December 2010

The Assocation of Real Property Owners in Łódź v Poland, ECtHR, App No 3485/02, Decision of 8 March 2011

Dimitrov and Hamanov v Bulgaria, ECtHR, App. No. 48059/06 and 2708/09, Judgment on Merits and Just Satisfaction of 10 May 2011

Al-Khawaja and Tahery v the United Kingdom, ECtHR (Grand Chamber), App Nos 26766/05 and 22228/06, Judgment on Merits and Just Satisfaction of 15 December 2011

Ananyev and Others v Russia, ECtHR, App No 42525/07 and 60800/08, Judgment on Merits and Just Satisfaction of 10 January 2012

Olaru and Others v the Republic of Moldova, ECtHR, App Nos 476/07, 22539/05, 17911/08 and 13136/07, Judgment on Merits of 28 July 2009; *Balan v the Republic of Moldova*, ECtHR, App No 44746/08, Decision of 24 January 2012

Von Hannover v Germany (No 2), ECtHR (Grand Chamber), App No 40660/08, Judgment on Merits and Just Satisfaction of 7 February 2012

Ümmühan Kaplan v Turkey, ECtHR, App No 24240/07, Judgment on Merits and Just Satisfaction of 20 March 2012

Ilyushkin and Others v Russia, ECtHR, App. Nos. 5734/08 and Others, Judgment on Merits and Just Satisfaction of 17 April 2012

Taron v Germany, ECtHR, App No 53126/07, Decision of 29 May 2012

Torreggiani and Others v Italy, ECtHR, App No 43517/09 and Others, Judgment on Merits and Just Satisfaction of 8 January 2013

Müdür Turgut and Others v Turkey, ECtHR, App No 4860/09, Decision of 26 March 2013

Valcheva and Abrashev v Bulgaria, ECtHR, App Nos 6194/11 and 34887/11, Decision of 18 June 2013

Techniki Olympiaki A E v Greece, ECtHR, App No 40547/10, Decision of 1 October 2013

Kurić and Others v Slovenia, ECtHR (Grand Chamber), App No 26828/06, Judgment on Just Satisfaction of 12 March 2014

The National Union of Rail, Maritime and Transport Workers (RMT) v. the United Kingdom, ECtHR, App No 31045/10, Judgment on Merits and Just Satisfaction of 8 April 2014 (Concurring Opinion of Judge Wojtyczek)

Preda and Others v Romania, ECtHR, App Nos 9584/0 and Others, Judgment on Merits and Just Satisfaction of 29 April 2014

SAS v France, ECtHR (Grand Chamber), App No 43835/11, Judgment on Merits and Just Satisfaction of 1 July 2014 (Partly Dissenting Opinion of Judges Angelika Nußberger and Helena Jäderblom)

Zornić v Bosnia and Herzegovina, ECtHR, App No 3681/06, Judgment on Merits and Just Satisfaction of 15 July 2014

Cyprus v Turkey, ECtHR (Grand Chamber), App No 25781/94, Judgment on Just Satisfaction of 12 May 2014 (Joint Concurring Opinion of Judges Zupančič, Gyulumyan, Davíd Thór Björgvinsson, Nicolaou, Sajó, Lazarova Trajkovska, Power-Forde, Vučinić and Pinto de Albuquerque)

Stella and Others v Italy, ECtHR, App Nos 49169/09 and Others, Decision of 16 September 2014

Neshkov and Other v Bulgaria, ECtHR, App Nos 36925/10 and Other, Judgment on Just Satisfaction of 27 January 2015

Varga and Others v Hungary, ECtHR, App Nos 14097/12 and Others, Judgment on Merits and Just Satisfaction of 10 March 2015

Rohlena v Czech Republic, EctHR (Grand Chamber), Appl. no. 59552/08, Judgment on Merits and Just Satisfaction of 27 January 2015 (Concurring Opinion of Judge Ziemele)

Pilav v Bosnia and Herzegovina, ECtHR, App No 41939/07, Judgment Merits and Just Satisfaction of 9 June 2016

Anastasov and Others v *Slovenia*, ECtHR, App No 65020/13, Decision of 10 October 2016

*Hiernaux v Bel*gium, ECtHR, App No 28022/15, Judgment on Merits and Just Satisfaction of 24 January 2017

Dakir v Belgium, ECtHR App No 4619/12, Judgment on Merits and Just Satisfaction of 11 July 2017

Belcacemi v Belgium, ECtHR, App No 37798/13, Judgment on Merits and Just Satisfaction of 11 July 2017

Correia de Matos v Portugal, ECtHR (Grand Chamber), App no 56402/12, Judgment on Merits and Just Satisfaction of 4 April 2018 (Joint Dissenting Opinion of Judges Tsotsoria, Motoc and Mits; Dissenting opinion of Judge Pinto de Albuquerque joined by Judge Sajó)

GIEM SRL and others v Italy, ECtHR (Grand Chamber), App No 1828/06 and others, Judgment on Merits of 28 June 2018 (Partly Concurring, Patly Dissenting Opinion of Judge Paulo Pinto de Albuquerque)

Advisory Opinion Concerning the Recognition in Domestic Law of a Legal Parent-child Relationship between a Child Born through a Gestational Surrogacy Arrangement Abroad and the Intended Mother, Advisory Opinion (Protocol 16) of 10 April 2019

Savelyev v Russia, ECtHR, App No 42982, Decision of 21 May 2019

Ilgar Mammadov v Azerbaijan, ECtHR (Grand Chamber), App No 15172/13, Judgment on Article 46(4) of 29 May 2019 (Joint Concurring Opinion of Judges Zupančič, Gyulumyan, David Thór Björgvinsson, Nicolaou, Sajó, Lazarova Trajkovska, Power-Forde, Vučinić and Pinto de Albuquerque)

Baralija v Bosnia and Herzegovina, ECtHR, App No 30100/18, Judgment on Merits and Just Satisfaction of 29 October 2019

Shmelev and Others v Russia, ECtHR, App Nos 41743/17 and Others, Decision of 17 March 2020

[Others]

The Parliamentary Assembly of the CoE, Resolution 1226 (2000), Execution of judgments of the European Court of Human Rights

Explanatory Report to Protocol No 14 to the Convention for the Protection of Human Rights and Fundamental Freedoms, amending the control system of the Convention, 13 May 2004

Explanatory Report to Protocol No 16 to the Convention for the Protection of Human Rights and Fundamental Freedoms, 5 June 2013

High Level Conference on the Future of the European Court of Human Rights Interlaken Declaration 19 February 2010

High Level Conference on the Future of the European Court of Human Rights, Izmir, Turkey 26 – 27 April 2011

High Level Conference on the Future of the European Court of Human Rights Brighton Declaration 19–20 April 2012

Venice Commission, Opinion on the Draft Amendments to the Constitution (as Signed by the President of the Russian Federation on 14 March 2020) Related to the Execution in the Russian Federation of Decisions by the European Court of Human Rights, CDL-AD(2020)009, 18 June 2020.

Organization of American States

[Advisory Opinion of the Inter-American Court of Human Rights (Series A)]

"Other Treaties" Subject to the Consultative Jurisdiction of the Court (Art. 64 American Convention on Human Rights), IACtHR, Series A No 1, OC-1/82, Advisory Opinion of 24 September 1982

Compulsory Membership in an Association Prescribed by Law for the Practice of Journalism (Arts. 13 and 29 American Convention on Human Rights), IACtHR, Series A No 5, Advisory Opinion of 13 November 1985

Habeas Corpus in Emergency Situations (Arts 27(2), 25(1) and 7(6) ACHR), IACtHR, Series A No 7, Advisory Opinion of 30 January 1987

Restrictions to the Death Penalty (Arts 4(2) and 4(4) American Convention on Human Rights), IACtHR, Series A No 8, Advisory Opinion of 8 September 1983

Certain Attributes of the Inter-American Commission on Human Rights (Arts. 41, 42, 44, 46, 47, 50 and 51 of the American Convention on Human Rights), IACtHR, Advisory Opinion OC-13/93 of 16 July 1993,

The Right to Information on Consular Assistance in the Framework of the Guarantees of Due Process of Law, IACtHR, Series A No 16, Advisory Opinion OC-16/99 of 1 October 1999

Juridical Condition and Human Rights of the Child, IACtHR, Series A No17, Advisory Opinion OC-17/02 of 28 August 2002

Rights and Guarantees of Children in the Context of Migration and/or in Need of International Protection, IACtHR, Series A No 21, Advisory Opinion OC-21/14 of 19 August 2014

Entitlement of Legal Entities to Hold Rights under the Inter-American Human Rights System (Interpretation and scope of Article 1(2), in relation to Articles 1(2), 8, 11(2), 13, 16, 21, 24, 25, 29, 30, 44, 46 and 62(3) of the American Convention on Human Rights, as well as of Article 8(1)(A) and (B) of the Protocol of San Salvador), IACtHR, Series A No 22, Advisory Opinion OC-22/16 of 26 February 2016

Gender Identity, and Equality and Non-discrimination with Regard to Same-sex Couples, State Obligations in Relation to Change of Name, Gender Identity, and Rights Deriving from a Relationship between Same-sex Couples, IACtHR, Series A No 24, Advisory Opinion OC-24/17 of 24 November 2017

The Institution of Asylum, and Its Recognition as a Human Right under the Inter-American System of Protection (interpretation and scope of Arts 5, 22(7) and 22(8) in Relation to Art 1(1) of the American Convention on Human Rights), IACtHR, Series A No. 25, Advisory Opinion OC-25/18 of 3 May 2018

Denunciation of the American Convention on Human Rights and the Charter of the Organization of American States and the consequences for State human rights obligations (interpretation and scope of articles 1, 2, 27, 29, 30, 31, 32, 33 a 65 and 78 of the American Convention on Human Rights and 3(l), 17, 45, 53, 106 and 143 of the Charter of the Organization of American States), Series A No 26, Advisory Opinion OC-26/20 of 9 November 2020

[Judgements of the Inter-American Court of Human Rights (Series C)]

Aloeboetoe and Others v Suriname, IACtHR, Series C No 15, Judgment on Reparations and Costs of 10 September 1993

Caballero-Delgado and Santana v Colombia, IACtHR, Series C No 22, Judgment on Merits of 8 December 1995

Velásquez-Rodríguez v Honduras, Series C No 4, Judgment on Merits of 29 July 1988

Castillo-Páez v Peru, IACtHR, Series C, No. 34, Judgment on Merits of 3 November 1997

Bámaca-Velásquez v Guatemala, IACtHR, Series C No 70, Judgment on Merits of 25 November 2000

Barrios Altos v Peru, IACtHR, Series C No 75, Judgment on Merits of 14 March 2001

The Mayagna (Sumo) Awas Tingni Community v Constantine and Ohters v Trinidad and Tobago, IACtHR, Series C, No 82 Judgment on Preliminary Objections of 1 September 2001

Bámaca-Velásquez v Guatemala, IACtHR, Series C No. 91, Judgment on Reparations and Costs of 22 February 2002

Baena-Ricardo Others v Panama, IACtHR, Series C No 104, Judgment on Preliminary Objections of 28 November 2003

Nicaragua, IACtHR, Series C No 79, Judgment on Merits, Reparations and Costs of 31 August 2001

The Yakye Axa Indigenous Community v Paraguay, IACtHR, Series C No 125, Judgment on Merits, Reparations and Costs of 17 June 2005

The Mapiripán Massacre v Colombia, IACtHR, Series C No 134, Judgment on Merits, Reparations and Costs of 15 September 2005

Sawhoyamaxa Indigenous Community v Paraguay, IACtHR, Series C No 146, Judgment on Merits, Reparations and Costs. Judgment of 29 March 2006

The Ituango Massares v Colombia, IACtHR, Series C No 148, Judgment on Preliminary Objections, Merits, Reparations and Costs of 1 July 2006

Claude Reyes v Chile, IACtHR, Series C No 151, Judgment on Merits, Reparations and Costs of 19 September 2006

Almonacid-Arellano and Others v Chile, IACtHR, Series C No 154, Judgment on Preliminary Objections, Merits, Reparations and Costs of 26 September 2006

The Dismissed Congressional Employees (Aguado-Alfaro and Others) v Peru, IACtHR, Series C No 158, Preliminary Objections, Merits, Reparations and Costs, Judgment of 24 November 2006

La Cantuta v Peru, IACtHR, Series C No 162, Judgment on Merits, Reparations and Costs 29 November 2006 (Separate Opinion of Judge Sergio García-Ramírez)

The Saramaka People v Suriname, IACtHR, Series C No 172, Judgment on Preliminary Objections, Merits, Reparations and Costs of 28 November 2007

Radilla Pacheco v Mexico Series C No 209, IACtHR, Judgment on Preliminary Objections, Merits, Reparations and Costs of 23 November 2009

The 'Las Dos Erres' Massacre v Guatemala, IACtHR, Series C No 211, Judgment on Preliminary Objection, Merits, Reparations, and Costs of 24 November 2009

Cepeda Vargas v Colombia, IACtHR, Series C, No 213, Judgment on Preliminary Objections, Merits, Reparations and Costs of 26 May 2010 (Concurring opinion of Judge Diego García-Sayán)

Vélez Loor v Panama, IACtHR, Series C No 218, Judgment on Preliminary Objections, Merits, Reparations, and Costs of 23 November 2010

Gelman v Uruguay, IACtHR, Series C No 221, Judgment on Merits and Reparations of 24 February 2011

Cabrera Garcia and Montiel Flores v Mexico, IACtHR, Series C No 220, Judgment on Preliminary Objection, Merits, Reparations and Legal Costs of 26 November 2010 (Concurring Opinion of Judge *ad hoc* MacGregor Poisot)

Dimitrov and Hamanov v Bulgaria and *Finger v Bulgaria*, App Nos 48059/06 and 2708/09, Judgment on Merits and Just Satisfaction of 10 May 2011

Finger v Bulgaria, App No 37346/05, Judgment on Merits and Just Satisfaction of 10 May 2011

Fontevecchia and D'Amico v Argentina, IACtHR, Series C No 238, Judgment on Merits, Reparations and Costs of 29 November 2011

Atala Riffo and Daughters v. *Chile*, IACtHR, Series C No. 239, Merits, Reparations and Costs, Judgment of 24 February 2012

Kichwa Indigenous People of Sarayaku v. Ecuador, IACtHR, Series C No. 245, Judgment on Merits and Reparations 27 June 2012

The Massacres of El Mozote and Surrounding Areas v El Salvador, IACtHR, Series C No 252, Judgment on Merits, Reparations and Costs of 25 October 2012 (Concurring Opinion of Judge Diego García Sayán)

The Santo Domingo Massacre v Colombia, IACtHR, Series C No 259, Judgment on Preliminary Objections, Merits and Reparations of 30 November 2012

Artavia Murillo and Othres ('in vitro Fertilization') v Costa Rica, IACtHR, Seiries C No 257, Judgement on Preliminary Objections, Merits, Reparations and Costs of 28 November 2012

The Afro-descendant Communities Displaced from the Cacarica River Basin (Operation Genesis) v Colombia, IACtHR, Series C No 270, Judgment on Preliminary Objections, Merits, Reparations and Costs, Judgment of 20 November 2013

The Pacheco Tineo Family v Plurinational State of Bolivia, IACtHR, Series C No 272, Judgment on Preliminary Objections, Merits, Reparations and Costs of 25 November 2013

Rodríguez Vera and others (the Disappeared from the Palace of Justice) v Colombia, IACtHR, Series C No 287, Judgment on Preliminary Objections, Merits, Reparations and Costs of 14 November 2014

Norín Catrimán and Others (Leaders, Members and Activist of the Mapuche Indigenous People) v Chile, IACtHR, Series C No 279, Judgment on Merits, Reparations and Costs of 29 May 2014

Expelled Dominicans and Haitians v. Dominican Republic, IACtHR, Series C No 282, Judgment on Preliminary Objections, Merits, Reparations and Costs of 28 August 2014

Liakat Ali Alibux v Surinam, IACtHR, Series C No 276, Judgment on Preliminary Objections, Merits, Reparations and Costs of 30 January 2014 (Concurring Opinion of Judge Eduardo Ferrer MacGregor Poisot)

Duque v Colombia, IACtHR, Series C No 310, Judgment on Preliminary Objections, Merits, Reparations and Costs of 26 February 2016

Andrade Salmón v Bolivia, IACtHR, Series C No 330, Judgment on Merits, Reparations and Costs of 1 December 2016

Vásquez Durand and Others v Ecuador, Series C No 332, Judgment on Preliminary Objections, Merits, Reparations and Costs 15 of February 2017

The Employees of the Fireworks Factory of Santo Antônio de Jesus v Brazil, IACtHR, Series C No 407, Judgment on Preliminary Objections, Merits, Reparations and Cost of July 15, 2020, para 156. See also, *Lagos del Campo v Peru*, IACtHR, Series C No 340, Judgment on Preliminary Objections, Merits, Reparations and Costs of 31 August 2017

Amrhein y otros v Costa Rica, IACtHR, Serie C No 354, Judgment of Preliminary Objections, Merits, Reparations and Costs of 25 April 2018

Colindres Schonenberg v El Salvador, IACtHR, Series C No. 373, Judgment of Merits, Reparations and Costs of 4 February 2019

Rosadio Villavicencio v Peru, IACtHR, Series C No 388, Judgment of Preliminary Objections, Merits, Reparations and Costs of 14 October 2019

The National Association of Discharged and Retired Employees of the National Tax Administration Superintendence (ANCEJUB-SUNAT) v Peru, IACtHR, Series C No 394, Judgment on Preliminary Objections, Merits, Reparations and Costs of 21 November 2019

The Indigenous Communities of the Lhaka Honhat Association (Our Land) v Argentina, IACtHR, Series C No 400, Judgment on Merits, Reparations and Costs of 6 February 2020

[**Orders of the Inter-American Court of Human Rights**]

Almonacid-Arellano and Others vs Chile, IACtHR, Monitoring Compliance with Judgment, Order of 18 November 2010

Radilla Pacheco v Mexico, IACtHR, Monitoring Compliance with Judgment, Order of 19 May 2011

Apitz-Barbera and Others ('First Court of Administrative Cisputes') v Venezuela, IACtHR, Monitoring Compliance with Judgment, Order of 23November 2012

Gelman v Uruguay, IACtHR, Monitoring Compliance with Judgment, Order of 20 March 2013

Radilla Pacheco v Mexico, IACtHR, Monitoring Compliance with Judgment, Order of 14 May 2013

Artavia Murillo and Others (In Vitro Fertilization) v Costa Rica, IACtHR, Monitoring Compliance with Judgments, Order of 26 February 2016 (Individual Dissenting Opinion of Judge Eduardo Vio Grossi)

The Massacres of El Mozote and Surrounding Areas v El Salvador, IACtHR, Order on Monitoring Compliance with Judgment of 31 August 2017

Fontevecchia and D'Amico v Argentina, IACtHR, Monitoring Compliance with Judgment, Order of 18 October 2017

Norín Catrimán and Others (Leaders, Members and Activist of the Indigenous Mapuche People) v Chile, IACtHR, Monitoring Compliance with Judgment, Order of 28 November 2018

Artavia Murillo and Others (In Vitro Fertilization) and Case of Gómez Murillo and Others v Costa Rica, Monitoring Compliance with Judgments. Order of the Inter-American Court of Human Rights of 22 November 2019

Fontevecchia and D'Amico v Argentina, IACtHR, Monitoring Compliance with Judgment, Order of 11 March 2020

Gelman v Uruguay, IACtHR, Monitoring Compliance with Judgment, Order of 19 November 2020

[Others]

IACHR, Press Release: IACHR Notes Uruguay Court Decision Limiting the Application of Statute of Limitations to Crime Committed during the Dictatorship, June 24, 2019, available at https://www.oas.org/en/iachr/media_center/PReleases/2019/158.asp.

Intervención del Presidente de la Corte Interamericana de Derechos Humanos, Juez Antonio Augusto Cançado Trindade, ante el Plenario de la Asamblea General de la Organización de los Estados Americanos, Barbados, 4 de junio de 2002

Court of Justice of the European Union

Case 6/64 *Costa v ENEL* [1964] ECR 585

Case 11/70 *Internationale Handelsgesellschaft v Einfuhr- und Vorratsstelle für Getreide und Futtermittel* [1970] ECR 1125

Case 106/77, *Amministrazione delle Finanze dello Stato v. Simmenthal SpA* [1978] ECR 629

Case 106/77 Amministrazione delle Finanze dello Stato v Simmenthal SpA [1978] ECR 629

Cases C-188/10 and C-189/10, *Aziz Melki and Sélim Abdeli*, CJEU, Judgment of 22 June 2010

Case C 571/10, *Servet Kamberaj v Istituto per l'Edilizia sociale della Provincia autonoma di Bolzano (IPES) and Others*, CJEU, Judgment of 24 April 2012

Case C-399/11, *Stefano Melloni v Ministerio Fiscal*, CJEU, Judgment of 26 February 2013

Case C-617/10, *Åklagaren v Hans Åkerberg Fransson*, CJEU, Judgment of 26 February 2013

Case C-112/113, *A v B and others*, CJEU, Judgment of 11 September 2014

Case C-105/14, *Taricco and Others*, CJEU, Judgment of 8 September 2015

Case C-42/17 M A S, M B, CJEU, Judgment of 5 December 2017

Opinion 2/13 of 18 December 2014

Opinion of Advocate General Bot in Case C-42/17 M A S, M B, para 166.

National Practices

[Argentine]

Suprema Corte de Justicia de la Nación de Argentina, *Simón, Julio Héctor y otros*, Causa No 17.768, Sentencia de 17 de junio de 2005

Suprema Corte de Justicia de la Nación de Argentina, Resolución 4015/17 de 5 diciembre de 2017

Suprema Corte de Justicia de la Nación de Argentina, Fallos 329:2265, Sentencia de 20 junio 2006

[Austria]

Bundesverfafssungsgesetz vom 4. März, mit dem Bestimmungen des Bundesverfassungsfesetzes in der Fassung von 1929 über Staatsverträge abgeändert und ergänzt weden, 59/1964

Verfassungsgerichtshof Österreich, U 466/11–18 und U 1836/11–13, Erkenntnis vom 14 März 2012

[Belgium]

Cour de Cassation belge, *Fromagerie franco-suisse Le Ski. État Belge c SA*, arrêt du 27 mai 1971

Cour Constitutionnelle belge, Arrêt n° 195/2009 du 3 décembre 2009

Cour constitutionnelle belge, Arrêt n° 159/2004 du 20 octobre 2004

[Bolivia]

Tribunal Constitucional de Bolivia, Exp 2009–20768–42-AL, Sentencia 1907/2011-R de 7 de noviembre 2011

[Bosnia and Herzegovina]

Constitutional Court of Bosnia and Herzegovina, Decision of No. U 9/09 of 26 November 2010

[Brasil]

Supremo Tribunal Federal do Brasil, Recurso Extraordinário Nº 466,343, Julgamento do 3 de Dezembro de 2008

[Chile]

Corte Suprema de Justicia de Chile, Sentencia 740–07-CDS de 18 abril 2008

Corte Suprema de Justicia de Chile, Sentencia AD 1386–2014 de 16 de mayo de 2019

[Colombia]

Corte Constitucional de Colombia, Exp T-357702, Sentencia T-1319–01 de 7 de diciembre de 2001

Corte Constitucional de Colombia, Exp D-7473, Sentencia C-372/09 de 27 mayo 2009

Corte Constitucional de Colombia, Exp T-3005221, Sentencia SU712/13 de 17 octubre de 2013

[Costa Rica]

Sala Constitucional de la Corte Suprema de Justicia de Costa Rica, Exp 0421-S-90, Res N° 2313–95 de 9 mayo de 1995

Sala Constitucional de la Corte Suprema de Justicia de Costa Rica, Exp 08–012101–0007-CO, Res Nº 2008018884 de 19 deciembre 2008

Sala Constitucional de la Corte Suprema de Justicia de Costa Rica, Exp 15–013929–0007, Res Nº 01692/2016 de 3 febrero 2016

Sala Constitucional de la Corte Suprema de Justicia de Costa Rica, Exp 15–013971–0007-CO, Res Nº 2018012782 de 8 de agosto del 2018

[Dominican Republic]

Corte Suprema de Justicia de República Dominicana, Res Nº 1920–2003 de 13 de noviembre de 2003

Tribunal Constitucional de República Dominicana, Exp TC-01–2005–0013, Sentencia de TC/0256/14 de 4 de noviembre de 2014

[Ecudador]

Corte Constitucional del Ecuador, Caso 0003–08-IS, Sentencia 0001–09-SIS-CC de 19 de mayo de 2009

[El Salvador]

Sala de lo Constitucional de la Corte Suprema de Justicia de El Salvador, Sentencia 52–2003/56–2003/57–2003 de 1 abril 2004

Sala de lo Constitucional de la Corte Suprema de Justicia de El Salvador, Sentencia 31–2004/34–2004/38–2004/6–2005/9–2005 de 6 de junio de 2008

Sala de lo Constitucional de la Corte Suprema de Justicia de El Salvador, Inconstitucionalidad 44–2013/145–2013, Sentencia de 13 de julio de 2016

[Germany]

BVerfG, *Solange I*, 2 BvL 52/71, Entscheidung vom 29. Mai 1974

BVerfG, *Solange II*, 2 BvR 197/83, Entscheidung vom 22. Oktober 1986

BVerfG, *Görgülü*, 2 BvR 1481/04, Entscheidung vom 14. Oktober 2004

BVerfG, 2 BvR 2365/09, Entscheidung vom 4. Mai 2011

BVerfG, 2 BvL 1/12, Entscheidung vom 15. Dezember 2015

BVerfG, 2 BvR 2735/14, Entscheidung vom 15. Dezember 2015

BVerfG, 2 BvR 1738/12 et al, Entscheidung vom vom 12. Juni 2018

[France]

Conseil constitutionnel de la République Française, Décision n° 74–54 DC du 15 janvier 1975

[Honduras]

Sala de lo Constitucional de la Corte Suprema de Justicia de Honduras, Recurso de inconstitucionalidad (acumulado), Nos. 55 y 88, 13 de noviembre de 2007

[Hungary]

Hungarian Constitutional Court, Decision 22/2016. (XII. 5.) AB of 30 November 2016

[Italy]

Corte costituzionale italiana, *Frontini v. Ministerio delle Finanze*, Sentenza № 183 del 27 dicembre 1973

Corte constituzionale italilana, Sentenza № 317 del 3 novembre 2007

Corte constituzionale italilana, Sentenze № 348 e 349 del 24 ottobre 2007

Corte costituzionale italiana, Sentenza № 238 del 22 ottobre 2014

Corte costituzionale italiana, Sentenza № 49 del 1 maggio 2015

Corte costituzionale italiana, Sentenza № 24/2017 del 23 novembre 2016

Corte costituzionale italiana, Sentenza № 269 del 7 novembre 2017

[Malawi]

High Court of Malawi, Moyo v Attorney General, Constitutional Review, Constitutional Case No 12 of 2007, Judgment of 26th August 2009 (ILDC 1370 (MW 2009) analysed by Mwiza Jo Nkhata)

[Mexico]

Suprema Corte de Justicia de la Nación de México, *Radilla-Pacheco v Estados Unidos Mexicanos*, Exp Varios 912/2010, 4, 5, 7, 11, 12 y 14 julio 2011

Contradicción de Tesis 293/2011, SCJN de México, Sentencia de 3 septiembre de 2013

[**Norway**]

Norges Høyesterett, HR-2011–00182-A, 26. januar 2011 (for Engish translation Mads Andenas and Eirik Bjorge, 'The Norwegian Court Applies the ECHR by Building upon Its Underlying Principles' (2013) 19 *European Public Law* 241–248)

[Peru]

Tribunal Constitucional de Perú, Exp. 1417–2005-AA/TC, Sentencia de 8 julio 2005

Tribunal Constitucional de Perú, Exp 0047–2004-AI/TC, Sentencia de 24 de abril de 2006

Tribunal Constitucional de Perú, *Colegio de Abogados del Callao c. Congreso de la República*, Perú, Causa N° 00007–2007-PI-TC, Sentencia de 19 de Junio, 2007; ILDC 961 (PE 2007), reported by Salmón Gárate, E

[Poland]

Poland, the Chancellery of the Prime Minister, the White Paper on the Reform of the Polish Judiciary, 7 March 2018

[Russia]

The Russian Constitutional Court, Decision No. 21-П/2015 of 14 July 2015.

The Russian Constitutional Court, Decision No 1-Z of 16 March 2020 (for English translation, Venice Commission's unofficial translation, CDL-REF(2020)022, 30 April 2020)

[South Africa]

Constitutional Court of South Africa, Government of South Africa and ors v Grootboom, Appeal to Constitutional Court, [2000] ZACC 19, 2001 (1) SA 46, 2000 (11) BCLR 1169 (CC), 4 October 2000, paras 26–31 (ILDC 285 (ZA 2000) analysed by Waruguru Kaguongo)

[Spain]

Tribunal Constitucional español, Sentencia STC 1/1981 de 26 de febrero

Tribunal Constitucional español, Declaración 1/2004 de 13 diciembre 2004 (Voto particular concurrente que formula la Magistrada doña Encarnación Roca Trías)

Tribunal Constitucional español, Sentencia 91/2000 de 4 de mayo de 2000

Tribunal Constitucional español, Sentencia 26/2014 de 13 febrero 2014

[The Netherlands]

Hoge Raad der Nederlanden, NJ 2002/278, 10 augustus 2001 (for English translation, Nick S Efthymiou and Joke C de Wit, 'The Role of Dutch Courts in the Protection of Fundamental Rights', (2013) 9 *Utrecht Law Review* 75–88)

[The United Kingdom]

Trendtex Trading Corporation v Central of Bank of Nigeria [1977] 1 QB 529

Ghaidan v Mendoza [2004] 3 WLR 113

R(Miller) v Secretary of State for Exiting the European Union [2017] UKSC 5

R (on the application of Ullah) v Special Adjudicator [2004] UKHL 26, [2004] 2 AC 323

R v Horncastle and others [2009] UKSC 14

[The United States of America]

Murray v Charming Betsy, 6 U.S. (2 Cranch) 64 (1804), 18.

Medellín v Texas, 552 US 491 (2008)

[Uruguay]

Corte Suprema de Justicia de Uruguay, *Sabalsagaray Curutchet, Blanca Stela. Denuncia de Excepción de Inconstitucionalidad*, Sentencia Nº 365 de 19 de octubre de 2009

Corte Suprema de Justicia de Uruguay, *Gelman*, Caso 20/2013, Proceso de Inconstitucionalidad. Sentencia de 22 de febrero de 2013

[Venezuela]

Sala Constitucional del Tribunal Supremo de Justicia de Venezuela, Sentencia Nº 1942 de 13 noviembre 2003, at consideraciones para decidir I.

Sala Constitucional del Tribunal Supremo de Justicia de Venezuela, Sentencia Nº 87 de 14 de marzo de 2000 (81 *Revista de Derecho Público* (2000) 157)

Sala Constitucional del Tribunal Supremo de Justicia de Venezuela, Sentencia Nº 1942

Miscellaneous

Prosecutor v. Tadić, ICTY, Case No. IT-94–1, Appeals Chamber, Interlocutory Appeal on Jurisdiction, Judgment of 2 October 1995

Guidelines: The Obligations of a State and Its Domestic Courts with Respect to a Decision Issued by an International Judicial or Quasi-judicial Body Involving International Human Rights Law, annexed to *Johannesburg Conference Resolution No 2/2016*, the Committee on International Human Rights Law, the 77th Conference of the International Law Association, held in Johannesburg, South Africa, 7–11 August 2016

The Final Report of the ILA Study Group on Principles on the Engagement of Domestic Courts with International Law, the 77th Conference of the International Law Association, held in Johannesburg, South Africa, 7–11 August 2016

United Nations Conference on Trade and Development (UNCTAD), 'Denunciation of the ICSID Convention and BITs: Impact on Investor-State Claims' (2010) 2 *IIA Issues Note* 1–10

Amnesty International, *The State of African Regional Human Rights Bodies and Mechanisms 2019–2020*, 41–42

Contesse, Jorge, 'The Supreme Court of Chile as an inter-American Tribunal' I·CONnect (Blog of the International Jounal of Constitutional Law, 31 May 2019, available at: http://www.iconnectblog.com/2019/05/the-supreme-court-of-chile-as-an-inter-american-tribunal

Fachin, Melina Girardi and Nowak, Bruna, *The Joint Declaration to the Inter-American System of Human Rights: Backlash or Contestation?* Internationall Journal of Constitutional Law Blog, 12 December 2019, at: http://www.iconnectblog.com/2019/12/the-joint-declaration-to-the-inter-american-system-of-human-rights-backlash-or-contestation/

Peters, Anne, *Let Not Triepel Triumph – How To Make the Best Out of Sentenza No. 238 of the Italian Constitutional Court for a Global Legal Order*, EJIL: *Talk!*, 22 December 2014, available at http://www.ejiltalk.org/let-not-triepel-triumph-how-to-make-the-best-out-of-sentenza-no-238-of-the-italian-constitutional-court-for-a-global-legal-order-part-i/

Smirnova, Maria, Russian Constitutional Court Affirms Russian Constitution's Supremacy over ECtHR Decisions' EJIL: *Talk!*, 15 July 2015, available at http://www.ejiltalk.org/russian-constitutional-court-affirms-russian-constitutions-supremacy-over-ecthr-decisions/

Report of the International Law Commission, 70th sess, UN Doc A/73/10, 64–70.

Yearbook of International Law Commission, 1973 Vol. II, A/CN.4/SER.A/1973/Add.1, 253.

Literature

Acosta-López, Juana I, 'The Inter-American Human Rights System and the Colombian Peace: Redefining the Fight Against Impunity' (2016) 110 *American Journal of International Law* 178–182

Aguilar Cavallo, Gonzalo, 'El control de convencionalidad; análisis en derecho comparado' (2013) 9 *Revista Direito GV* 721–754

Akinkugbe, Olabisi, 'Towards an Analysis of the Mega-Political Jurisprudence of the ECOWAS Community Court of Justice' in James Thuo Gathii (eds), The Performance of Africa's International Courts: Using Litigation for Political, Legal, and Social Change (Oxford University Press 2020) 149–177

Alter, Karen J and Helfer, Laurence R, *Transplanting International Courts: The Law and Politics of the Andean Tribunal of Justice* (Oxford University Press 2017), 187; Salvatore Caserta, *International Courts in Latin America and the Caribbean: Foundations and Authority* (Oxford University Press 2020) 230–235

Alter, Karen J and Helfer, Laurence R (eds), *Transplanting International Courts: The Law and Politics of the Andean Tribunal of Justice* (Oxford University Press 2017)

Alter, Karen J, Gathii, James T and Helfer, Laurence R, 'Backlash against International Courts in West, East and Southern Africa: Causes and Consequences' (2016) 27 European Journal of International Law 293–328

Alter, Karen J, Laurence R Helfer and Osvaldo Saldías, 'Transplanting the European Court of Justice: The Experience of the Andean Tribunal of Justice' (2012) 60 *American Journal of Comparative Law* 629–664

Alter, Karen, 'The Multiple Roles of International Courts and Tribunals: Enforcement, Dispute Resolution, Constitutional and Administrative Review' in Jeffrey L Dunoff and Mark A Pollack (eds), *Interdisciplinary Perspectives on International Law and International Relations: The State of the Art* (Cambridge University Press 2012) 345–370

Amaya Villarreal, Álvaro Franciscco, 'El principio *pro homine*: Interpretación extensiva vs. el consentimiento del Estado' (2005) *Revista Colombiana de Derecho Internacional* 337–380

Amos, Merris, 'The Dialogue between United Kingdom Courts and the European Court of Human Rights' (2012) 61 Int'l & Comp. LQ 557.

Andenas, Mads and Bjorge, Eirik, '"Preventive Detention." No. 2 BvR 2365/09' (2011) 105 *American Journal of International Law* (2011) 768–774

Andenas, Mads and Bjorge, Eirik, 'National Implementation of ECHR Rights', in Andreas Føllesdal, Birgit Peters and Geir Ulfstein (eds), *Constituting Europe: The European Court of Human Rights in a National, European and Global Context* (Cambridge University Press 2013) 181–262

Antkowiak, Thomas M, 'An Emerging Mandate for International Courts: Victim Centered Remedies and Restorative Justice' (2011) 47 Stanford Journal of Internationall Law 270–332

Anzilotti, Dionisio, 'La responsabilité internationale des États à raison des dommages soufferts par des étrangers' (1906) 13 *Revue générale de droit international public* 5–29 and 284–309

Anzilotti, Dionisio, *Cours de droit international, Premier Volume: Introduction : Théorie génerales*, traduit par Gilbert Gidel) (Sirey 1929)

Arai-Takahashi, Yutaka, 'Disharmony in the Process of Harmonisation? – The Analytical Account of the Strasbourg Court's Variable Geometry of Decision-Making Policy Based on the Margin of Appreciation Doctrine' in Mads Andenas and Camilla Baasch Andersen (eds), *Theory and Practice of Harmonization* (Edward Elgar 2011) 95–114

Arai-Takahashi, Yutaka, The Margin of Appreciation Doctrine and the Principle of Proportionality in the Jurisprudence of the ECHR (Intersentia 2002)

Arias López, Boris Wilson, 'Entre la Constitución y los tratados de derechos humanos' (2014) 38 *Derecho y Cambio Social* 1–13

Arnardóttir, Oddný Mjöll, '*Res Interpretata*, *Erga Omnes* Effect and the Role of the Margin of Appreciation in Giving Domestic Effect to the Judgments of the European Court of Human Rights' (2017) 28 *European Journal of International Law* 819–843

Avbelj, Matej and Komárek, Jan, 'Introduction' in Matej Avbelj and Jan Komárek (eds), *Constitutional Pluralism in the European Union and Beyond* (Hart 2012) 1–15

Ayala Corao, Carlos, *Del diálogo jurisprudencial al Control de Convencionalidad* (Editorial Jurídica Venezolana 2012)

Baillet, C. M, 'Measuring Compliance with the Inter-American Court of Human Rights: The Ongoing Challenge of Judicial Independence in Latin America' (2013) 31 *Nordic Journal of Human Rights* 31 (2013) 477–495, 478–480

Baillet, Cecilia M, 'Measuring Compliance with the Inter-American Court of Human Rights: The Ongoing Challenge of Judicial Independence in Latin America' (2013) 31 *Nordic Journal of Human Rights* 477–495

Barraud, Boris, *Repensar la pyramide des normes à l'ère des réseaux : Pour une conception pragmatique du droit* (L'Harmattan 2012)

Barsotti, Vittoria, Paolo G Carozza, Marta Cartabia and Andrea Simoncini, *Italian Constitutional Justice in Global Context* (Oxford University Press 2016)

Basch, Fernando, Filippini, Leonardo, Laya, Ana, Nino, Mariano, Rossi, Felicitas and Schreiber, Bárbara, 'The Effectiveness of the Inter-American System of Human Rights Protection: A Quantitative Approach to Its Functioning and Compliance with Its Judgments' (2010) 7 *International Journal of Human Rights* 9–35

Bates, Ed, *The Evolution of the European Convention on Human Rights: From its Inception to the Creation of a Permanent Court of Human Rights* (Oxford University Press 2010)

Bates, Ed, *The Evolution of the European Convention on Human Rights: From its Inception to the Creation of a Permanent Court of Human Rights* (Oxford University Press 2010)

Bazán, Víctor, 'La interacción del derecho internacional de los derechos humanos y el derech interno en Argentina' (2007) 5 *Estudios Constitucionales* 137–183

Benvenisti, Eyal, 'Margin of Appreciation, Consensus, and Universal Standards' (1999) 31 *New York Journal of International Law and Policy* 834–854

Bernhardt, Rudolf, 'Just Satisfaction under the European Convention on Human Rights' in Maurizio Ragazzi (ed), *International Responsibility Today: Essays in Memory of Oscar Schachter* (Martinus Nijhoff Publishers 2005) 243–252

Besselink, Leonard F M, 'The Proliferation of Constitutional Law and Constitutional Adjudication or How American Judicial Review Came to Europe After All' (2013) 9 Utrecht Law Review 19–35

Besson, Samantha, 'The *Erga Omnes* Effect of Judgments of the European Court of Human Rights: What's in a Name?' in Samantha Besson (ed), *La Cour européenne des droits de l'homme après le Protocole 14: Premier bilan et perspectives* (Schulthess 2011) 125–175

Besson, Samantha, 'The Reception in Ireland and the United Kingdom' in Helen Keller and Alec Stone Sweet (eds), *A Europe of Rights: The Impact of the ECHR on National Legal Systems* (Oxford University Press 2008) 31–106

Bessson, Samantha, 'State Consent and Disagreement in International Law-making: Dissolving the Paradox' (2016) 29 *Leiden Journal of International Law* 289–316

Bessson, Samantha, 'The Authority of International Law: Lifting the State Veil' (2009) 31 *Sydney Law Review* 343–380

Beyani, Chaloka, 'Reconstituting the Universal: Human Rights as a Regional Idea' in Conor Gearty and Costas Douzinas (eds), *The Cambrdige Companion to Human Rights Law* (Cambridge University Press 2012) 173–190

Biaggini, Giovanni, 'Switzerland' in Dawn Oliver and Carlo Fusaro (eds), *How Constitutions Change: A Comparative Study* (2011) 303–328

Bianco, Giuseppe and Martinico, Giuseppe, 'Dialogue or Disobedience? On the Domestic Effects of the ECHR in Light of the *Kamberaj* Decision' (2014) 20 *European Public Law* 435–450

Bickel, Alexander M, *The Least Dangerous Branch: The Supreme Court at the Bar of Politics*, 2nd ed (Yale University Press 1986)

Biondi dal Monte, Francesca and Fontanelli, Filippo, 'The Decisions No. 348 and 349/2007 of the Italian Constitutional Court: The Efficacy of the European Convention in the Italian Legal System' (2008) 9 *German Law Journal* 889–932

Bjorge, Eirik, *The Evolutionary Interpretation of Treaties* (Oxford University Press 2014); Katharina Böth, *Evolutive Auslegung völkerrechtlicher Verträge: Eine Untersuchung zu Voraussetzungen und Grenzen in Anbetracht der Praxis internationaler Streitbeilegungsinstitutionen* (Duncker & Humbolt 2013)

Bodnar, Adam, '*Res Interpretata*: Legal Effect of the European Court of Human Rights' Judgments for other States Than Those Which Were Party to the Proceedings' in Yves Haeck and Eva Brems (eds), *Human Rights and Civil Liberties in the 21st Century* (Springer 2014) 223–262

Bonelli, Matteo, 'The Taricco Saga and the Consolidation of Judicial Dialogue in the European Union CJEU' (2018) 25 *Maastricht Journal of European and Comparative Law* 357–373, 364–365.

Bossuyt, Marc and Verrijdt, Willem, 'The Full Effect of EU Law and of Constitutional Review in Belgium and France after the *Melki* Judgment' (2011) 7 *European Constitutional Law Review* 355–391, 366–375.

Boudouhi, El, 'The National Judge as an Ordinary Judge of International Law? Invocability of Treaty Law in National Courts' (2015) 28 *Leiden Journal of International Law* 283–301

Brems, Eva, 'Positive Subsidiarity and Its Implications for the Margin of Appreciation Doctrine' (2019) 37 *Netherlands Quarterly of Human Rights* 210–227

Breuer, Marten, 'Principled Resistance' to ECtHR Judgments: An Appraisal' in Marten Breuer (ed), *Principled Resistance to ECtHR Judgments: A New Paradigm?* (Springer 2019) 323–350

Brewer-Carías, Allan R, *Constitutional Protection of Human Rights in Latin America: A Comparative Study of Amparo Proceedings* (Cambridge University Press 2009)

Bricker, Kristin, 'Military Justice and Impunity in Mexico's Drug War' (2011) 3 *CIGI Security Sector Reform Issue Paper* 2–13

Broude, Tomer, 'The Constitutional Function of Contemporary International Tribunals, or Kelsen's Visions Vindicated' (2012) 4 *Göttingen Journal of International Law* 519–549

Burgorgue-Larsen, Laurence, 'Exhaustion of Domestic Remedies' in Laurence Burgorgue-Larsen and Amaya Úbeda de Torres (eds), *The Inter-American Court of Human Rights: Case Law and Commentary* (Oxford University Press 2011) 129–145

Burgorgue-Larsen, Laurence, 'Interpreting the European Convention: What Can the African Human Rights System Learn from the Case Law of the European Court of Human Rights on the Interpretation of the European Convention?' (2012) 5 *Inter-American and European Human Rights Journal* 90–123

Burgorgue-Larsen, Laurence, 'La Corte Interamericana de Derechos Humanos como tribunal constitucional' in Armin von Bogdandy, Héctor Fix-Flerro and Mariela Morales Antoniazzi (eds), *Ius Constitutionale Commune en América Latina: Rasgos, Potencialidades y Desafios* (Universidd Nacional Autótonoma de México 2014) 421–457

Burgorgue-Larsen, Laurence, '*Nothing is Perfect* : Libres propos sur la méthodologie interpretative de la Cour européenne' in *L'homme et le droit : En hommage au Professeur Jean-François Flauss* (Pedone 2014) 129–143

Burke-White, William W, 'Proactive Complementarity: The International Criminal Court and National Courts in the Rome System of International Justice' (2008) 49 Harvard International Law Journal 53–108

Caballero Ochoa, José Luis, 'La cláusula de interpretación conforme y el principio *pro persona* (artículo 1º., segundo párrafo, de la Constitucion)' in Miguel Carbonell and Pedro Salazar (eds), *La reforma constitucional de derechos humanos: un nuevo paradigma* (Instituto de Investigaciones Jurídicas de la Universidad Nacional Autónoma de México 2012) 103–133

Cabranes, José A, 'Human Rights and Non-Intervention in the Inter-American System' (1967) 65 *Michigan Law Review* 1147–1182

Caflisch, Lucius and Cançado Trindade, Antonio Augusto, 'Les conventions américaine et européenne des Droits de l'Homme et le droit international général' (2004) 108 *Revue générale de droit international public* 5–62

Çalı, Başak, 'From Flexible to Variable Standards of Judicial Review: The Responsible Domestic Courts Doctrine at the European Court of Human Rights', in Oddný Mjöll Arnardóttir and Antoine Buyse (eds), Shifting Centres of Gravity in Human Rights Protection: Rethinking Relations between the ECHR, EU, and National Legal Orders (Routledge 2016) 144–161.

Çalı, Başak, *The Authority of International Law: Obedience, Respect, and Rebuttal* (Oxford University Press 2015)

Cançado Trindade, Antonio Augusto, *International Law for Humankind: Towards a New Jus Gentium* (Brill 2010)

Cançado Trindade, Antonio Augusto, *Reflexiones sobre el Futuro del Sistema Interamericano de Protección de los Derechos Humanos*, in Juan E Méndez and Francisco Cox (eds), El futuro del sistema interamericano de protección a los derechos humanos (IIDH 1998) 573–603

Candela Soriano, Mercedes, 'The Reception Process in Spain and Italy' in Keller and Stone Sweet Helen Keller and Alec Stone Sweet (eds), *A Europe of Rights: The Impact of the ECHR on National Legal Systems* (Oxford University Press 2008) 393–450

Cannizzaro, Enzom 'Proportionality and Margin of Appreciation in the Whaling Case: Reconciling Antithetical Doctrines?' (2017) 27 *European Journal of International Law* 1061–1069

Cappelletti, Mauro, 'Judicial Review in Comparative Perspective' (1970) 58 *California Law Review* 1017–1053

Carcano, Andrea, 'Uses and Possible Misuses of a Comparative International Law Approach' (2018) 54 *Questions of International Law* 21–38

Carozza, Paolo G, 'Subsidiarity as a Structural Principle of International Human Rights Law' (2003) American Journal of International Law 38–79

Carozza, Paolo G, 'Subsidiarity as a Structural Principle of International Human Rights Law' (2003) 97 *American Journal of International Law* 38–79

Casanovas y La Rosa, Oriol, *Unity and Pluralism in Public International Law* (Martinus Nijhoff The Hague 2001)

Caserta, Salvatore, *International Courts in Latin America and the Caribbean: Foundations and Authority* (Oxford University Press 2020)

Cassel, Douglas, 'The Expanding Scope and Impact of Reparations Awarded by the Inter-American Court of Human Rights' in Koen De Feyter, Stephan Parmentier, Marc Bossuyt and Paul Lemmens (eds), *Out of the Ashes: Reparation for Victims of Gross and Systematic Human Rights Violations* (Intersentia 2005) 191–223

Cassese, Antonio, 'Towards a Moderate Monism: Could International Eventually Acquire the Force to Invalidate Inconsistent National Law?' in in Antonio Cassese (ed), *Realizing Utopia: The Future of International Law* (Oxford University Press 2012) 187–199

Castañeda, Mireya, *El principio pro persona: experiencias y expectativas* (Comisión Nacional de los Derechos Humanos 2014)110–129

Cavallaro, James L and Brewer, Stephanie Erin, 'Reevaluating Regional Human Rights Litigation in the Twenty-First Century: The Case of the Inter-American Court' (2008) 102 *American Journal of International Law* 768–827

Cede, Philip, 'Report on Austria and Germany' in Giuseppe Martinico and Oreste Pollicino (eds), *The National Judicial Treatment of the ECHR and EU Laws: A Comparative Constitutional Perspective* (Europa Law Publishing 2010) 55–80

Cerna, Christina M, 'The Inter-American System for the Protection of Human Rights' (2004) 16 *Florida Journal of International Law* 195–212, 201–203.

Chang, Wen-Chen and Yeh, Jiunn-Rong, 'Internationalization of Constitutional Law' in Michel Rosenfeld and A András Sajó (eds), *The Oxford Handbook of Comparative Constitutional Law* (Oxford University Press 2012) 1165–84

Chowdhury, Nupur, *European Regulation of Medical Device and Pharmaceutical: Regulatee Expectations of Legal Certainty* (Springer 2014)

Christiano, Thomas, 'Democratic Legitimacy and International Institutions' in Samantha Besson and John Tasioulas (eds), *The Philosophy of International Law* 119–138

Christoffersen, Jonas, 'Individual and Constitutional Justice: Can the Power Balance of Adjudication be Reversed?' in Jonas Christoffersen and Mikael Rask Madsen (eds), *The European Court of Human Rights between Law and Politics* (Oxford University Press 2011) 181–203

Claes, Monica, *The National Courts' Mandate in the European Constitution* (Hart 2006)

Claes, Monica, *The National Courts' Mandate in the European Constitution* (Hart Publishing 2006)

Clayton, Richard, 'Should the English Courts under the HRA Mirror the Strasbourg Case Law?', in Katja S Ziegler, Elizabeth Wicks and Loveday Hodson (eds), *The UK and European Human Rights: A Strained Relationship?* (Hart 2015) 95–114, 105

Cohen, Jean L, *Globalization and Sovereignty: Rethinking Legality, Legitimacy, and Constitutionalism* (Cambridge University Press 2012)

Colandrea, Valerio, 'On the Power of the European Court of Human Rights to Order Specific Non-Monetary Measures: Some Remarks in Light of the *Assanidze, Broniowski* and *Sejdovic* Cases' (2007) 7 *Human Rights Law Review* 396–411

Collings, Justin, 'Introduction' in Matthias Jestaedt, Oliver Lepsius, Christoph Schönberger, Christoph Möllers (eds), *The German Federal Constitutional Court: The Court Without Limits* (Oxford University Press 2020) xv–xvi

Contesse, Jorge, 'Sexual Orientation and Gender Identity in Inter-American Human Rights Law' (2019) 44 *North Carolina Journal of International Law* 353–385.

Contreras, Pablo, 'National Discretion and International Deference in the Restriction of Human Rights: A Comparison between the Jurisprudence of the European and the Inter-American Court of Human Rights' (2012) 11 *Northwestern Journal of International Human Rights* 28–82

Corten, Olivier, 'Les techniques reproduites aux aritlces 31 à 33 des conventions de Vienne : approche objectivistte ou approche volontariste de l'interprétation?' (2011) 115 *Revue Générale de Droit International Public* 351–366

Cot, Jean-Pierre, 'Margin of Appreciation' in Rüdiger Wolfrum (ed), *Max Planck Encyclopedia of Public International Law* (Oxford University Press) updated in 2007

Cowell, Frederick, 'The Death of the Southern African Development Community Tribunals Human Rights Jurisdiction' (2013) 13 *Human Rights Law Review* 153–165

Crawford, James, *Brownlie's Principles of Public International Law*, 8th ed (Oxford University Press 2012)

Crawford, James, *Brownlie's Principles of Public International Law*, 8th ed (Oxford University Press 2012)

Crema, Luigi, 'Disappearance and New Sightings of Restrictive Interpretation(s)' (2010) 21 *European Journal of International Law* 681–700

Cuenca Gómez, Patricia, 'La incidncia del derecho interncional de los derechos humanos en el derecho interno: la interpretación del Artículo 10.2 de la Constitución española' (2012) 12 *Revista de Estudios Jurídicos* 1–24

Cuenca Gómez, Patricia, 'La incidncia del derecho interncional de los derechos humanos en el derecho interno: la interpretación del Artículo 10.2 de la Constitución española' (2012) 12 *Revista de Estudios Jurídicos* 1–24

D'Aspremont, Jean, 'Comparativism and Colonizing Thinking in International Law' (2019) 57 *Canadian Yearbook of International Law* 89–112

D'Aspremont, Jean, *Formalism and the Sources of International Law: A Theory of the Ascertainment of Legal Rules* (Oxford University Press 2011)

De Búrca, Gráinne, 'After the EU Charter of Fundamental Rights: The Court of Justice as a Human Rights Adjudicator?' (2013) 13 *Maastricht Journal of European and Comparative Law* 168–184

de Londras, Fiona and Dzehtsiarou, Kanstantsin, *Great Debates on the European Convention on Human Rights* (Macmillan International Higher Education, 2018) 61–62.

De S-O-l'E Lasser, Mitchel, *Judicial Transformations: The Rights Revolution in the Courts of Europe* (Oxford University Press 2009)

De Visser, Maartje, *Constitutional Review in Europe: A Comparative Analysis* (Hart 2014)

De Wet, Erika, 'The Reception Process in the Netherlands and Belgium' in Helen Keller and Alec Stone Sweet (eds), *A Europe of Rights: The Impact of the ECHR on National Legal Systems* (Oxford University Press 2008) 229–310

De Wet, Erika, 'The Reception Process in the Netherlands and Belgium' in Keller and Stone Sweet Helen Keller and Alec Stone Sweet (eds), *A Europe of Rights: The Impact of the ECHR on National Legal Systems* (Oxford University Press 2008) 229–310

Del Mar, Maksymilian, 'Legal Reasoning in Pluralist Jurisprudence: The Practice of The Relational Imagination' in Nicole Roughan and Andrew Halpin (eds), *In Pursuit of Pluralist Jurisprudence* (Cambridge University Press 2017) 40–63

Del Toro Huerta, Mauricio Iván, 'La aperture constitucional al derecho internacional de los derechos humanos en la era de la Mundialización y sus consecuencias en la práctica judicial' (2005)112 *Boletín Mexicano de Derecho Comparado* 325–363

Delmas-Marty, Mireille, *Le pluralisme ordnné : Les forces imaginantes du droit (tome 2)* (Le Seuil 2006) 28 (*Ordering Pluralism: A Conceptual Framework for Understanding the Transnational Legal World* (Hart 2009))

Dhommeaux, Jean, 'Hiérarchie et conflits en droit international des droits de l'homme' (2009) 4 *Annuaire international des droits de l'homme* 55–62

Dickson, Brice, *Human Rights and the United Kingdom Supreme Court* (Oxford University Press 2013) 43

Dominigo, Rafael, *The New Global Law* (Cambridge University Press 2010)

Dougan, Michael, 'The Vicissitudes of Life at the Coalface: Remedies and Procedures for Enforcing Union Law before the National Courts' in Paul Craig and Gráinne de Búrca (eds), *The Evolution of EU Law*, 2nd ed (Oxford University Press 2015) 407–438

Drzemczewski, Andrew, 'The Parliamentary Assembly's Involvement in the Supervision of the Judgments of the Strasbourg Court' (2010) 28 *Netherlands Quarterly of Human Rights* 164-178

Dulitzky, Ariel, 'An Inter-American Constitutional Court? The Invention of the Conventionality Control by the Inter-American Court of Human Rights' (2015) 50 *Texas International Law Journal* 45–93

Dupuy, Pierre-Marie, 'Dionisio Anzilotti and the Law of International Law' (1992) 3 *European Journal of International Law* 139–148

Dupuy, Pierre-Marie, 'Evolutionary Interpretation of Treaties: Between Memory and Prophecy' in Enzo Cannnizzaro (ed), *The Law of Treaties Beyond the Vienna Convention* (Oxford University Press 2011) 123–137

Dzehtsiarou, Kanstantsin, *European Consensus and the Legitimacy of the European Court of Human Rights* (Cambridge University Press 2015)

Enabulele, Amos O, 'Incompatibility of National Law with the African Charter on Human and Peoples' Rights: Does the African Court on Human and Peoples' Rights Have the Final Say' (2016) 16 African *Human Rights Law Journal* 1–28

Endo, Ken, 'The Principle of Subsidiarity: From Johannes Althusius to Jacques Delors' (1994) 46 *Hokudai Hogaku Ronsyu* 2064–1965

Fabbrini, Federico, *Fundamental Rights in Europe: Challenges and Transformations in Comparative Perspective* (Oxford University Press 2014)

Farahat, Anuscheh, 'The German Federal Constitutional Court' in Armin von Bogdandy, Peter Huber and Christoph Grabenwarter (eds), *The Max Planck Handbooks in European Public Law: Volume III: Constitutional Adjudication: Institutions* (Oxford University Press 2020) 320–324.

Faúndez Ledesma, Héctor, *The Inter-American System for the Protection of Human Rights: Institutional and Protection Aspects*, 1st ed in English, trans of 3rd ed in Spanish (Inter-American Institute of Human Rights 2007)

Feichtner, Isabel, 'Subsidiarity' in Rüdiger Wolfrum (ed), *Max Planck Encyclopedia of Public International Law* (Oxford University Press), updated in 2007

Ferdinandusse, Ward, 'Out of the Black-Box? The International Obligation of State Organs' (2003) 29 *Brooklyn Journal of International Law* 45–127

Ferrer Mac-Gregor, Eduardo and Sánchez Gil, Rubén, 'Mexico: Struggling for an Open View in Constittuional Adjudcation' in Tania Groppi and Marie-Claire Ponthoreau (eds), *The Use of Foreign Precedents by Constituional Judges* (Hart Publishing 2013) 301–320

Ferrer Mac-Gregor, Eduardo, 'Interpretación conforme y control difuso de convencionalidad: El nuevo paradigma para el juez mexicano' (2011) 9 *Estudioos Constitucionales* 531–622, 620.

Ferreres Comella, Víctor, 'The Rise of Specialized Constitutional Courts' in Tom Ginsburg and Rosalind Dixon (eds), *Comparative Constitutional Law: Research Handbooks in Comparative Law* (Edward Edgar 2011) 265–277

Ferreres Comella, Víctorm *Constitutional Courts and Democratic Values: A European Perspective* (Yale University Press 2009)

FikFak, Veronika, 'Non-pecuniary Damages before the European Court of Human Rights: Forget the Victim: It's All about the State' (2020) 33 *Leiden Journal of International Law* 335–369

Fitzmaurice, Gerald, 'The General Principles of international Law: Considered from the Standpoint of the Rule of Law' (1957-II) 92 *Recueil des cours* 1–228

Fitzmaurice, Malgosia, 'Interpretation of Human Rights Treaties' in Dinah Shelton (ed), *The Oxford Handbook of International Human Rights Law* (Oxford University Press 2013) 739–771

Flauss, Jean-François and Cohen-Jonathan, Gérard, 'Cour européenne des droits de l'homme et droit international général' (2008) 54 *Annuaire français de droit international* 529–546

Føllesdal, Andreas, 'The Principle of Subsidiarity as a Constitutional Principle in International Law' (2013) 2 *Global Constitutionalism* 37–62

Fouarge, Didier, *Poverty and Subsidiarity in Europe: Minimum Protection from an Economic Perspective* (Edward Elgar 2004)

Frankenberg, Günter, 'Democracy' in Michel Rosenfeld and A András Sajó (eds), *The Oxford Handbook of Comparative Constitutional Law* (Oxford University Press 2012) 250–258

Friedmann, Wolfgang, *The Changing Structure of International Law* (Columbia University Press 1964)

Furuya, Syuichi, 'The Image of International Legal Order in International Criminal Adjudicative System: The Exteriorisation of "International Law as Intervention" [Kokusai Keiji Sisutem no Kokusaiho Chitsujozo: "Kainyu no Kokusaiho" no Kenzaika]' (2013) 11 *Horitsu Jiho* 32–36 (in Japanese).

Fyrnys, Markus, 'Expanding Competences by Judicial Lawmaking: The Pilot Judgment Procedure of the European Court of Human Rights' (2011) 12 *German Law Journal* 1231–1259

Garay Boza, Norberto E, 'Gobernar desde abajo: Del control de convencionalidad a la instrumentalización de la inversión estructural de la pirámide kelseniana' (2012) 5 *Inter-American and European Human Rights Journal* 124–147

Garlicki, Lech, 'Broniowski and After: On the Dual Nature of 'Pilot Judgments' in Lucius Caflisch, Johan Callewaert, Roderick Liddell, Paul Mahoney and Mark Villiger (eds), *Liber Amicorum Luzius Wildhaber: Human Rights: Strasbourg Views* (N P Engel 2007) 177–192

Garlicki, Lech, 'Constitutional Courts versus Supreme Courts' (2007) 5 *International Journal of Constitutional Law* 44–68

Garlicki, Lech, 'Contrôle de constitutionnalité et contrôle de conventionnalité : sur le dialogue des juges' in *La conscience des droits : Mélanges en l'honneur de Jean-Paul Costa* (Dalloz 2011) 271–280

Garlicki, Lech, 'Cooperation of Courts: The Role of Supranational Jurisdictions in Europe' (2008) 6 International Journal of Constitutional Law 509–530

Gerards, Janneke and Fleuren, Joseph, 'The Netherlands' in Janneke Gerards and Joseph Fleuren (eds), *Implementation of the European Convention on Human Rights and of the Judgments of the ECtHR in National Case-Law: A Comparative Analysis* (Intersentia 2014) 217–260

Gerards, Janneke, 'Advisory Opinion: European Court of Human Rights (ECtHR)' in Hélène Ruiz Fabri (ed), *Max Planck Encyclopedia of International Procedural Law* (Oxford University Press 2018)

Gerards, Janneke, 'Pluralism, Deference and the Margin of Appreciation Doctrine' (2011) 17 *European Law Journa*l 80–120

Ghandhi, Sandy, 'Human Rights and the International Court of Justice: The Ahmadou Sadio Diallo Case' (2011) 11 *Human Rights Law Review* 527–555

Giannopoulos, Christos, 'The Reception by Domestic Courts of the *Res Interpretata* Effect of Jurisprudence of the European Court of Human Rights' (2019) *Human Rights Law Review* 537–559

Ginsburg, Tom, 'The Global Spread of Constitutional Review', in Gregory A Keleman, R Daniel Kelemen and Keith E Whittington (eds), *Oxford Handbook of Law and Politics* (Oxford University Press 2008) 81–98

Gisbert, Bustos, 'Elementos constitucionales en la red global' (2012) 60 *Estudios de Deusto* 21–43

Glas, Lize R, 'The European Court of Human Rights supervising the execution of its judgments' (2019) 37 *Netherlands Quarterly of Human Rights* 228–244

Gonenc, Levent and Esen, Selin 'The Problem of the Application of Less Protective International Agreements in Domestic Legal Systems: Article 90 of the Turkish Constitution' (2007) 8 *European Journal of Law Reform* 485–500

Góngora Mera, Manuel Eduardo, 'La diffusion del bloque de constitucionalidad en la jurisprudencia latinoamericana y su potencial en la construcción del *ius constitutionale commune* latinoamericano' in Armin von Bogdandy, Héctor Fix-Fierro and Mariela Morales Antoniazzi (eds), *Ius constitututionale commune en América Latina: Rasgos, potencialidades y desafíos* (UNAM —IIJ/Institut Max Planck de Derecho Público comparado y Derecho Internacional 2014) 301–324

Góngora Mera, Manuel Eduardo, *Inter-American Judicial Constitutionalism: On the Constitutional Rank of Human Rights Treaties in Latin America through National and Inter-American Adjudication* (Inter-American Institute of Human Rights 2011)

González Pascal, María Isabel, 'El CEDH como parte del Derecho Constitucional Europeo' in Queralt Jiménez (ed), *El Tribunal de Estrasburgo en el Espacio Judicial Europeo* (2013) 109–130

González-Domínguez, Pablo, *The Doctrine of Conventionality Control: Between Uniformity and Legal Pluralism in the Inter-American Human Rights System* (Intersentia 2018)

Graf-Brugère, Anne-Laurence, '*A lex favorabilis*? Resolving Norm Conflicts between Human Rights and Humanitarian Law' in Robert Kolb and Gloria Gaggioli (eds), *Research Handbook of Human Rights and Humanitarian Law* (Edward Elgar 2013) 251–270

Gragl, Paul, *Legal Monism: Law, Philosophy, and Politics* (Oxford University Press 2018)

Groppi, Tania, 'Constitutional Reasoning in the Italian Constitutional Court' (2014) *Rivista dell'Associazione Italiana dei Costituzionalisti* 1–45

Gros Espiell, Héctor, 'L'appplication du droit international dans le droit interne en amérique latine' in Studi di diritto internazionale in onore di Gaetano Arangio-Ruiz, Vol I (Editoriale Scientifica 2004) 529–549

Gruszczynski, Lukasz and Werner, Wouter (eds), *Deference in International Courts and Tribunals: Standard of Review and Margin of Appreciation* (Oxford University Press 2014)

Guggenheim, Paul, *Traité de droit international public*, 2e éd., (Tome I, Librairie de l'Université, Georg & Cie S. A. 1967)

Gutmann, Amy and Thompson, Dennis, *Why Deliberative Democracy*? (Princeton University Press 2004)

Häberle, Peter, *Der kooperative Verfassungsstaat aus Kultur und als Kultur: Vorstudien zu einer universalen Verfassungslehre* (Duncker & Humblot GmbH 2013)

Habermas, Jürgen, 'Constitutional Democracy: A Paradoxical Union of Contradictory Principles?' (2001) 29 *Political Theory* 766–781

Habermas, Jürgen, *Faktizität und Geltung: Beiträge zur Diskurstheorie des Rechts und des demokratischen Rechtsstaats* (Suhrkamp 1992)

Halberstam, Daniel, 'It's the Autonomy, Stupid!' A Modest Defense of Opinion 2/13 on EU Accession to the ECHR and a Way Forward' (2015) Public Law and Legal Theory Research Paper Series (University of Michigan), 19 <http://papers.ssrn.com/sol3/papers.cfm?abstract_id=2567591> accessed 30 March 2015.

Haljan, David, *Separating Powers: International Law before National Courts* (Springer 2013)

Halmai, Gábor, 'Abuse of Constitutional Identity. The Hungarian Constitutional Court on Interpretation of Article E (2) of the Fundamental Law' (2018) 43 *Review of Central and East European Law* 23–42

Hawkins, Darren and Jacoby, Wade, 'Partial Compliance: A Comparison of the European and Inter-American Courts of Human Rights' (2010) 6 *Journal of International Law & International Relations* 35–85

Heinrich, Andrew, 'Sub-Regional Courts as Transitional Justice Mechanisms: The Case of the East African Court of Justice in Burundi' in James Thuo Gathii (eds), The Performance of Africa's International Courts: Using Litigation for Political, Legal, and Social Change (Oxford University Press 2020) 88–105

Helen Keller, 'Reception of the European Convention for the Protection of Human Rights and Fundamental Freedoms (ECHR) in Poland and Switzerland' (2005) 65 *Zeitschrift für ausläandisches öffentliches Recht und Völkerrecht* 283–349

Helfer, Laurence R, 'Redesigning the European Court of Human Rights: Embeddedness as a Deep Structural Principle of the European Human Rights Regime' (2008) 19 *European Journal of International Law* 125–159

Henderson, Humberto, 'Los tratados internacionales de derechos humanos en el orden interno: la importancia del principio *pro homine*' (2004) 39 *Revista IIDH* 71–99

Hennebel, Ludovic, 'The Inter-American Court of Human Rights: The Ambassador of Universalism' (2011) *Quebec Journal of International l Law (Special Edition)* 57–97

Hentrei, Simon,'Generalising the Principle of Complementarity: Framing International Judicial Authority' (2013) 4 *Transnational Legal Theory* 419–435

Hernández Castaño, Diana P, *Legitimidad democrática de la Corte Interamericana de Derechos Humanos en el control de convencionalidad* (Universidad Externado de Colombia 2015)

Hernández, Gleider, '*E Pluribus Unum?* A Divisible College?: Reflections on the International Legal Profession' (2018) 29 *European Journal of International Law* 1003–1022

Higgins, Rosalyn, 'The Concept of 'The State': Variable Geometry and Dualist Perceptions' in Laurence Boisson de Chazournes and Vera Gowlland-Debbas (eds), *The International Legal System in Quest of Equity and Universality* (Martinus Nijhoff 2001) 547–561

Hillebrecht, Courtney, *Domestic Politics and International Human Rights Tribunals: The Problem of Compliance* (Cambridge University Press 2014).

Huneeus, Alexandra, 'Courts Resisting Courts: Lessons from the Inter-American Court's Struggle to Enforce Human Rights' (2011) 44 Cornell International Law Journal 493–533

Isiksel, Turkuler 'Global Legal Pluralism as Fact and Norm' (2013) 2 *Global Constitutionalism* 160–195

Iwasawa, Yuji, 'Domestic Application of International Law' (2016) 378 Recueil des Cours 9–261

Jowell, Jeffery, *The Changing Constitution* (Oxford University Press 2015)

Kahn, Jeffrey, 'The Relationship between the European Court of Human Rights and the Constitutional Court of the Russian Federation: Conflicting Conceptions of Sovereignty in Strasbourg and St Petersburg' (2019) 30 *European Journal of International Law* 933–959

Kattan, Victor, 'Jadhav Case (India v. Pakistan)' (2020) 114 *American Journal of International Law* 281–287

Kavanagh, Aileen, *Constitutional Review under the UK Human Rights Act* (2009)

Kavanagh, Aileen, *Constitutional Review under the UK Human Rights Act* (Cambridge University Press 2009)

Kelemen, R Daniel and Pech, Laurent, 'The Uses and Abuses of Constitutional Pluralism: Undermining the Rule of Law in the Name of Constitutional Identity in Hungary and Poland' (2019) 21 *Cambridge Yearbook of European Legal Studies* 59–74

Keller, Helen and Stone Sweet, Alec, 'Assessing the Impact of the ECHR on National Legal Systems' in Helen Keller and Alec Stone Sweet (eds), *A Europe of Rights: The Impact of the ECHR on National Legal Systems* (Oxford University Press 2008) 677–710

Kelsen, Hans, *Principles of International Law,* 2nd ed. (Revised and Edited by Robert W Tucker) (Holt, Rinehart and Winston 1967)

Kelsen, Hans, *Reine Rechtslehre*, 2nd ed (Deuticke 1960)

Kingsbury, Benedict, 'International Law as Inter-Public Law', in Henry S Richardson and Melissa Williams (eds), *Nomos XLIX: Moral Universalism and Pluralism* (New York University Press 2009) 167–204

Klabbers, Jan, 'Constitutionalism Lite' (2004) 1 *International Organizations Law Review* 31–58

Klabbers, Jan, 'International Legal Positivism and Constitutionalism', in Jean d'Aspremont and Jörg Kammerhofer (eds), *International Legal Positivism in a Post-Modern World* (Cambridge University Press 2014) 264–290

Kleinlein, Thomas, 'Alfred Verdross as a Founding Father of International Constitutionalism?' (2012) 4 *Goettingen Journal of International Law* 385–416

Koller, David, '... and New York and The Hague and Tokyo and Geneva and Nuremberg and...: The Geographies of International Law' (2012) 23 *European Journal of International Law* 97–119

Komárek, Jan, 'National Constitutional Courts in the European Constitutional Democracy' (2014) 12 *International Journal of Constitutional Law* 525–544, 528 (emphasis added).

Korhonen, Outi, 'New International Law: Silence, Defence or Deliverance?' (1996) 7 *European Journal of International Law* 1–28

Koskenniemi, Martti, The Case for Comparative International Law' (2009) 20 *Finnish Yearbook of International Law* 1–8

Krisch, Nico, 'Global Administrative Law and the Constitutional Ambition' in Petra Dobner and Martin Loughlin (eds), *The Twilight of Constitutionalism?* (Oxford University Press 2010) 245–266

Krisch, Nico, *Beyond Constitutionalism: The Pluralist Structure of Postnational Law* (Oxford University Press 2010) Chap 4. It is suggestive that Greer and Wildhaber, who had advocated the ECtHR's constitutional justice, altered their position incorporating these pluralists' perspectives. Steven Greer and Luzius Wildhaber, 'Revisiting the Debate about "Constitutionalising" the European Court of Human Rights' (2012) 12 Human Rights Law Rreview 655–687

Kühn, Zdeněk, 'Wachauf and ERT: On the Road from the Centralized to the Decentralized System of Judicial Review' in Miguel Poiares Maduro and Loïc Azoulai (eds), *The Past and Future of EU Law. The Classics of EU Law Revisited on the 50th Anniversary of the Rome Treaty* (Hart 2010) 151–162

Kumm, Matthias, 'The Legitimacy of International Law: A Constitutionalist Framework of Analysis' (2004) 15 *European Journal of International Law* 907–931

Kunz, Raffaela, *Richter über internationale Gerichte? Die Rolle innerstaatlicher Gerichte bei der Umsetzung der Entscheidungen von EGMR und IAGMR* (Springer 2020)

Lageot, Céline, 'France' in Janneke Gerards and Joseph Fleuren (eds), *Implementation of the European Convention on Human Rights and of the Judgments of the ECtHR in National Case-Law: A Comparative Analysis* (Intersentia 2014) 145–184

Lalisan, Samantha, 'Classifying Systems of Constitutional Review: A Context-Specific Analysis' (2020) 5 *Indiana Journal of Constitutional Design* 1–24

Lamarque, Elisabetta, 'Interpreting Statutes in Conformity with the Constitution: The Role of the Italian Constitutional Court and Ordinary Judges' (2010) 1 *Italian Journal of Public Law* 87–120

Langer, Magnus Jesko and Hansbury, Elise, 'Monitoring Compliance with the Decisions of Human Rights Courts: The Inter-American Particularism' in Laurence Boisson de Chazournes, Marcelo G Kohen and Jorge E Viñuales (eds), *Diplomatic and Judicial Means of Dispute Settlement* (Martinus Nijhoff 2013) 213–245

Langer, Magnus Jesko and Hansbury, Elise, 'Monitoring Compliance with the Decisions of Human Rights Courts: The Inter-American Particularism' in Laurence Boisson de Chazournes, Marcelo Gustavo Kohen, Jorge E Viñuales (eds), *Diplomatic and Judicial Means of Dispute Settlement* (Martinus Nijhoff 2013) 213–245, 230–236

Lawson, Rick, 'Beyond the Call of Duty? Domestic Courts and the Standards of the European Court of Human Rights', in Henk Snijders and Stefan Vogenauer (eds), *Content and Meaning of National Law in the Context of Transnational Law* (Sellier European Law Publishers 2010) 21–38

Lazzerini, Nicole, 'Dual Preliminarity Within the Scope of the EU Charter of Fundamental Rights in the Light of Order 182/2020 of the Italian Constitutional Court', European Papers 25 November 2020, 1–14. See also the list of decisions coherent with and diverging from the Italian Constitutional Court Judgment No 269/2017, available at https://www.cir.santannapisa.it/observatory-practices-inter-legality-italian-high-courts.

Leach, Philip, 'No Longer Offering Fine Mantras to a Parched Child? The European Court's Developing Approach to Remedies' in in Andreas Føllesdal, Birgit Peters and Geir Ulfstein (eds), *Constituting Europe: The European Court of Human Rights in a National, European and Global Context* (Cambridge University Press 2013) 142–180

Legg, Andrew, *The Margin of Appreciation in International Human Rights Law: Deference and Proportionality* (Oxford University Press 2012)

Leiter, Andrea, 'Review Essay: Is International Law International? by Anthea Roberts' (2018) 19 *Melbourne Journal of International Law* 413–422

Letsas, George, 'The ECHR as a Living Instrument: Its Meaning and Legitimacy' in Andreas Føllesdal, Birgit Peters and Geir Ulfstein (eds), *Constituting Europe: The European Court of Human Rights in a National, European and Global Context* (Cambridge University Press 2013) 106–141

Letsas, Goerge, 'Two Concepts of the Margin of Appreciation' (2006) *Oxford Journal of Legal Studies* 705–732

Lixinski, Lucas, 'The Consensus Method of Interpretation by the Inter-American Court of Human Rights' (2017) 3 *Canadian Journal of Comparative and Contemporary Law* 65–95

Lixinski, Lucas, 'Treaty Interpretation by the Inter-American Court of Human Rights: Expansionism at the Service of the Unity of International Law' (2010) 21 *European Journal of International Law* 585–604

Lopes Saldanha, Jânia M and Pacheco Vieira, Lucas, 'Controle jurisdictional de convencionalidade e reenvio prejudicial interamericano: Um diálogo de ferramentas processuais em favor da efetivação do direito internacional dos direitos humanos' (2013) 19 *Anuario de derecho constitucional latinoamericano* 435–466

Lopes Saldanha, Jânia Maria and Pacheco Vieira, Lucas, 'Controle jurisdictional de convencionalidade e reenvio prejudicial interamericano: Um diálogo de ferramentas processuais em favor da efetivação do direito internacional dos direitos humanos' (2013) 19 *Anuario de derecho constitucional latinoamericano* 435–460

Lovat, Henry, 'International Criminal Tribunal Backlash' in Kevin Heller, Frédéric Mégret, Sarah Nouwen, Jens Ohlin, and Darryl Robinson (eds), *The Oxford Handbook of International Criminal Law* (Oxford University Press 2020) 601-625

Mac Amhlaigh, Cormac, 'Back to a Sovereign Future?: Constitutional Pluralism after Brexit' (2019) 21 *Cambridge Yearbook of European Legal Studies* 41–58

MacCormick, Niel, 'Beyond the Sovereign State' (1993) 56 *Modern Law Review* 1–18

MacCormick, Niel, *Questioning Sovereignty* (Oxford University Press 1999)

Malarino, Ezequiel, 'Judicial Activism, Punitivism and Supranationalisation: Illiberal and Antidemocratic Tendencies of the Inter- American Court of Human Rights' (2012) 12 *International Criminal Law Review* 665–695

Malinverni, Giorgio, 'La compétence de la Cour pour surveiller l'exécution de ses propres arrêts' in Dean Spielmann, Marialena Tsirti, Panayotis Voyatzis (eds), *La Convention européenne des droits de l'homme, un instrument vivant : Mélanges en l'honneur de Chirstos L. Rozakis* (Bruylant 2011) 361–375

Mälksoo, Lauri, 'International Legal Theory in Russia: A Civilizational Perspective, or: Can Individuals Be Subjects of International Law?' in Florian Hoffmann and Anne Orford (eds), *The Oxford Handbook on the Theory of International Law* (Oxford University Press 2016) 257–275

Mälksoo, Lauri, 'Russia's Constitutional Court Defies the European Court of Human Rights: Constitutional Court of the Russian Federation Judgment of 14 July 2015, No 21-П/2015' (2016) 12 *European Constitutional Law Review* 377–395

Maringele, Sarah, *European Human Rights Law: The Work of the European Court of Human Rights Illustrated by an Assortment of Selected Cases* (Anchor Academic Publishing 2014)McKenna, Miriam Bak, 'Decentering the Universal: Comparative International Law and Decolonizing Critique' (2018) 12 *ESIL Conference Paper Series* 1–25

Martineau, Anne-Charlotte, 'The Rhetoric of Fragmentation: Fear and Faith in International Law' (2009) 22 *Leiden Journal of International Law* 1–28

Martínez Estay, José Ignacio, 'The Impact of the Jurisprudence Inter-American Court of Human Rights on the Chilean Constitutional System' in Rainer Arnold (ed), *The Universalism of Human Rights* (Springer 2013) 63–79

Martinico, Giuseppe and Repetto, Giorgio, 'Fundamental Rights and Constitutional Duels in Europe: An Italian Perspective on Case 269/2017 of the Italian Constitutional Court and Its Aftermath' (2019) 15 *European Constitutional Law Review* 731–751

Martinico, Giuseppe, 'Constitutionalism, Resistance and Openness: Comparative Law Reflections on Constitutionalism in Global Governance' (2016) 35 *Yearbook of European Law* 318–340

Martinico, Giuseppe, 'Corti constituzionali (o supreme) e "disobbedienza funzionale": Critica, dialogo e conflitti nel rapporto fra diritto interno e diritto delle Convenzioni (CEDU e Convenzione americana sui diritti umani)' *Diritto Penale Contemporaneo*, 28 Aprile 2015

Martinico, Giuseppe, 'Is the European Convention Going to Be "Supreme"? A Comparative-Constitutional Overview of ECHR and EU Law before National Courts' (2012) 23 *European Journal of International Law* 401–424

Martinico, Giuseppe, 'Is the European Convention Going to Be "Supreme"? A Comparative-Constitutional Overview of ECHR and EU Law before National Courts' (2012) 23 *European Journal of International Law* 401–424

Matringe, Jean, 'L'exécution par le juge étatique des décisions judiciares internationales' (2013) 117 *Revue Générale de Droit International Public* 555–578

Matsuda, Hiromichi, 'International Law in Japanese Courts' in Curtis Bradley (ed), *The Oxford Handbook of Comparative Foreign Relations Law* (Oxford University Press 2019) 537–548

Maus, Didier, 'Nouveux regards sur le contrôle de constitutionnalité par voie d'exception' in Dnys de Béchillon, Pierre Brunet, Véronique Champeil-Desplats and Éric Millard (eds), *L'architecture du droit : Mélanges en l'honneur de Michel Troper* (Economica 2006) 665–678

Maxeiner, James R, 'Legal Certainty: A European Alternative to American Legal Indeterminacy?' (2006–2007) 15 *Tulane Journal of International and Comparative Law* 541–607

Mazzuoli, Valerio De Oliveira and Ribeiro, Dilton, 'The *Pro Homine* Principle as an Enshrined Feature of International Human Rights Law' (2016) 3 *Indonesian Journal of International & Comparative Law* 77–99

Medellín Urquiaga, Ximena, *Principio pro persona* (Comisión de Derechos Humanos del Distrito Federal, Suprema Corte de Justicia de la Nación y Oficina en México del Alto Comisionado de las Naciones Unidas para los Derechos Humanos 2013) 16–17

Miara, Lucja and Prais, Victoria, 'The Role of Civil Society in the Execution of Judgments of the European Court of Human Rights' (2012) 5 *European Human Rights Law Review* 528–537

Michaels, Ralf, 'Law and Recognition: Towards a Relational Concept of Law' in Nicole Roughan and Andrew Halpin (eds), *In Pursuit of Pluralist Jurisprudence* (Cambridge University Press 2017) 90–115

Michelman, Frank I, 'The Interplay of Constitutional and Ordinary Jurisdiction' in Tom Ginsburg and Rosalind Dixon (eds), *Comparative Constitutional Law: Research Handbooks in Comparative Law* (Edward Edgar 2011) 278–297

Milanovic, Marko, 'Sejdić &Finci v Bosnia and Herzegovina' (2010) 104 *American Journal of International Law* 636–641

Möllers, Christoph, *The Three Branches: A Comparative Model of Separation of Powers* (Oxford University Press 2015)

Morales Antoniazzi, Mariela,'El nuevo paradigma de la apertura de los órdenes constitucionales: una perspectiva sudamericana', in Armin von Bogdandy and José María Serna de la Garza (eds), *Soberanía y Estado abierto en América Latina y Europa* (Biblioteca Jurídica Virtual 2014) 233–282.

Moreira Maués, Antonio, 'Supra-Legality of International Human Rights Treaties and Constitutional Interpretation' (2013) 18 *SUR – International Journal on Human Rights* 205–223

Mowbray, Alastair, 'An Examination of the European Court of Human Rights' Indication of Remedial Measures' (2017) 17 *Human Rights Law Review* 451–478

Negishi, Yota, 'Relative Authorities: Constitutional Reasonable Resistances against Inter-American Court's Doctrines' (2018) 21 *Iuris Dictio* 49–61

Negishi, Yota, 'The *Pro Homine* Principle's Role in Regulating the Relationship between Conventionality Control and Constitutionality Control' (2017) 28 *European Journal of International Law* 457–481

Negishi, Yota, 'Conventionality Control of Domestic 'Abuse of Power' Influencing Human Rights and Democracy' (2016) 26 *Italian Yearbook of International Law* 243–264

Negishi, Yota, 'The Subsidiarity Principle's Role in Allocating Competences Between Human Rights Courts and States Parties: The Hybrid Model of Centralized and Diffused Conventionality Control of Domestic Law' in Armin von Bogdandy, Flávia Piovesan e Mariela Morales Antoniazzi (eds), *Ius Constitutionale Commune na América Latina, Volume III, Diálogos Jurisdicionais e Controle de Convencionalidade: Coleção Direitos Humanos e Constitucionalismo Regional Transformador* (Juruá Editora 2016) 125–160

Negishi, Yota, 'Distribution of Powers for the Conventionality Control of Domestic Law between Constitutional and Ordinary Courts: Decentralisation and Recentralisation' (2016) 1 *Turkish Journal of Legal Studies* 77–101

Neuman, Gerald L, 'Import, Export and Regional Consent in the Inter-American Court of Human Rights' (2008) 19 *European Journal of International Law* 101–123

Neuman, Gerald L, 'Subsidiarity' in Dinah Shelton (ed), *The Oxford Handbook of International Human Rights Law* (Oxford University Press 2013) 360–378

Nickel, Rainer, 'Private and Public Autonomy: Jürgen Habermas' Concept of Co-Originality in Times of Globalisation and the Militant Security State' in Martin Loughlin and Neil Walker (eds), *The Paradox of Constitutionalism* (Oxford University Press 2007) 147–167

Nijman, Janne E and Nollkaemper, André, 'Beyond the Divide', in Janne E Nijman and André Nollkaemper (eds), *New Perspectives on the Divide Between National and International Law* (2007) 341–360

Nogueira Alcalá, Humberto, 'Diálogo interjurisdiccional, control de convencionalidad y jurispurdencia del Tribunal Constitucional en período 2006–2011' (2012) 10 *Estudios Constitucionales* 57–140

Nogueira Alcalá, Humberto, 'El control de convencionalidad y el diálogo interjurisdiccional entre tribunales nacionales y Corte Interamericana de Derechos Humanos' (2013) 19 *Revista de Derecho Constitucional Europeo* 221–270

Nollkaemper, André, 'Conversations among Courts: Domestic and International Adjudicators' in Cesare P R Romano, Karen Alter and Yuval Shany (eds), *The Oxford Handbook of International Adjudication* (Oxford University Press 2014) 523–549

Nollkaemper, André, 'The Duality of Direct Effect of International Law' (2014) 25 *European Journal of International Law* 105–125

Nollkaemper, André, 'Rethinking the Supremacy of International Law' (2010) 65 *Zeitschrift für öffentliches Recht* 65–85

Nollkaemper, André, 'The Power of Secondary Rules to Connect the International and National Legal Order' in Tomer Broude and Yuval Shany (eds), Multi-Sourced Equivalent Norms in International Law (Hart 2011) 45–67

Nollkaemper, André, *National Courts and the International Rule of Law* (Oxford University Press 2012)

Nolte, Georg, *Treaties and Subsequent Practice* (Oxford University Press 2013)

O'Donoghue, Aoife, *Constitutionalism in Global Constitutionalisation* (Cambridge University Press 2014)

Kaoru Obata, 'The Emerging Principle of Functional Complementarity for Coordination Among National and International Jurisdictions: Intellectual Hegemony And Heterogeneous World' in Takao Suami, Anne Peters, Mattias Kumm and Dimitri Vanoverbeke (eds.), *Global Constitutionalism from European and East Asian Perspectives* (Cambridge University Press 2018) 451–469

Okafor, Obiora C and Effoduh, Okechukwu J, 'The ECOWAS Court as a (Promising) Resource for Pro-Poor Activist Forces: Sovereign Hurdles, Brainy Relays, and "Flipped Strategic Social Constructivism"' in James Thuo Gathii (eds), The Performance of Africa's International Courts: Using Litigation for Political, Legal, and Social Change (Oxford University Press 2020) 106–148

Oklopčić, Zoran, *Beyond the People: Social Imaginary and Constituent Imagination* (Oxford University Press 2018)

Omerdić, Dženeta and Halilović, Harun, 'The Case of Baralija v Bosnia and Herzegovina: A new Challenge for the State Authorities of Bosnia and Herzegovina?' (2020) 4 *Društvene i humanističke studije* 217–238

ONUMA Yasuaki, *International Law in a Transcivilizational World* (Cambridge University Press 2017)

Oscar Schachter, 'The Invisible College of International Lawyers' (1977–78) 72 Northwestern University Law Review 217–226

Ost, François and van de Kerchove, Michel, *De la pyramide au réseau? Pour une théorie dialectique du droit* (Publications des Facultés universitaires Saint-Louis 2002)

Palombino, Fulvio M, 'Compliance with International Judgments: Between Supremacy of International Law and National Fundamental Principles' (2015) 75 *Heidelberg Journal of International Law* (2015) 503–529

Panoussis, Ioannis, 'L'obligation générale de protection des droits de l'homme dans la jurisprudence des organes internationaux' (2007) 70 *Revue trimestrielle des droits de l'homme* 427–461

Paris, Davide, 'Constitutional Courts as Guardians of EU Fundamental Rights? Centralized judicial Review of Legislation and the Charter of Fundamental Rights of the EU: European Court of Justice (Fifth Chamber), Judgment of 11 September 2014, Case C-112/13, *A v B and Others*' (2015) 11 *European Constitutional Law Review* 389–407

Pascual Vives, Francisco, 'Consenso e interpretación evolutiva de lots tratados regionales de derechos humanos' (2014) 66 *Revista Española de Derecho Internacional* 113–153

Pasqualucci, Jo M, *The Practice and Procedure of the Inter-American Court of Human Rights* (2nd ed, Cambridge University Press 2013)

Paulus, Andreas L, 'Subsidiarity, Fragmentation and Democracy: Towards the Demise of General International Law?' in Tomer Broude and Yuval Shany (eds), *The Shifting Allocation of Authority in International Law: Considering Sovereignty, Supremacy and Subsidiarity: Essays in Honour of Professor Ruth Lapidoth* (Hart 2008) 193–213

Paunio, Elina, 'Beyond Predictability: Reflections on Legal Certainty and the Discourse Theory of Law in the EU Legal Order' (2009) 10 *German Law Journal* 1469–1493

Pavoni, Riccardo, '*Simoncioni v. Germany*' (2015) 109 *American Journal of International Law* 400–406

Peat, Daniel and Windsor, Matthew, 'Playing the Game of Interpretation: On Meaning and Metaphor in International Law' in Andrea Bianchi, Daniel Peat, and Matthew Windsor (eds), *Interpretation in International Law* (Oxford University Press 2015) 3–33

Pernice, Ingolf, 'The Treaty of Lisbon: Multilevel Constitutionalism in Action' (2009) 15 *Columbia Journal of European Law* 349–407 (emphasis added). See also, Ingolf Pernice, 'Theorie und Praxis des Europäischen Verfassungsverbundes' in Calliess (ed), *Verfassungswandel im europäischen Staaten- und Verfassungsverbund* (Mohr Siebeck 2007) 61–92

Peters, Anne, 'Fragmentation and Constitutionalization' in Anne Orford and Florian Hoffmann (eds), *The Oxford Handbook of the Theory of International Law* (Oxford University Press 2016) 1011–1032

Peters, Anne, 'Realizing Utopia as a Scholarly Endeavour' (2013) 24 *European Journal of International Law* 533–552

Peters, Anne, 'Supremacy Lost: International Law Meets Domestic Constitutional Law' (2009) 3 Vienna *Online Journal of International Constitutional Law* 170–198

Petzold, Herbert, 'The Convention and the Principle of Subsidiarity' in Ronald St J MacDonald, Franz Matscher and Herbert Petzold (eds), *The European System for the Protection of Human Rights* (Martinus Nijhoff 1993) 41–62

Philipp Aust, Helmut, Rodiles, Alejandro and Staubach, Peter, 'Unity or Uniformity? Domestic Courts and Treaty Interpretation', 27 *Leiden Journal of International Law* (2014) 75–112

Pinto, Mónica, 'El principio *pro homine*: criterios de la hermenéutica y pautas para la regulación de los derechos humano', in Martín Abregú and Christian Courtis (eds), *La aplicación de los tratados sobre derechos humanos por los tribunales locales* (Centro de Estudios Legales y Sociales 1997) 163–171

Piovesan, Flávia, 'Direitos humanos e diálogo entre juridições' (2012) 19 *Revista Brasileira de Direito Constitucional* 67–93

Pisillo-Mazzeschi, Riccardo, 'Responsabilité de l'État pour violation des obligations positives relatives aux droits de l'homme' (2009) Recoueil des cours 177–506

Pizzolo, Calogero, 'Los mechanismos de protección en el sistema interamericano de derechos humanos y el derecho interno de los países miembros: El caso argentino', in R. Méndez Silva (ed.), *Derecho internacional de los derechos humanos. Memoria del VII Congreso Iberoamericano de Derecho Constitucional* (2002) 505–519

Pollicino, Oreste, 'The Italian Constitutional Court at the Crossroads between Constitutional Parochialism and Co-operative Constitutionalism. Judgments Nos. 348 and 349 of 22 and 24 October 2007' (2008) 4 *European Constitutional Law Review* 363–382

Popelier, Patricia and Patiño Álvarez, Aída Araceli, 'Deliberative Practices of Constitutional Courts in Consolidated and Non-consolidated Democracies' in Patricia Popelier, Armen Mazmayan and Werner Vandenbruwaene (eds), *The Role of Constitutional Courts in Multilevel Governance* (Intersentia 2013) 199–231

Porto, Sierra, 'La Corte Constitucional colombiana frente al control de convencionalidad' in Edgar Corzo Sosa, Jorge Ulises Carmona Tinoco and Pablo Saavedra Alessandri (eds), *Impacto de las sentencias de la Corte Interamericana de Derechos Humanos* (Tirant lo Blanch México 2013) 427–447, 440–446.

Prost, Mario, *The Concept of Unity in International Law* (Hart 2012)

Quesada, Jimena, *Jurisdicción nacional y control de convencionalidad: A propósito del diálogo judicial global y de la tutela multinivel de derechos* (Aranzadi 2013)

Rachovitsa, Adamantia, 'Fragmentation of International Law Revisited: Insights, Good Practices and Lessons to be Learned from the Case Law of the European Court of Human Rights' (2015) 28 *Leiden Journal of International Law* 863–885

Roberts, Anthea, *Is International Law International?* (Oxford University Press 2017)

Rodiles, Alejandro, 'The Law and Politics of the *Pro Persona* Principle in Latin America' in Helmut Philipp Aust and Georg Nolte (eds), *The Interpretation of International Law by Domestic Courts: Unity, Diversity, Convergence* (Oxford University Press 2015) 153–174

Rodley, Nigel, 'The International Court of Justice and Human Rights Treaty Bodies' in James A Green and Christopher PM Waters (eds), *Adjudicating International Human Rights: Essays in Honour of Sandy Ghandhi* (Martinus Nijhoff Publishers 2014) 12–33

Roughan, Nicole, *Authorities: Conflict, Cooperation, and Transnational Legal Theory* (Oxford University Press 2016)

Rousseau, Charles, 'Principes de droit international public' (1958-I) 93 *Recueil des cours* 369–550

Rt Hon Lady Justice Arden DBE, 'Peaceful or Problematic? The Relationship between National Supreme Courts and Supranational Courts in Europe' (2010) 29 *Yearbook of European Law* 3–20, 14.

Ruiz González, Ana María, 'Supreme Court of Justice of Costa Rica (Corte Suprema de Justicia de Costa Rica) Costa Rica [cr]' in Rainer Grote, Frauke Lachenmann, Rüdiger Wolfrum (eds), *Max Planck Encyclopedia of Comparative Constitutional Law* (Oxford University Press 2019), updated in 2019

Ruiz-Chiriboga, Oswaldo, 'The Conventionality Control: Examples of (Un)Successful Experiences in Latin America' (2010) 3 *Inter-American and European Human Rights Journal* 200–219

Saavedra Alessandri, Pablo, 'The Role of the Inter-American Court of Human Rights in Monitoring Compliance with Judgments' (2020) 12 *Journal of Human Rights Practice* 178–184

Sadat-Akhavi, *Methods of Resolving Conflicts between Treaties* (Brill 2004)

Sadurski, Wojciech, *Constitutionalism and the Enlargement of Europe* (Oxford University Press 2012)

Sagüés, Néstor Pedro, 'El "control de convencionalidad" en el sistema interamericano, y sus anticipos en el ámbito de los derechos económico-sociales: concordancias y diferencias con el sistema europeo' in Armin von Bogdandy, Héctor Fix-Fierro, Mariela Morales Antoniazzi and Eduardo Ferrer Mac-Gregor (eds), *Construcción y papel de los derechos sociales fundamentales: Hacia un ius constitucionale commune en América Latina* (Instituto de Investigaciones Jurídicas 2011) 993–1030

Sauer, Heiko, 'Principled Resistance to and Principled Compliance with ECtHR Judgments' in Marten Breuer (ed), *Principled Resistance to ECtHR Judgments: A New Paradigm?* (Springer 2019) 55–88

Schönsteiner, Judith, 'Dissuasive Measures and the 'Society as a Whole': A Working Theory of Reparations in the Inter-American Court of Human Rights' (2007) 23 *American University International Lwe Review* 127–164

Schroth, Peter W, 'Marbury and Simmenthal: Reflections on the Adoption of Decentralized Judicial Review by the Court of Justice of the European Community' (1979) 12 *Loyola of Los Angeles Law Review* 869–902

Seibert-Fohr, Anja, 'Judicial Engagement in International Human Rights Comparativism' in August Reinisch, Mary E Footer and Christina Binder (eds), *International Law and...: Select Proceedings of the European Society of International Law*, Vol 5, (Hart 2014) 7–24

Seminara, Letizia, *Les effets des arrêts de la Cour interaméricaine des droits de l'homme* (Bruylant/Nemesis 2009)

Shai Dothan, *International Judicial Review: When Should International Courts Intervene?* (Cambridge University Press 2020) 41–60

Shany, Yuval, '*Dédoublement fonctionnel* and the Mixed Loyalties of National and International Judges' in Filippo Fontanelli, Giuseppe Martinico and Paolo Carrozza (eds), *Shaping Rule of Law Through Dialogue* (Europa Law Publishing 2010) 27–44

Shany, Yuval, 'Toward a General Margin of Appreciation Doctrine in International Law?' (2005) 16 *European Journal of International Law* 907–940

Shelton, Dinah and Huneeus, Alexandra, '*In re* Direct Action of Unconstitutionality Initiated Against the Declaration of Acceptance of the Jurisdiction of the Inter-American Court of Human Rights' (2017) 109 *American Journal of International Law* 866–872

Shelton, Dinah, 'Form, Function, and the Powers of International Courts' Chin. J. Int'l L. 9 (2009), 537–571

Shelton, Dinah, 'Subsidiarity and Human Rights Law' (2006) 27 *Human Rights Law Journal* 4–11

Sijniensky, Romina I, 'From the Non-Discrimination Clause to the Concept of Vulnerability in International Human Rights Law: Advancing on the Need for Special Protection of Certain Groups and Individuals' in Yves Haeck, Brianne MacGonigle Leyh, Clara Burbano-Herrera and Diana Contreras-Garduño (eds), *The Realization of Human Rights: When Theory Meets Practice: Studies in Honour of Leo Zwaak* (Intersentia 2013) 259–272

Singh, Sahib, 'The Potential of International Law: Fragmentation and Ethics' (2011) 24 *Leiden Journal of International Law* 23–43

Soley, Ximena and Steininger, Silvia, 'Parting Ways or Lashing Back? Withdrawals, Backlash and the Inter-American Court of Human Rights' (2018) 14 *International Journal of Law in Context* 237–257; Jorge Contesse, 'Resisting the Inter-American Human Rights System' (2018) 44 Yale Journal of International Law 179–237

Spano, Robert, 'Universality or Diversity of Human Rights? Strasbourg in the Age of Subsidiarity' (2014) 14 *Human Rights Law Review* 487–502

Steiner, Henry J, Philip Alston and Ryan Goodman, *International Human Rights in Context: Law, Politics, Morals : Text and Materials*, 3rd ed (Oxford University Press 2008)

Stone Sweet, Alec, 'A Cosmopolitan Legal Order: Constitutional Pluralism and Rights Adjudication in Europe' (2011) 1 *Global Constitutionalism* 53–90

Stone Sweet, Alec, 'Sur la constitutionalisation de la Convention européenne des droits de l'homme : cinquante ans après son installation, la Cour européenne des droits de l'homme conçue comme une cour constitutionnelle' (2009) 77 *Revue trimestrielle des droits de l'homme* 923–944

Storme, Matthias E, 'The Struggle Concerning Interpretative Authority in the Context of Human Rights: The Belgian Experience' in Rainer Arnold (ed), *The Universalism of Human Rights* (Springer 2013) 223–235

Storme, Matthias E, 'The Struggle Concerning Interpretative Authority in the Context of Human Rights: The Belgian Experience' in Rainer Arnold (ed), *The Universalism of Human Rights* (Springer 2013) 223–236

Sudre, Frédéric, 'L'interpretation constructive de la liberté syndicale, au sens de l'article 11 de la Convention EDH' (2009) 5 *JCP/La semaine juridique, édition générale* 30–33

Sudre, Frédéric, 'Question préjudicielle de constitutionnalité et Convention européenne des droits de l'homme' (2009) 3 *Revue du droit public et de la science politique en France et a l'etranger* 671–684

Susi, Mart, 'The Definition of a "Structural Problem" in the Case-Law of the European Court of Human Rights Since 2010' (2012) 55 *German Yearbook of International Law* 1–51

Szymezak, David, 'Question prioritaire de constitutionnalité et Convention européenne des droits de l'homme : L'européanisation « heurtée » du Conseil constitutionnel français' (2012) 7 *Jus Politicum* 1–23

Szymezak, David, 'Question prioritaire de constitutionnalité et Convention européenne des droits de l'homme : L'européanisation « heurtée » du Conseil constitutionnel français' (2012) 7 *Jus Politicum* 1–23

Teagu, Elizabeth, 'Russia's Constitutional Reforms of 2020' (2020) 5 *Russian Politics* 301–328

Teraya, Koji, 'Shijinkan Koryoku to "Kokusaiho" no Siko Yoshiki: Kenpogaku to Kokusaihogaku no Dosyoimu [Horizontal Application Theories and "International Law" Thinking: Strange Bedfellows in the Disciplines of Constitutional Law and International Law]' (2012) 23 *Kokusai Jinken [Human Rights International]* 9–15 (in Japanese)

Teubner, Gunther, *Constitutional Fragments: Societal Constitutionalism and Globalization* (Oxford University Press 2012)

Thirlway, Hugh, *The Sources of International Law* (Oxford University Press 2014)

Thürer, Daniel, 'Kosmopolitische Verfassungsentwicklungen' in Daniel Thürer (ed), *Kosmopolitisches Staatsrecht*, Vol 1 (Schulthess Zurich 2005) 3–39

Thürer, Daniel, 'Verfassungsrecht und Völkerrecht' in Daniel Thürer, Jean-François Aubert, Jörg Paul Müller (eds), *Verfassungsrecht der Schweiz* (Schulthess 2001) 179–206

Thurnherr, Daniela, 'The Reception Process in Austria and Switzerland' in Helen Keller and Alec Stone Sweet (eds), *A Europe of Rights: The Impact of the ECHR on National Legal Systems* (Oxford University Press 2008) 311–391

Tigroudja, Hélène, 'La satisfaction et les garanties de non-répétition de l'illicite dans le contentieux interaméricain des droit de l'homme' in Elisabeth Lambert Abdelgawad and Kathia Martin-Chenut (eds), *Réparer les violations graves et massives des droits de l'homme: la Cour interaméricaine, pionnière et modèle?* (Société de Législation Comparée 2010) 69–89

Tigroudja, Hélène, 'The Inter-American Court of Human Rights and International Humanitarian Law' in Robert Kolb and Gloria Gaggioli (eds), *Research Handbook of Human Rights and Humanitarian Law* (Edward Elgar 2013) 466–479

Tojo, Liliana y Elizalde, Pilar, 'Artículos 44–47: Competencia de la Comisión Interamericana de Derechos Humanos' in Christian Steiner and Patricia Uribe (eds), *Convención Americana sobre Derechos Humanos: Comentarios* (Konrad Adenauer Stiftung 2014) 765–784

Torres Pérez, Aida, 'Melloni in Three Acts: from Dialogue to Monologue' (2014) 10 *European Constitutional Law Review* (2014) 308–331

Torres Zúñiga, Natalia, *El control de convencionalidad: Deber complementario del juez constitucional peruano y el juez interamericano (similitudes, deferencias y convergencias)* (Editorial Académica Española 2013)

Torres Zúñiga, Natalia, *El control de convencionalidad: Deber complementario del juez constitucional peruano y el juez interamericano (similitudes, deferencias y convergencias)* (Editorial Académica Española 2013)

Triepel, Heinrich 'Les rapports entre le droit interne et le droit international' (1923) 1 *Recueil des cours* 73–122, 82–87

Trispiotis, Ilias, 'Two Interpretations of "Living Together" in European Human Rights Law' (2016) 75 *Cambridge Law Journal* 580–607

Tzanakapoulos, Antonios, 'Domestic Courts in International Law: The International Judicial Function of National Courts' (2011) 34 *Loyola of Los Angeles International and Comparative Law Review* 133–168

Tzanakopoulos, Antonios, 'Domestic Courts in International Law: The International Judicial Function of National Courts' (2011) 34 *Loyola of Los Angeles International and Comparative Law Review* 133–168

Ulfstein, Geir, 'The International Judiciary' in Jan Klabbers, Anne Peters and Geir Ulfstein, *The Constitutionalization of International Law* (Oxford University Press 2009) 126–152

Uprimny Yepes, Rodrigo y Saffon, María Paula, 'Reparaciones transformadoras, justicia distributiva y profundización democrática' in Catalina Díaz Gómez, Nelson Camilo Sánchez, Rodrigo Uprimny Yepes (eds), *Reparar en Colombia: los dilemas en contextos de conflicto, pobreza y exclusión* (Centro Internacional para la Justicia Transicional y Centro de Estudios de Derecho, Justicia y Sociedad 2009) 31–70

Valticos, Nicolas and Potobsky, Gerald W von, *International Labour Law*, 2nd ed (Kluwer 1995)

Van Aaken, Anne, 'Defragmentation of Public International Law through Interpretation: A Methodological Proposal' (2009) 16 *Indiana Journal of Global Legal Studies* 483–512

Van Bockel, Bas and Wattel, Peter, 'New Wine into Old Wineskins: The Scope of the Charter of Fundamental Rights of the EU after *Åkerberg Fransson*' (2013) 38 *European Law Review* 866–883

Van de Heyning, Catherine, 'Constitutional Courts as Guarantees of Fundamental Rights: The Constitutionalisation of the Convention through Domestic Constitutional Adjudication' in Patricia Popelier, Armen Mazmayan and Werner Vandenbruwaene (eds), *The Role of Constitutional Courts in Multilevel Governance* (Intersentia 2013) 21–48

Van de Heyning, Catherine, 'No Place like Home: Discretionary Space for the Domestic Protection of Human Rights' in Patricia Popelier, Catherine Van de Heyning and Piet Van Nuffel (eds), *Human Rights Protection in the European Legal Order: The Interaction between the European and National Courts* (Intersentia 2011) 65–96

Van de Heyning, Catherine, 'The Natural "Home" of Fundamental Rights Adjudication: Constitutional Challenges to the European Court of Human Rights' (2012) 31 *Yearbook of European Law* 128–161

Van den Eynde, Laura 'The Consensus Argument in NGOs' *Amicus Curiae* Briefs Defending Minorities Through A Creatively Used Majoritarian Argument' in Panos Kapotas and Vassilis P Tzevelekos (eds), *Building Consensus on European Consensus: Judicial Interpretation of Human Rights in Europe and Beyond* (Cambridge University Press 2019) 96–119

Van der Schyff, Gerhard, 'Constitutional Review by the Judiciary in the Netherlands' (2010) 11 *German Law Journal* 275–290

Van Hoecke, Mark, 'Constitutional Courts and Deliberative Democracy' Patricia Popelier, Armen Mazmayan and Werner Vandenbruwaene (eds), *The Role of Constitutional Courts in Multilevel Governance* (Intersentia 2013) 183–198

Vereshchetin, Vladen S, 'On the Expanding Reach of the Rulings of the International Court of Justice' in Pierre-Marie Dupuy, Bardo Fassbender, Malcolm N Shaw and Karl-Peter Sommermann (eds), *Völkerrecht als Wertordnung: für Christian Tomuschat* (N P Engel 2006) 621–633

Villagrán Sandoval, Carlos Arturo and Carvalho Veçoso, Fabia Fernandes, 'A Human Rights' Tale of Competing Narratives' (2016) 8 *Revista Direito e Práxis* 1603–1651.

Villiger, Mark E, 'The Principle of Subsidiarity in the European Convention on Human Rights' in Marcelo G Kohen (ed), *Promoting Justice, Human Rights and Conflict Resolution through International Law: Liber Amicorum Lucius Caflisch* (Martinus Nijhoff 2007) 623–637

Vítolo, Alfredo M, 'Una novedosa categoría jurídica: el «querer ser». Acerca del pretendido carácter normativo erga omnes de la jurisprudencia de la Corte Interamericana de Derechos Humanos. Las dos caras del «control de convencionalidad»' (2013) 18 *Pensamiento Constitucional* 357–380

Voeten, Erik, 'Populism and Backlashes against International Courts' (2020) 18 Perspectives on Politics 407–422

Vogel, Klaus, *Die Verfassungsentscheidung des Grundgesetzes für die internationale Zusammenarbeit* (Mohr Siebeck 1964)

Von Bogdandy, Armin and Venzke, Ingo, 'On the Functions of International Courts: An Appraisal in Light of Their Burgeoning Public Authority' (2013) *Leiden Journal of International Law* 49–72

Von Bogdandy, Armin, 'Founding Principles' in Armin von Bogdandy and Jürgen Bast (eds), *Principles of European Constitutional Law* (Hart Publishing 2010) 93–111

Von Bogdandy, Armin, 'Pluralism, Direct Effect, and the Ultimate Say: On the Relationship between International and Domestic Constitutional Law' (2008) 6 *International Journal of Constitutional Law* 397–413

Von Staden, Andreas, 'The Democratic Legitimacy of Judicial Review beyond the State: Normative Subsidiarity and Judicial Standards of Review' (2012) 10 *International Journal of Constittuional Law* 1023–1049

Wachsmann, Patrick, 'Réflexions sur l'interprétation 'globalisante' de la Convention européenne des droits de l'homme' in *La conscience des droits : Mélanges en l'honneur de Jean-Paul Costa* (Dalloz 2011) 667–676

Wagnerova, Eliska, 'The Direct Applicability of Human Rights Treaties' in Council of Europe (ed), *The Status of International Treaties on Human Rights* (2006) 111–128

Wählisch, Martin, *Peacemaking, Power-sharing and International Law: Imperfect Peace* (Bloomsbury 2019)

Wendel, Mattias, 'Lisbon Before the Courts: Comparative Perspectives' (2011) 7 *European Constitutional Law Review* 96–137

Wendel, Mattias, *Permeabilität im europäischen Verfassungsrecht: Verfassungsrechtliche Integrationsnormen auf Staats- und Unionsebene im Vergleich* (Mohr Siebeck 2011)

Wheatley, Steven, *The Democratic Legitimacy of International Law* (Bloomsbury Publishing 2010)

Wiener, Antje and Oeter, Stefan, 'Introduction: Who recognizes the emperor's clothes anymore?' (2016) 14 *International Journal of Constitutional Law* 608–621

Wiklund, Ola, 'The Reception Process in Sweden and Norway' in Keller and Stone Sweet Helen Keller and Alec Stone Sweet (eds), *A Europe of Rights: The Impact of the ECHR on National Legal Systems* (Oxford University Press 2008) 165–228

Yamamoto, Hajime and Negishi, Yota, 'Japan' in Fulvio M Palombino (ed), *Duelling for Supremacy: International vs. National Fundamental Principles* (Cambridge University Press 2019) 210–233

Yourow, Howard Charles, 'The Margin of Appreciation Doctrine in the Dynamics of European Human Rights Jurisprudence' (1987) 3 *Connecticut Journal of International Law* 111–159

Yourow, Howard Charles, *The Margin of Appreciation Doctrine in the Dynamics of European Human Rights Jurisprudence* (Brill 1996) 193.

Zglinski, Jan, *Europe's Passive Virtues: Deference to National Authorities in EU Free Movement Law* (Oxford University Press 2020)

Ziemele, Ineta, 'European Consensus and International Law' in Anne van Aaken and Iulia Motoc (eds), *The European Convention on Human Rights and General International Law* (Oxford University Press 2018) 23–39

Zurn, Christopher F, *Deliberative Democracy and the Institutions of Judicial Review* (Cambridge University Press 2007)